FV

WITHDRAWN

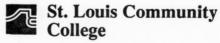
St. Louis Community College

Forest Park
Florissant Valley
Meramec

Instructional Resources
St. Louis, Missouri

GAYLORD

SEDUCTIVE CINEMA

SEDUCTIVE CINEMA

THE ART OF SILENT FILM

James Card

ALFRED A. KNOPF

New York 1994

THIS IS A BORZOI BOOK
PUBLISHED BY ALFRED A. KNOPF, INC.

Copyright © 1994 by James Card

All rights reserved under International and Pan-American Copyright Conventions. Published in the United States by Alfred A. Knopf, Inc., New York, and simultaneously in Canada by Random House of Canada Limited, Toronto. Distributed by Random House, Inc., New York.

Library of Congress Cataloging-in-Publication Data
Card, James.
   Seductive cinema / by James Card. — 1st ed.
      p.   cm.
   Includes index.
   ISBN 0-394-57218-1
   1. Silent films—History and criticism.   I. Title.
PN1995.75.C37   1993
791.43'09—dc20   93-15431
                                          CIP

Manufactured in the United States of America
First Edition

To Jeannie, Callista and Priscilla

CONTENTS

FOREWORD

We have become an alarmingly endangered species, those of us who enjoyed silent films throughout the 1920s. We know that we are not alone in admiring the best of the surviving predialogue movies, but understandably, some misconceptions have crept into histories of the early period, written by those who were not around to see first-run prints of the acknowledged masterpieces, or could not have visited the resplendent palaces or the cozy neighborhood houses of more than half a century ago.

As there are today, there were those who took the existence of cinema very much for granted, saw only an occasional film because it was being discussed. And there were even a few (I never met one) who hated pictures. But there were some of us with an addiction, with fierce passion for the medium. We were militant and protective and we didn't want it to change in any way. We loved its silence. We were devoted to the aspect ratio of the frame. As collectors, we were even enchanted by the unique scent of nitrate of cellulose.

There are even fewer of us left who not only had this almost insane, passionate affection for film, but became involved in hands-on work with motion pictures, shooting, editing and screening as well as simply watching. When dialogue arrived and the silent film almost vanished, some of us were so infuriated that we actually refused, for many months, to even look at a talkie.

Before it is too late and there are none of us left, I want to write informally about those halcyon days. Although I have been professorially involved with film history since 1936, I assure the reader that this is not a scholarly work. Historians may find information in these pages that will enrich their knowledge of film history. But if they do, it will be inadvertent enhancement, for this work is not organized academically. I promise no semiotic obscurities and no murky intellectual game playing.

An index is provided, but you will look in vain for a section of notes of the sort that try to validate every statement the author makes throughout the text. Have faith. This writer was there.

SEDUCTIVE CINEMA

INTRODUCTION

After Adam was separated from his first wife, Lilith, and did not have to work for his food in the Garden of Eden, he had an inordinate amount of time on his hands. Until Eve was constructed, he embarked on the not inconsequential project of naming all the animals and plants in the world. Undoubtedly and understandably, he was under the impression that they all belonged to him. After all, there was no one else to claim and possess them. Ever since, with this atavistic compulsion, men have insisted on collecting. Baseball cards, postage stamps, antique autos, money or women; a normal male human being must collect something.

For me there was never any question. I had to have film, motion picture film, of my own. Imagine, if you can, the homes of the world before 1920. They were without radio programs. Television was only the dream of scientists generally regarded as mentally unstable. Packaged, professional home entertainment was limited to phonograph records, player-piano rolls, stereographic views or slides projected from a magic lantern.

But downtown there were the movies! My home in the 1920s and before was Cleveland, Ohio, where there were 147 movie theatres with 123,320 seats. The film houses ranged from palatial first-run theatres of more than 3,000 seats to a few survivors of the nickelodeon days that had room for as few as 240.

The Elysian fields of the downtown film theatres were along the first twenty blocks of Euclid Avenue. Euclid of the 1880s had been one of those fabulous stretches of Victorian elegance, towering elms, luxurious mansions set far back from the road, the display route for the prancing thoroughbreds drawing glistening coaches up and down the avenue and into the long curving drives of the magnificent estates.

By the 1920s the savage erosion of commercial "progress" had destroyed all that beauty. What grandeur remained was confined within the enrapturing space of the picture palaces of Euclid Avenue. Starting up Euclid from the public square, one first encountered the Hippodrome. Its stage was probably the largest in the United States. The stage area was so vast that the road show of the theatrical *Ben-Hur* had room for the famous chariot race live with real horses galloping on treadmills. The stage could be opened up to expose a great water tank. Scaled down somewhat, naval battles were reenacted and the likes of an Annette Kellerman could exhibit the art of high diving.

Soon the glittering spectacles of Cecil B. DeMille on the silver screen so far outshone whatever could take place on the Hippodrome's stage that its spots and borders went dark forever and only the projectors' arcs illumined the theatre after the asbestos rose and the heavy curtains parted.

With four balconies, the Hippodrome seated 3,600. We couldn't know it then, but watching a movie from the back rows of the fourth balcony furnished us with a preview of seeing a movie on a television set.

The big commercial crossroads of Cleveland was at East Ninth and Euclid, a ten-minute walk up Euclid from the public square. Traffic was so heavy there that the cop with his semaphore had more than he could handle. The solution was to build a high traffic tower right in the middle of the crossroads. Perched in his glass-enclosed cage the policeman could see what was coming and attempt to deal with it. Walking up Euclid, if surviving the crossing at Ninth Street, one came to the Stillman right next to the Statler Hotel. This pleasant movie theatre was a handy refuge for visitors to Cleveland staying at the Statler, for of course in 1920 there were neither TV sets nor even radios in the hotel rooms.

Just a little bit farther up Euclid one arrived at the largest cluster of great entertainment establishments within a single block anywhere west of Broadway. Playhouse Square! There beckoned the State, the Allen, the Palace, the Ohio and the Hanna, together offering an aggregate of 17,600 seats for people out to be amused.

The State had a lobby longer than the whole interior of most of today's film theatres. It was decorated by a dazzling mural, *The Spirit of the Movies*. A small section of that work was once pictured on a fold-out cover of *Life*. Dominating the balcony of the foyer was one of a pair of giant Japanese bronze eagles alleged to have formerly guarded a temple. The other belonged to my grandfather, a collector of objets d'art; his genes in his grandson deteriorated to collecting movies. Grandfather's bronze eagle spreads its wings today in my living room. To what collector's den its mate may have flown I often wonder.

Naming the most resplendent of the Cleveland theatres—the Palace—was in no way hyperbole. In the first years of the Palace's life the imperial furnishings of the foyers were never tarnished by the ugly presence of soft-drink dispensers or candy and popcorn machines.

Patrons of these gorgeous establishments did not come to attend the program in casual clothes, and eating and drinking during the shows was unthinkable. Audiences dressed to watch Pola Negri, Gloria Swanson and Greta Garbo as they would to attend a concert of the Cleveland Orchestra under the direction of Nikolai Sokoloff or Artur Rodzinski. They were shown to their seats by rigidly trained, uniformed ushers who wore gleaming white gloves. Each usher carried a flashlight to seat patrons who arrived in the dark throughout the entire film. Starting times of the films were not advertised and few bothered to linger in the lobby until the next beginning of the feature. Thus every movie became something of a mystery picture; one did not know what had gone on before the moment of being seated. You just stayed there until the program reached the spot where your father said, "This is where we came in." If your father wasn't with you, if you were there with your mother, your grandmother or your aunt, or if you were alone, you could stay and see it through to the end again.

In the mid-1920s I was averaging more than five movies a week. There was probably only one man in the whole state of Ohio who came close to the record I was establishing. He was Ward Marsh, the distinguished film critic and movie reviewer who began his career with the *Cleveland Plain Dealer* in 1918, the very year I began my career as fanatic fan. Inevitably we became friends. Ward Marsh continued writing for the *Plain Dealer* well into the 1960s.

Obsession added to the normal impulse to collect soon pushed me far over the edge that separates a film watcher from, well, whatever kind of monomaniac I had become. The critical added dimension was the proselytizer's determination to inflict his enthusiasm on others.

Bill Everson, close friend of many decades, writer, historian and teacher, at a film festival announced that his notion of hell would be to have all the films in the world but no projector. My own hell would be to have a projector and all the films but no one around to see them with me.

That first life-defining projector came to me about 1921, when the Keystone Moviegraphs appeared for sale in the department stores of Cleveland. Those home movie-projectors were made in Boston, and some chemical in their manufacture endowed the machines with a characteristic scent not unlike mothballs. This endearing perfume, so utterly associated with my first projector, even today when I walk into a moth-proofed clothes closet, can send me into a transport of nostalgia. The early models, and of course I was the owner of one of those, used a loop of about twenty-five feet of 35mm film. That was enough for only one very short scene. The projector was hand-cranked and it showed the brief action of that short loop over and over as long as the operator turned the crank. My first film, the one that came with the projector, was a scene showing a naval officer looking out to sea through a pair of binoculars. Then he turns and focuses his glasses on a comely young lady passenger, her short white sailing skirt whipping about in the breeze. Many years later I was reminded of this 1921 vintage film loop when I watched W. C. Fields nautically clad in *The Big Broadcast of 1938*, similarly looking out over the ocean from the bridge of a liner. In the Fields version the comely young lady passenger plucks at his uniform sleeve for attention. Fields turns to her and says, "Never interfere with a mariner in the employment of his barnacles."

In the mid-1920s nearly every boy at one time or another, for Christmas or a birthday, got a Mechano set or an Erector set. With these one could build metal toys of machinery, some of them quite practical. I used my Erector set one inspired afternoon to construct extension arms on my Keystone Moviegraph so that it would hold 1,000-foot reels of 35mm film. With that I was really in business. Regular feature films then came on 1,000-foot reels. Eight or nine of those reels would constitute a full-length, professional movie. Thus equipped, I could set my sights on acquiring and showing whole feature films instead of the inadequate little excerpts.

Around the neighborhood were other Keystone Moviegraph owners. Collections began by swapping one's less than favorite items for those of fellow collectors. In our Shaker Heights group, king of the movie collectors was Wilbur Lang. He had the best collection of all. Wilbur's father was a city court judge. At that time movies were heavily censored. State boards were paid to hack out nasty stuff from every film that crossed the state line. Most areas had county censors getting into the act and cities had their own watchdogs with eager shears. In Illinois the board decided that no film subtitle could carry the word "sin." When DeMille's *King of Kings* came along with Jesus saying "Let him who is without sin cast the first stone," the Illinois board censored the Saviour's admonition. It was miraculous that any film ever reached a

The "greasy man" was the most censored actor in Hollywood: Erich von Stroheim with Miss Du Pont in *Foolish Wives* (1922).

theatre with enough left to make up a normal show time. An eleven-reel epic could easily wind up with only nine reels left and some obvious gaps in the story line.

But Wilbur's good father would bring home rolls and rolls of film that were deemed unfit for public viewing and had been clipped out of the movies of the week. A tolerant fellow, Judge Lang saw no hazard in turning over the censored material for his son's Moviegraph and, ultimately, for his son's trading partners.

An Erich von Stroheim film was always sure to provide ample rolls of invidious material, just right for Wilbur and his collector friends. That was the time when Stroheim exulted in his fame as "the man you love to hate." Only many years later did I realize that the copious scenes involving a uniformed character we called "the greasy man" was Erich von Stroheim acting in his own film *Foolish Wives*. All Stroheim had to do in that film to qualify for inclusion in the Shaker Heights collections was to look lustfully at another man's susceptible wife.

As months went by, my collection kept growing and so did the avidity that inspired constant searching for film. There were rumors about an old, former cowboy showman living in Cleveland with cans and cans of seasoned nitrate film in his tool shed. I tracked him down, and, sure

In *The Great Train Robbery* (1903) George Barnes fired his Colt right at the camera lens.

enough, that retired cowboy had gold for my collection, including a glorious melodrama called *Kidnapped in New York*. That film has never been listed in the *Film Daily Yearbooks* nor is it to be found in the American Film Institute's catalogues. My vivid memory of it can attest to its being one of the most spectacular of the many tinted features coaxed through my modified Moviegraph.

That same cowboy had beguiling tales of his days touring the West with *The Great Train Robbery*. He claimed he had to keep replacing his screen. With a reflex action induced by the film's final close-up of the train robber firing directly at the spectators, half a dozen real pistols would leap from their holsters and the screen would suffer multiple punctures at every showing.

My growing awareness that movies were not solely a manifestation of North American production was heated to a new passion by two events. The first was the appearance in *The New York Times* of a piece by Kirk Bond. It was titled "Lament for the Cinema Dead." The article appeared at the time dialogue films were just beginning their struggle to eclipse silent movies. One of the great "dead" films Bond was lamenting (quite prematurely for sure) was *The Cabinet of Dr. Caligari*. I had never heard of this film before. The very title, in print, evoked a delightful chill. The name Caligari was sinister enough by itself but what delicious terror must lurk in the cabinet of a fiendish doctor named Caligari. That film, all unseen, became a beckoning ideal for me, and if it were indeed "dead," I vowed to devote an obsessive determination to resurrecting it.

The next step in my conversion to international cinema happened in my fifteenth year. Still in high school, I was absolutely dedicated to the motion picture. My circle of film devotees resented the advent of dialogue in 1930 and we tended to boycott the early talkies. But with some reluctance, we dropped in to see *All Quiet on the Western Front*. The film was far from quiet. It was discussed so much that we had to lower our standards to look at it. The puerile dialogue confirmed our low opinion of movie talk, although much of the action was stirring and magnificently directed. But right across the street the other side of the World War I story was being exhibited. The German view was movingly presented by Georg Pabst's *Westfront 1918*, retitled *Comrades of 1918* in the United States. The superiority of Pabst, it seemed to me

His role in *All Quiet on the Western Front* (1930) made Lew Ayres a dedicated pacifist. Here he is with Louis Wolheim.

Pabst's *Westfront 1918* (1930) was memorable for its rare sensitivity. Here, Gustav Diesel as the infantryman is on leave back home in Berlin, with his mother and his unfaithful wife.

then, was overwhelming. From that moment on, *any* film made overseas I rated as infinitely better than whatever came from Hollywood.

Such an overreaction to the novelty of the European approach to filmmaking was immeasurably reenforced by the appearance of Paul Rotha's book *The Film Till Now*. There were engrossing stills and critical support for the value of films that had been made in France, Germany and Russia. In 1930 that first edition of Rotha became the gospel for every ardent film fan/critic.

In those days, being a film fan was a condition completely different from being a film buff today. There was an emotional involvement with the stars to a degree unimaginable now. Perhaps part of it was the hypnotic effect of sitting in a darkened theatre with only music to support the play of light and shadow and the not altogether human apparitions of the mute actors and actresses, shimmering images reflected from a silver screen.

Before I left high school, the mania to show and share wonderful films became an intense concern. In the *National Board of Review Magazine* I had read that Fritz Lang's *Siegfried* was "too beautiful for words." Using a theatrical group I belonged to as my organizational base, I

On the back lot of UFA's Berlin Studio an Odinwald was constructed that was as impressive as a sequoia forest. Paul Richter as the Nibelungen hero in Fritz Lang's *Siegfried* (1922).

arranged an evening showing of Lang's lovely film in the high school auditorium. I badgered teachers, colleagues and relations to come to see the film, insisting it was the greatest film ever made.

For one of our Theatre Guild sessions, I rented a film for the evening solely on the basis of its literary source. It was *The Fall of the House of Usher*, made in 1927 by Dr. J. Sibley Watson in Rochester, New York. The 35mm print was sent to us minus the last hundred feet. The Usher house never fell. If the house hadn't fallen, this entrepreneur certainly did. It was my first encounter with expressionism and it instigated my first hunt for an elusive film to keep as my own. After a long and usually frustrating search, I found a 16mm print with the satisfying fall intact. It was the beginning of what I thought of as a film collection, quite different from the Moviegraph films that had just been pictures to show.

Now I had tasted the wine of showmanship and I became a promoter, although a somewhat limited one since I was still in high school. But I kept busy renting films and cajoling audiences to see them. It was then that I learned the profound wisdom of Samuel Goldwyn's dictum: "If people won't come to see your picture, there's no way you can stop them."

My offerings included revivals of Douglas Fairbanks' *Robin Hood*, John Barrymore's *Tempest* and Fritz Lang's *By Rocket to the Moon*, this last one attended by a mysterious group of German rocket experts. There were even ambitious first-run showings: the Cleveland premieres of Reinhold Schuenzel's *Amphitryon* and Erik Charell's *Congress Dances* with Lilian Harvey, Conrad Veidt and Lil Dagover.

But there was one revival that changed my life and shaped what would ultimately become a kind of career. It was *The Cabinet of Dr. Caligari*.

CHAPTER 1

In the Beginning

I n most of the Western world, music by name and essence is easily recognizable. It is *musique*, or *Musik* or *musica* and has been so called for centuries. But movies have been written about as *Photographie Animée, Lichtbilder, Pantomimes Lumineuse, Lichtspiele, Kintopp, Cinéma, Kino, Shadow Plays, Picture Plays, Photoplays, Photodramas, Film* or just *Pictures*. The official or encyclopedia and dictionary designation has become *motion pictures*, a corruption of Thomas Edison's own nomenclature, *life-motion'd pictures*.

Little wonder then that historians have been in such chaotic disagreement over the origins of the medium; they've never settled on what it is they are writing about. Do they mean hand-drawn or painted figures in apparent action, or photographically obtained images in an illusion of natural movement?

Dictionary and encyclopedia notwithstanding, now in the 1990s in this country we talk about "movies." If we're buffs, we discuss "film." But currently there's much more videotape around than there is film. Will cinema screens someday yield completely to television tubes and remain dark forever? A basic purpose of this book is to present some of the reasons that such a situation should not come about.

The men who brought about the essential magic of speechless cinema are few. They include Eadweard Muybridge, James Williamson, Louis Lumière, Georges Méliès, Thomas Edison and George Eastman. Fellow historians who may actually chance upon these lines may be horrified by my omissions. I myself am horrified by the need to include Edison and Eastman. I hasten to apologize for this sort of sacrilege. Some historians writing the account of the twentieth century I'm sure would like very much to exclude the names of Benito Mussolini and Adolf

Hitler. Their history, if they did, would be fatuous indeed and about as valuable as a tract by the Flat Earth Society.

Thomas Edison is one of those giants in the folklore and mythology of American history comparable to Mathew Brady. Although Brady was nearly blind at the time of the Civil War, he still endures as the brave photographic-buggy cameraman who documented scenes of the Civil War in the famous photographs that Ken Burns in his brilliant TV series has celebrated so successfully. But Mathew Brady no more made the pictures himself than Henry Ford stood in his factory personally assembling his enduring Model Ts. Edison was stymied in his efforts to devise a system of motion photography. He interviewed Muybridge, learned all he could about the Zoopraxiscope. Out of that knowledge came his Kinetoscope, a peep-box system that used a continuous strip of film, intermittently illuminated. His attempts at projection coming to nothing, Edison bought a projector invented by Thomas Armat, a Washington experimenter. It was the Edison-Armat Vitascope that projected the Edison films publicly at the undeservedly "historic" introduction of Edison movies at Koster & Bials Music Hall in New York.

As for George Eastman, early on he had legal problems with the Reverend Hannibal Goodwin of Newark, New Jersey. Eastman thought he had invented flexible film in celluloid strips for his Kodak camera. Goodwin, a dabbler in photography, had patented a flexible kind of film and felt that Eastman infringed on his patent. There were protracted suits, but it was Kodak film on which the history of motion pictures was recorded, not Goodwin's celluloid.

Eadweard Muybridge was projecting moving photographic images to spectators before Edison had finished playing with his phonographs. But the names and corporations of Thomas Edison and George Eastman were both formidable and so powerful in the making of motion pictures in this country that we *have* to acknowledge, however distastefully, their existence.

Muybridge was close enough to the real beginning of motion pictures to provide the most reasonable starting point in cinema's history. An incredible amount of nonsense has been published concerning the activities of Mr. Muybridge, who had been a distinguished British photographer long before he was able to bring motion pictures, enlarged, to a screen earlier than anyone else managed to do it.

Hostility toward Muybridge and a resulting determination to deny him credit for his accomplishments probably began with the writer

Terry Ramsaye in his 1926 book, *A Million and One Nights*, long considered a standard work in motion picture history.

Ramsaye titled one chapter "Muybridge in Myth and Murder" and devoted some six pages to the fact that the photographer had killed his wife's lover and, in a more romantic day, had been acquitted of the deed by a San Francisco jury.

Although this melodrama had nothing whatsoever to do with Muybridge's experiments that led to his invention of the Zoopraxiscope, Ramsaye, outraged over Muybridge's acquittal, characterized the eminent photographer as something of an untidy scalawag, implying in his account that he was a kind of con man exploiting the interest of Governor Leland Stanford of California in motion-study photography.

The facts are quite different indeed. Muybridge came to Stanford's attention by reason of his international reputation as an excellent photographer. No one aware of the maddeningly exacting nature of wet-collodion photography (the state of the art when Muybridge established his fame) would imply that a successful practitioner of photography might be in any way mechanically inept or careless. The photographer had to coat his glass plates on the spot, a manual operation that required extreme dexterity. The plates were sensitized and exposed while still wet. They had to be developed at once and the slightest accident, the action of dust or the use of any but the most meticulously cleaned equipment, would result not merely in a poor negative, but in a useless one.

Muybridge's negatives, some of which still exist, provided superb pictures. Moreover, working as a photographer with assignments from the United States government, he had to perform the trying tasks of wet-collodion photography in the most inaccessible regions. Glass plates, chemicals and a dark tent had to be packed along with the large camera and tripod. Yet many Muybridge pictures of the rugged crags and forbidding chasms of Yosemite were made on heavy glass plates measuring seventeen by twenty-two inches.

Muybridge had written in the preface to his fascinating book *Animals in Motion* that his own projector, the Zoopraxiscope, was "the first apparatus ever used or constructed, for synthetically demonstrating movements analytically photographed from life, and in its resulting effects is the prototype of all the various instruments which, under a variety of names, are used for a similar purpose at the present day." Muybridge copyrighted *Animals in Motion* in 1887.

On May 4, 1880, Muybridge projected moving pictures before spectators. That was a year before he'd gone to Paris to meet Dr. E. J. Marey, eminent scientist, and the painter Jean-Louis Meissonier. Some authors have pretended that Muybridge learned how to project his images from them!

No mention of the 1880 projection by Muybridge is to be found in any of the published chronologies of the important steps in motion picture history, even though that event is a matter of more than adequate public record. So utterly has the significant work of Muybridge been ignored by historians either malicious or incompetent, that the actual centennial of the beginning of motion pictures, May 4, 1980, was allowed to pass without even one single newspaper notice.

The historic first projection of motion pictures took place in San Francisco at a meeting of the San Francisco Art Association. That event was reported the next day, May 5, 1880, by the *San Francisco Alta*, the *San Francisco Call*, the *San Francisco Bulletin* and on May 8, 1880, by the *California Spirit of the Times*.

The account in the *San Francisco Alta* is wonderfully prophetic:

> Mr. Muybridge gave an interesting private exhibition last evening to a few critics and artists, showing the results of his recent experiments and studies in taking instantaneous photographs of animals in motion ... The most interesting new feature of the exhibition was the application of the series of instantaneous photographic pictures of animals in motion to the magic-lantern zoetrope. Horses of life size were represented running, trotting and jumping; men, deer, bulls and dogs ran with all the motions of life; horses were shown running past each other in different directions, and other wonderful and ludicrous movements were exhibited. Mr. Muybridge has laid the foundation of a new method of entertaining the people, and we predict that his instantaneous photographic magic-lantern zoetrope will make the rounds of the civilized world.

That historic demonstration of 1880 was repeated three evenings for the general public. For that series of shows, in order to project the images he had photographed on Governor Stanford's racetrack, Muybridge had devised a combination magic lantern and zoetrope that he called the Zoopraxiscope.

Five years later, Muybridge was busy at the University of Pennsylvania, engaged in a quasi-scientific project of motion analysis. His models were mostly nude women, athletes, himself and many of the animals of the Pittsburgh Zoo. Ostensibly his studies in "animal locomotion" were intended for the enlightenment of physiologists and the inspiration of artists.

The seriousness of his academic purpose was reenforced by the calibrated background that appeared in most of the photographs. But his choice of action for analysis suggests that entertainment (at least his own) was not a neglected factor. For instance, he titled three series of studies this way:

No. 406: Two models pouring bucket of water over one.
No. 464: Two models chasing another with a broom.
No. 977: Relinquishing drapery for nature's garb.

Although his work at the University of Pennsylvania was distinguished by adequate academic prestige, Muybridge's personal work books (now in the George Eastman House collection) reveal that he had not forsaken thoughts of showmanship. Notations in the "Remarks" column after some of his photo studies specify "Zoopraxiscope" or "Zoopraxiscopic." Examining these specially designated photographs, one finds that, unlike his other models, these were fully clothed and that they were photographed against a plain white background rather than the usual calibrated black wall.

Most of Muybridge's nude female models were recruited from among Pittsburgh's prostitutes. The photographer kept scrupulous records of the amount of time each model spent on his project. It is perhaps unworthy of note that the nude female models were employed much longer than any of the males.

Muybridge used his Zoopraxiscopic productions to liven up his show at the Chicago World's Fair of 1893. The fair included among its attractions an entire Zoopraxigraphical Hall.

The spectacular success of Muybridge's projections for the San Francisco Art Association and for the public in May of 1880 was widely reported. It was news that stimulated scientists throughout Europe. In Germany and Austria, Franz Uchatius, Ottomar Anschuetz, Max Skladanowski and Oskar Messter made pioneering advances as did Casimir Sivan in Switzerland.

As French scientists had seeded the development of photography itself, some of them assumed leading roles in motion picture history. Professor Marey, specialist in the study of movement, aided by his resourceful mechanic, Demeny, made significant progress. Léon Bouly

patented an apparatus he called the Cinématographe in 1893, two years
before the Lumières contributed their own Cinématographe.

Just as Daguerre in 1839 achieved the earliest effective and practical
system of photography, it was in France, thanks to the brothers
Lumière, Auguste and Louis, that workable and ingenious solutions to
the riddle of cinematography were devised.

The Lumière Cinématographe was at once a camera, a printer and
a projector using 35mm perforated film so good that some of it from
1898 still exists at Eastman House, unfaded and without deterioration.
The fact that the Lumières were established manufacturers of photographic materials placed them in a favorable position to pursue the challenge posed by Edison's rather incomplete Kinetoscope apparatus.

Louis Lumière was a man of exceptional ingenuity, with wide experience in experimental photography. The preeminence of his Cinématographe in the beginning years of the motion picture was soon
established although the international fame of Thomas Edison pro-
longed the life of the Kinetoscope far beyond its practical value.

The French public had an early look at moving pictures by the
Lumières in December 1895. On that initial Lumière program, the
alarming scene of a locomotive rushing at the spectators and the new
sensation of watching breaking waves and ocean spray while indoors,
comfortable in their chairs, provided the astonished Parisians with a
memorable experience. The Lumières had powerfully enhanced the
miracle provided the world by Daguerre fifty-six years before.

In their first year of film production, with most of their filming done
by Francis Doublier, the pioneer of pioneer cameramen, the Lumières
staked out most areas of cinema: reportage, sensation, comedy, personal
movies and "made-up" subjects. The second year would see them sending cameramen to various parts of the world recording such news events
as the coronation of the tsar in Russia and the inauguration of President
McKinley in Washington.

In 1895, the earliest year of its practical existence, cinema arrived at a
fateful crossroads in its destiny: two divergent directions that would forever separate its most enthusiastic supporters into opposite camps of pref-
erential interest. It was the Lumières' international hit film *L'Arroseur
Arrosé*, variously known as *Watering the Gardener* or *Sprinkling the Sprin-
kler*, that brought about the great schism. Up to the making of this film the
Lumières had produced only actualities. This time they decided to create
their own situation and to direct its participants; in short, it was a staged,
acted production, a story film. And a comedy.

The other Lumière films had provoked wonder, amazement, even fright. But *L'Arroseur Arrosé* evoked laughter and delight. The enduring source of devotion to cinema was born with this little movie; it was not just that it was a comedy, but that in its primitive way, it told a story that didn't *really* happen that way but that *could* have happened as it was imagined. Creativity came to the cinema with the Lumières' *L'Arroseur.*

In the world of magic, the name of France's Robert Houdin still designates the foremost wizard of the nineteenth century. In Paris it became the role of Georges Méliès to keep blazing the fires of imagination and the brilliance of the master's prestidigitatorial skills. Ambitious and resourceful, Méliès presided in the Théâtre Robert-Houdin as a formidable successor to the great magician.

The brothers Lumière had no magic in mind when they presented Paris with its first look at their Cinématographe. It was an urge to document reality that drove them to perfect their marvelous Cinématographe, which filmed images of such unimaginative events as the arrival of locomotives, the departure of rowboats, the charge of glitteringly uniformed cuirassiers and the Lumière baby at breakfast. But seeing photographs in movement, noting the spray of breaking ocean waves and the smoke curling from leaf fires, all larger than life on a picture screen, provided intense excitement to Parisians who had never before experienced "life-motion'd pictures." But Georges Méliès was the most excited Parisian of all. To him, as a professional conjuror, the newborn Cinématographe was the ideal magic box he'd long hoped for. It easily outstripped every magical device he or Robert Houdin had ever produced. With accurate foresight, he suspected that in the hands of a professional magician, the new movie machine could achieve wonders never dreamed of by its inventors.

Méliès implored the Lumières to sell him a Cinématographe. They declined, citing a benign concern for the eager proprietor of the Théâtre Robert-Houdin. Cinema, they insisted, would never amount to much theatrically, and Georges would go broke if he tried to make pictures himself.

Not to be put off, Méliès built his own movie camera and by 1898 he was busy making films. Before the century ended, he had already put his camera through every movie magic trick the medium was ever to learn. He did double and multiple exposures, animation, stop motion, slow and fast motion, wipes, fades and dissolves.

Early in his work, Méliès found there was a curious problem about camera illusion. It was during the shooting of a street scene that he discovered stop motion. He'd stopped cranking his camera for a few moments, then started again in the same setup. When he printed and projected the scene, there were horse-drawn cabs and pedestrians suddenly appearing right there on the Avénue de l'Opéra where, only an instant before, they hadn't been. He was delighted with the trick but was disappointed to find his audience didn't regard the effect as properly *magical.*

For magic, Méliès realized he had to take his movie camera back into his studio. Actual cabs and familiar buildings wouldn't do. He had to go back to painting backdrops with wild and improbable scenes. He had to set a stage with fantastic props and then let his camera perform all those glorious deceptions he found it could create. He called one of his early hits *Fantastic Illusions* and his patrons acclaimed those illusions as delightful magic. And none was more magical or more acclaimed than his amazing *l'Homme de Têtes* of 1898.

Méliès cast himself as a banjoist who removes his head and places it on a table where it keeps moving by itself. He grows other heads, finally having four separate tabled heads, each moving in a manner different from the others. Annoyed, perhaps by their lack of harmony, he bashes them all.

Firmly established by 1895, the great marvel of the nineteenth century made its way with the speed of a virus, amazing and exciting all parts of the world that could supply any kind of electrical current to operate projectors. In Britain there were inspired inventors and showmen who made their pioneering contributions. England had Robert Paul, who created some fine trick cinematography, like his *Motorist* of 1899 wherein an auto is driven along the ring around Saturn.

Only in Ireland did they seem indifferent to the furor of moving pictures. The everyday lives of the Irish were so filled with magic and illusions, with the commonplaces of banshees, pixies, gremlins and leprechauns, that they found nothing particularly remarkable about the illusory images of cinema. It is said that one who ventured inside a hopeful nickelodeon in Dublin to have a look at the vaunted new wonder of the world reported to one of the few idly curious Irishmen loitering outside with the comment "Aw, it ain't nothin'. Just a bunch of people walkin' on the walls."

Britain's most important contributor to filmmaking was unquestionably James Williamson, who stumbled on two of the most basic essentials of creative cinema: editing and the close-up. Williamson's twin discoveries happened in 1901 in the film he called *A Big Swallow*. In it he has a reluctant still-camera subject approaching nearer and nearer to the camera until he appears to swallow the camera and photographer, munching both as he retreats from the scene.

Williamson's trick film was outstandingly popular but regarded by competing cameramen of the time as being too difficult technically for the imitation, which was the usual procedure that resulted in the appearance of a successful picture. Without the follow-focus devices of modern cameras, it was necessary for Williamson to construct a bellows extension to achieve his famous close-up that becomes ever larger until the whole screen is filled only with the subject's mouth.

A Big Swallow consists of only three shots: the approaching, protesting man; the photographer and his portrait camera as both are seen toppling into blackness; and, third, the swallower backing off. According to Williamson, who responded to requests for an account of how he managed to achieve the effect, the middle scene was made some time after the shots of the advancing and retreating subject. The second scene, which had been shot last, was only put in its place when the negatives were prepared for making positive prints. Thus Williamson, by 1901, had discovered the principle of film editing, had created filmic time and had brought to the medium its earliest full-frame close-ups.

A decade later, David Wark Griffith believed that he had invented the close-up. And film editing and the moving camera and even restrained acting. Griffith staked out his claim to the "invention" of all these basic elements of cinematic art by taking out an ad in the *New York Dramatic Mirror* of December 3, 1913. And such is the power of the printed word, and so rarely have pre-1913, non-Griffith films figured in preserved study collections, that too many historians have believed Griffith's preposterous claim.

In considering the effectiveness of the silent film both in the past and in present-day reexamination, one can think of some great films deficient or even totally lacking in good cutting, in photographic quality, in lighting, in story construction; in short, lacking nearly every device known to cinema, save only one: the close-up.

Multiple exposures, dissolves, wipes, fades, crosscutting—all of these might never have come to the film, and without them but with the close-up alone, it is possible to think of the movies reaching the astonishing degree of emotional impact that they did. For if the technological achievements of photography and the intermittent movements of cameras and projectors were able to give the illusion of life to the screen, it was the close-up that gave the medium its soul. A mysterious soul exemplified by the shimmering images of a Greta Garbo, Clara Bow, Asta Nielsen or Louise Brooks.

I will even go so far as to suggest that there has never been a great film without close-ups. In fact, a great film was never made *until* close-ups came into general use. All that the silent film contributed, apart from what it borrowed from the theatre (settings, movement and arrangement of the players), from the graphic arts (composition, spatial concepts, lighting) and from music (rhythmic cutting), is embodied in the close-up.

In the close-up the motion picture is in its own world. Only in the close-up can the cinema practice the utter concentration, employ the power of emphasis, the artistry of selection and the magic of revelation, strengths that are all unique to the medium.

It is in the close-up that the film player enters a realm of acting undreamed of in the whole tradition of theatre. The pitiless demands of the enormously magnified image shattered the hopes of many of the theatre's best people when they turned to film. In a large measure it was the overpowering intimacy of the close-up that turned film watchers into something approaching drug addicts as they flowed, ninety million of them every week, to the movies of North America during the greatest years of the silent drama.

Carl Theodor Dreyer, the internationally acclaimed Danish director of *La Passion de Jeanne d'Arc* (1928)

Not that all other factors of filmic construction were unimportant, but they had less to do with the effectiveness of the silent film than did the close-up. Cutting, continuity and lighting all modified the motion picture but the close-up characterized it.

Carl Dreyer, the famous Danish director, was fully aware of this unique power. He wrote:

> Nothing in the world can be compared to the human face. It is a land one can never tire of exploring. There is no greater experience in a studio than to witness the expression of a sensitive face under the mysterious power of inspiration. To see it animated from inside and turning into poetry.

Thanks to the pioneering of Muybridge, Méliès, the Lumières and Williamson, the motion picture entered the twentieth century equipped with all its basic properties: editing, close-up, multiple exposures, speed alterations, sound and dialogue, moving camera, large screens, even surrounding screens. The essentials were all there. The next fifty years would be devoted only to refinements.

CHAPTER 2

An Art Déclassé

The movies had no trouble leaping from being a cheap novelty to becoming one of the world's biggest businesses. But film has had great difficulty in getting the serious attention of the academic world. It has been even harder to gain any kind of respect in the rarefied world of art. The motion picture was born on the wrong side of the tracks. In fact, it was born *on* the track, the one owned by Governor Leland Stanford. But consider the competing entertainments: drama, classical music, dance and, to some extent, painting. Their antecedents were connected with religion, with the mystic rituals of worship. When drama finally separated itself from the church and began to deal with raunchy representations of less-than-spiritual life, the theatre suffered from the reformers, those ever-negative individuals who frowned so forbiddingly on plays that eventually drama was banned completely and for survival had to disguise itself by hiding in clouds of formal music. Opera became surreptitious drama and in the sumptuous surroundings of the opera house, women and even their children could be exposed to tales of adultery, miscegenation and murder, all those overemphasized facets of sexuality. The dramatic evils were made acceptable as long as they were purified by music.

Consider the early differences in presentation, the contrast between the dingy nickelodeons and the concert halls and opera houses glittering in their bright lights, their architecture not too far removed from that of churches. How could the movies compete in respectability with the opulence of the symphony hall where the elite could meet, elegant in formal attire, women in their designer gowns, men in tails and white ties, more resplendently dressed than the performers.

The attitudes engendered by those contrasts in the formative years of cinema persisted for decades. As late as the mid-1930s, when I was going to school in Heidelberg, I remember the old professor, the head of the household where I was boarding, when he found out that I was very much concerned with motion pictures and was actually studying them, marveled at so curious a pursuit and boasted that he never went to the movies. When I asked him why, he replied, "Well, you go to a concert, you get all dressed up; you meet your friends in a brightly lighted

Twenty-seven years before *The Jazz Singer* there were talkies in Paris at the Expo of 1900.

hall. It's like going to a formal party; it's all so pleasant, a celebration. You go to a movie, you don't even take off your overcoat. People huddle in the dark. You never see one another, you don't know who's there. It's almost a shameful, furtive kind of activity." Obviously the good doctor hadn't been slinking into movies for a long time or he would have noticed that the picture palaces in Germany and much of Europe in the mid-1930s rivaled any of the most gaudy opera houses. He might have been impressed, too, by the fact that most of Europe's greatest theatre artists were much quicker to lend their talents to film than were their counterparts in the United States. Unlike its humble status here, film got some powerful boosts in Europe. Sarah Bernhardt and Coquelin, France's two greatest theatrical luminaries at the turn of the century, appeared in sound films at the 1900 Paris Exposition. Cléo de Mérode (popularly called Cléopold, as the alleged mistress of the king of Belgium) was seen to be doing a few delicate dance steps on film at the same expo. Giants of the Teutonic theatre such as Max Reinhardt, Albert Bassermann and Leopold Jessner all made early films.

But there was this feeling among self-professed intellectuals of both Europe and the United States throughout the 1930s and persisting into the 1940s that there was something not quite respectable about the medium of motion pictures. At least not when compared with the elegance and prestige enjoyed by classical music, by opera and dance. How did this come to be? Indeed, cinema had no illustrious antecedents. Movies were a mixture of science, physiology and illusion; they were suspect from their very beginning. Not only suspect. Films were underpriced. Imagine, an activity that cost the public only five cents for three hours of entertainment! Like shopping in Woolworth's five-and-dime instead of Bergdorf Goodman's. Imagine an entertainment that was immediately accessible to the illiterate, to the immigrants who hadn't yet learned the language of their new home but who were perfectly able to understand the nuances of pantomime that they encountered in the nicolets, the nickelodeons, those unpretentious little halls where the movies first met their public.

As for those elaborately mounted concerts, probably one out of ten who attends a concert really isn't devoted to music, but is concerned instead about establishing a respectable position in the community. If one aspires to become a prestige leader in his city, there are certain things he is required to do. Regular church attendance is one of them, along with supporting the Philharmonic and making a soigné appearance regularly in the concert hall. It's strange what with all that peer pressure that symphony orchestras are always in financial trouble, teetering on the edge of bankruptcy and ever begging for contributions beyond the price of admission. Has the motion picture ever had to beg the public for that kind of support? "The most wanted art," as someone has called film, has needed no help other than in the area of acceptance in the fields of arts and letters.

Such support came rarely. It was an extraordinary boost when one of America's most popular poets, Vachel Lindsay, was audacious enough to publish a book in 1915 that he called *The Art of the Moving Picture*. Not only did he dare to discuss film as an art form, but he actually included a poem he had written extolling the artistry of film actress Blanche Sweet. He went even further, comparing the film image of Mary Pickford to a Botticelli angel!

Lindsay's book challenged the literary world and the art world by respecting cinema sufficiently to suggest its inclusion within the precious band of arts. The appearance of *The Art of the Moving Picture* marked the beginning of a controversy that was to endure for many years. Before 1920 there were few champions of the idea of considering the movies as a form of art. Filmmakers themselves were uneasy with the idea. "The movies are simply an entertainment," insisted many spokesmen of the industry who didn't want to find themselves involved in the rarefied atmosphere of "is it or isn't it art." As long as people kept coming to see their films, they didn't care what they were called by the poets or the professors. But many who went regularly to the predialogue movies did so without having much respect for them, calling films everything from "moom pitchas" to "the flicks," "galloping tintypes" or "Old-Time movies." General benign contempt even showed up in the lyrics of popular music. Irving Berlin wrote a song called "If That's Your Idea of a Wonderful Time, Take Me Home." The cover of the sheet music showed a girl standing in front of a nickelodeon box office, protesting to her date. When the talkies began to appear, there was a song called "I Can't Sleep Anymore in the Movies." A big hit was "Take Your Girlie to the Movies If You Can't Make Love at Home" that suggested not much attention was being paid to what was on the screen.

Silent movies? Before sound films nobody called motion pictures "silent movies." In those days the term "talkies" was already in use, but it referred only to plays on the stage to differentiate them from photoplays. As Lillian Gish never tired of pointing out, the "silent" film was never silent. Even in the primitive period, there was a pianist or an organist putting music to the film. The big downtown theatres usually began continuous showings at 10:00 a.m. Until the two evening performances, the film would be accompanied by a skillful organist seated at the mighty Wurlitzer. The evening shows boasted full orchestral accompaniment. The musicians were fine, well-paid professionals led by experts who knew very much what they were about. The top Cleveland movie orchestra was conducted by Maurice Spitalny in gleaming full dress, his exquisitely prepared profile turned toward the audience and bathed in his own special spotlight as his orchestra played the overture before the film began. Maurice was one of three Russian-born Spitalnys, all musicians. Brother Phillip conducted a famous all-girl orchestra in Manhattan. He went to Cleveland often to see his brother, whose greeting to Phillip became a local catchphrase: "Hallo, Pheel! How you fill?"

Leo Spitalny, after radio broadcasting came into being, was involved with directing studio orchestras. In broadcasting, of course, time became a crucial factor, and Morrie Secon, one of Leo's musicians for a time, tells about the Spitalny system for making the music come out just right. "The second ending we call it when we play it faster. When I put it up just one finger, it means dun't play the second ending. If I put it up two fingers, dun't play the first ending."

For sure, music belonged with the movies, and music of some sort *always* went with them in public presentations. Not so, alas, anymore. Professors often presume to show their film classes what the predialogue film was like by exhibiting seventh-generation, pallid dupes of 16mm prints run at the wrong speed on a small screen and without music. They might as well look at a videotape on a TV set and imagine that they're seeing something like the original work.

There are some major ingredients that militate against the chance of present-day film students being able to appreciate the strengths of silent cinema. One of the two most formidable hazards is the projection of early films at speeds far slower than their makers intended to have them shown.

But there is a factor even more damaging to the acceptance and appreciation of the really creative achievements reached by some directors working with silent films. It is unfortunately true that in the early days of movies there existed widespread cynicism in the film industry about the average intelligence of the audience. The main concern then of popular filmmaking was to ensure that the audience, considered

Even on location for *A Woman of the World* (1925), Pola Negri is kept in the mood by the studio trio.

something less than cretinous, should have every development in the plot laid out in utterly unmistakable terms. Should there be the slightest possibility of doubt, ambiguity was removed with an explanatory title.

Since film is still "the most wanted art," today's average film student is a cinematically sophisticated being. Today's filmmakers are aware of this and are no longer contemptuous of their prospective audiences. Quite the reverse. A "classy" film is now crammed with ambiguities and audience-flattering inferences. Nurtured on such fare, the college film student comes to class, is shown a Griffith "masterpiece" and is told by his instructor that the film is the greatest work the silent era produced. The student must conclude either that his professor is incompetent or that, if the Griffith represents the best, the competition must surely be unwatchable.

Writers and professors have long been guilty of perpetuating absolutely false perspectives regarding the films of D. W. Griffith and Erich von Stroheim so utterly irrational as to be comparable only to religious fanaticism. This statement is no wild exaggeration. Consider the statements made by the late Theodore Huff, then professor of American film history at New York University, on the occasion of the thirtieth anniversary of Griffith's 1916 *Intolerance*. Professor Huff wrote,

> *Intolerance* is the greatest motion picture ever produced. In its original form, and properly presented, it is a masterpiece of creative conception and execution which ranks with such works of art as Beethoven's Ninth Symphony, Rembrandt's Descent from the Cross, DaVinci's Mona Lisa, the sculptures of the Parthenon, or with the works of literature such as Tolstoy's *War and Peace*, the poetry of Walt Whitman, Thomas Hardy's *The Dynasts* or Shakespeare's *Hamlet*.

For many years the British publication *Sight and Sound* has been one of the most respected (and sensible) of the journals devoted to motion pictures. In a special index series, Seymour Stern, formerly editor of *Experimental Cinema*, in the April 1944 issue did an index to the films of Griffith. His work is inundated with hyperbole. For example:

> David Wark Griffith, the most influential and prolific genius this medium has yet known, exercised the most profound and far-reaching influence on both motion picture and motion picture audiences that has so far been achieved by any one single person.

The near-hysterical devotion to Griffith has not slackened over the years. As recently as 1980, Anthony Slide in *Fifty Great Silent Films* went way overboard:

> There can be little question that *Intolerance* is the greatest motion picture of the silent era if not the greatest motion picture in the history of the cinema. That one man could have conceived of a production such as *Intolerance* is staggering: that one man could have brought the conception to fruition despite tremendous odds, both technical and financial, seems impossible. It has stood the test of time and will continue to stand the test of time as a monument to a man who first understood that film was not just an industry but an art, a man with unswerving faith in human decency and a firm understanding of human frailty, a self-taught man with a message, and a man who was the first to present a film audience not with what it wanted to know, but what it should experience and should be aware of. *Intolerance* is *the* milestone of the silent film and D. W. Griffith *the* milestone director.

The truth about *Intolerance* is quite the opposite. In fact, not until Michael Cimino's *Heaven's Gate* in 1980 would there be such a mon-

Miriam Cooper was unforgettable in Griffith's *The Mother and the Law* (1916).

strous and epic failure. At its time *Intolerance* was reviled by most critics and ignored by a public that was repeatedly warned away by contemporary reviews. *Intolerance* includes two complete feature films, *The Mother and the Law* and *The Fall of Babylon*. Griffith scrambled them together with a short section about the Saint Bartholomew Day massacre in France and a quickie version of the Crucifixion.

With his *Sun Play of the Ages*, as he subtitled his film, Griffith hoped to present an epic denunciation of modern and historical intolerance as a kind of overkill answer to the thousands of intolerant protesters who,

with some notable successes, sought to prevent the showing of his preceding film, *The Birth of a Nation.*

Many critics who had exhausted all their store of hyperbole in prais-
ing *The Birth of a Nation* expressed either hostility or disappointment on
seeing *Intolerance. Intolerance* suffered a fate much worse than the still
prevailing controversies that discourage the showing of *The Birth of a
Nation;* the public failed to turn out to watch *Intolerance* while they
fought to be admitted to *The Birth of a Nation.*

Seen as a separate film *The Mother and the Law* was as good as anything Griffith had ever created. *The Fall of Babylon* was spectacle that
dwarfed in sheer size any movie sets ever built before it, outnumbered
the gigantic crowds assembled by the Italians in their vast movie mob
scenes. But Griffith's notion that he could stir bits and pieces of both
these films together with shots of Protestants being slaughtered by
Catholics and Jesus Christ being crucified, all under a blanket indict-
ment of "intolerance," was an error in both philosophy and aesthetics.

The Mother and the Law was about struggles between capital and
labor and the injustice of the legal system. Any concept of blaming those
problems, along with the fall of Babylon, on intolerance had to stretch a
definition of that term as far as it had to be extended to include what
happened to Jesus Christ.

In any case, such of the public as did go to see *Intolerance* found the
intercutting of all those stories more confusing than exciting.

No question but that in the popular mind, as well as in the opinion
of most film people, David Wark Griffith did occupy a position of
unchallenged supremacy reaching to the extreme notion of being "the
father of motion picture art." By now he has arrived at the godlike status of such national monuments as Thomas Edison, who is thought to
have invented not only electric light but the phonograph and moving
pictures, along with George Eastman, who "invented" cameras and film;
Mathew Brady, who "photographed" the Civil War; Benjamin Franklin,
who discovered bathtubs and electricity and George Washington, who
invented not telling lies.

There are factors that brought Griffith to this legendary status quite
apart from the cumulative reputation of his cinematic creations. First of
all and many months before the appearance of *The Birth of a Nation* in
1915, there was that December 3, 1913, Griffith ad in the *New York Dramatic Mirror.* That extravagant ad, unabashedly proclaiming his own
greatness with all the cavalier disregard of facts that one usually associ-

D. W. Griffith and his veteran cameraman, Billy Bitzer, are in the snows of New Jersey.

ates with political campaign claims, was noticed by most persons involved in any way with making or marketing motion pictures.

Since Griffith was not running for any office, there was little reason for anyone to seriously doubt the claims Griffith was making for himself—other than the grandiose nature of the statements. In 1913 filmgoers were unaware of the names of any motion picture directors. Griffith's ad was designed to change that.

The copy began with "D. W. Griffith" alone, on the top line, in heavy boldface. Then followed this introduction:

> Producer of all great Biograph successes, revolutionizing Motion Picture drama and founding the modern technique of the art

Did the "great Biograph successes" really revolutionize "Motion Picture drama"? Certainly Griffith's present-day biographers and admirers would have us think so. But it has been my own good fortune to have seen almost every Biograph film that has been preserved, starting with releases from the summer of 1908, when Griffith began directing. I have had in my own collection some Griffith Biographs that are still not present in the Museum of Modern Art collection, which has been the largest single archive of Biograph films. Examining the Biograph films that appeared from the summer of 1908 and comparing them with the films from Denmark, Germany and France simply does not show them to be anything like revolutionizing vehicles.

Granted, some of the Biograph titles were outstanding and showed their maker had exceptional gifts of visual showmanship. But there were just as many foolish, routine and crude Biograph releases as there were primitive and ludicrous productions coming from other American sources at the time.

In one area Griffith did seem to be ahead of his contemporaries: by either good luck or superior perception, he was able to recruit a cadre of fantastic players. With his theatre orientation, he had confidence in even the actresses who had been professionals from childhood, so that Mary Pickford, the Gish sisters and Blanche Sweet became Biograph stars. Experience in the theatre was cachet sufficient for Griffith to hire Lionel Barrymore, Tom Ince and Mack Sennett, all of whom graduated from Biograph to major film careers that endured for many years.

There were indeed some truly impressive Biographs. As early as 1909 Griffith had Pickford, Owen Moore and James Kirkwood acting in

The Restoration, an involved psychological drama concerned with memory loss. But on the other hand, as late as 1913 in *Broken Ways* with Blanche Sweet and Harry Carey, Griffith directed Henry B. Walthall in an acrobatic death scene as crudely hilarious as anything ever captured on motion picture film. An ironic achievement from the director who that very year in his ad claimed that he had introduced "restraint in expression" to the motion picture.

Was Griffith unaware that his somewhat obsessive direction of his actresses was damagingly lacking in restraint? His heroines were made to simper, scamper and skitter. As Mary Pickford put it, "He always wanted us to jump around, finding rabbits behind trees." Nor were critics of the day blind to this peculiar weakness of the great director. In reviewing *The Greatest Thing in Life* in the March 1919 issue of *Motion Picture*, Hazel Simpson Clark wrote:

> In producing another war picture Griffith does nothing big or unusual enough to justify our confidence in his being the greatest director . . . Little Lillian Gish is shown to beautiful advantage in three or four closeups . . . The rest of the time she jumps "ingenuishly" all over the place. The charm of Lillian is a very poignant thing and should not be tampered with in this manner, no matter how great the director.

Without making the arbitrary distinction between feature films and shorts, the predialogue history of cinema readily sorts itself into two periods: the 1895 to 1912 era when single-reel productions dominated the field, and the years after 1912, when multireel works became ever more common until they commanded a major portion of critical and popular attention.

During the years from 1908 to 1914 Griffith certainly did create many impressive works and his heroines were not always scampering "ingenuishly." In 1912 Griffith had Claire McDowell, Mary Pickford and Dorothy Bernard in his *Female of the Species* playing memorably tough and dangerous women close to becoming murderous until the saving presence of an abandoned baby reminds them of their maternal selves. In that same year he did *A Feud in the Kentucky Hills*, again with Pickford, supported by Henry Walthall and the handsome Walter Miller, Harry Carey and even young Jack Pickford. It was a vigorous, intelligent film, as was *The Informer*, also in 1912, with Pickford, Walthall, Lionel Barrymore and Lillian Gish. Indeed, 1912 was a zenith year for Griffith, notwithstanding an occasional grotesquerie like his 1913 *Broken Ways* which had Henry Walthall shot and dying as though

he were doing a ballet solo. The important point is that the best of Griffith was no better than Thanhouser's *Cry of the Children* or Edison's *Land
Beyond the Sunset*.

In 1911 Asta Nielsen's pictures began to arrive in this country. The
contribution of Asta Nielsen to the art of acting was profound and lasting; she was the first great actress of the screen whose work commanded
the respect accorded to talented performers of the theatre.

Before World War I, Asta Nielsen, a Dane, with her husband, the
director Urban Gad, were making films in Germany. Early signs of
maturity and primary examples of naturalistic acting had appeared in
Danish and Russian films a good ten years before such qualities could be
found in any abundance in the primitive movies of the rest of the world.
The Danish group in Berlin (directors Stellan Rye and Urban Gad and
the players Viggo Larsen, Olaf Foenss and Asta Nielsen) helped rescue
the German film from the infantilism that marked its tardy beginnings.
Apparently *Gypsy Blood* in 1911 was the first of Neilsen's films to arrive
in this country. Reviewers hailed its Danish star as "the German Bernhardt." In 1914 *The Girl Without a Fatherland*, which had been made in
1912, was shown in this country under the title *A Romany Spy*. It is significant that in the United States the Nielsen films of 1912 were being
seen along with the best of Griffith in 1914. At that period in film history, a difference of two years could be enormous. Yet the Nielsen films
of 1912 were described by reviewers as masterpieces. In the *Moving Picture World* of March 12, 1914, W. Stephen Bush wrote of *A Romany Spy*:
"the part of the gypsy girl was taken by Asta Nielsen and it may safely be
said that this gifted woman never played with more art. She portrays the
awakening of love in a woman's heart with an inspiration which amounts
to genius. This is indeed a masterpiece."

Earlier in 1914, Hanford Judson, in the *Moving Picture World*,
reviewed *Behind Comedy's Mask*, which had been made in 1913. Mr. Judson was almost moved to lyricism:

> Miss Nielsen has put the naturalness of truth into her picture . . . with
> one emotion in it opening the door to another. In her clown's queer
> dress she has not a whisper of direct help in her portrayal of grief. Her
> dress and make-up are both against her; but as Asta Nielsen makes the
> grief-stricken mother rush from the theater to the bedside and pray in
> her agony, it is like a cry from the depths of the spirit. The impression
> rings true with no counter suggestions and is carried to us solely by
> facial expressions. Here is passion without the rags. There is no clawing
> of the air; but a soul being wound up on the wheel of pain before us.

(Left) Asta Nielsen of Denmark was an international star by 1911; (below) as Hamlet, 1920

The Danish *Atlantis* (1913) was a grim reenactment of the 1912 sinking of the *Titanic*.

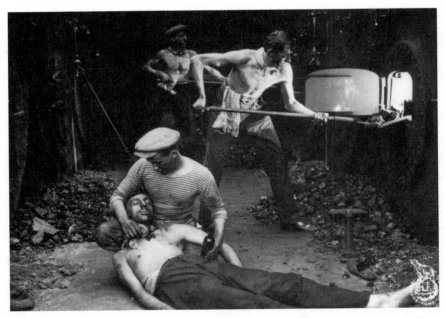

Blom's *Atlantis* from Denmark was adapted by Gerhardt Hauptmann. The film had no rival in 1913 for its effective visuals.

Asta Nielsen created more than forty-five film roles; many of them are glowing performances that still illumine the motion picture's past. She appeared as Strindberg's Julie and Wedekind's Lulu. For the silent drama she acted the complex characters created by Stendhal and Ibsen. It is not surprising that students seeing her early films are struck with their Garboesque quality, for in Pabst's *Joyless Street*, Garbo, in her second film, shared honors with veteran Asta Nielsen, whose films Garbo had been admiring for ten years.

For me, Asta Nielsen's performance as Hamlet is far more moving than that of Laurence Olivier. Even with the advantages of Shakespeare's verse, Olivier seemed to me far less a haunted and melancholy Dane than was Asta Nielsen in her silent *Hamlet* of 1920.

In 1913 August Blom in Denmark filmed *Atlantis* in eight reels. The cinematography in this super production makes the film look as though it had been made in 1928. The Gerhardt Hauptmann script calls for the sinking of a passenger liner and the handling of that disaster is as skillful as was achieved in any of the much later films dealing with the sinking of the *Titanic*. Blom's shots of the grimy stokers coaling the boilers in the smoky hold are in every way comparable in lighting and camera angles to the superb rendering of those Dantean scenes by Josef von Sternberg in his magnificent 1928 *The Docks of New York*.

But the real trailblazer, better than all the above, was a French triumph: Léonce Perret's astounding *Child of Paris*, made in 1910. This vigorous tale of a kidnapping and rescue featured startling depth of focus, moving camera shots and low-angle interiors with ceilings. It continues a dramatic pace for a full ninety minutes!

Brainwashed as they were by the myth of Griffith's greatness, American critics still marvelled at the brilliance of many of the films arriving from France, Germany and Scandinavia in those early and formative years. Present-day writers should make a point of looking at them before declaring that D. W. Griffith was the greatest director of the silent period. The fact is that some Griffith admirers *refuse* to examine existing prints that might bring Griffith's superiority into question. Although the Museum of Modern Art holds negatives of Collins' *The Stoning* with Viola Dana and Edison's *Land Beyond the Sunset*, *Land Beyond the Sunset* was made in 1912 by an anonymous director. It is a haunting film of an abused slum child who is finally reached by a social worker, bemused by her tales of some glorious land of peace and hope somewhere just over the horizon and sets sail in a tiny boat alone on the empty ocean. The film prompted wild enthusiasm and wonder among

the viewers, especially from Bill Everson, who has never tired of prais-
ing the poetic work. In that first viewing group, only Eileen Bowser of
the Museum of Modern Art, indefatigable admirer and biographer of
Griffith, professed to detest the film. Why? She gave no reasons, but
obviously it weakened the Griffith myth and all but destroyed the then
prevailing feeling that Edison films were dull and unimportant when
compared with the Biograph releases.

Along with *The Birth of a Nation* and *Intolerance, Broken Blossoms* of
1919 is one of Griffith's major efforts on which much of his fame rests.
The original release print of the film was elaborately colored with the
use of variously tinted base stock. The Museum of Modern Art Film
Library people arranged to undertake the demanding and expensive
project of copying the film and restoring the delicately colored version
to something very much like the original.

In a significant departure from routine filmmaking, Griffith rehearsed
the cast for weeks before the camera ever turned. His aim was to create a
film that he thought would be as fine and important as a great play on
the stage—his first love. However well intentioned his plan, his theatrical orientation lured him into a major aesthetic error that militates
against one's acceptance of the film today as a great work. Richard
Barthelmess, cast as a Chinese in London's Limehouse district, is made
up as a stereotyped stage Chinaman, eyes narrowed to tiny slits, hands
tucked into his sleeves and made to walk hunched over with teetering
steps. All perfectly acceptable as a nineteenth-century theatrical cliché.
But Griffith made the mistake of surrounding Barthelmess with real
Chinese, none of whom looked anything like the chief protagonist. In
The Birth of a Nation, Griffith was betrayed by this stagecraft into the
same aesthetic error. His principal players cast as blacks are white actors
and actresses, their faces smeared not too carefully with blackface makeup. Neither of his villains, George Siegmann and Walter Long, have
negroid features. Well and good had he been producing a minstrel show,
but again, extras in the film are real blacks bearing no resemblance to
Tom Wilson, George Siegmann or Walter Long.

The unfortunate effect for *Broken Blossoms* is that the film is neither
realistic drama nor effective theatre make-believe. The famous performance of Lillian Gish's almost rescues the film from being a grotesquerie rather than simply a very much dated melodrama with Donald
Crisp as the savage child beater, shown in enormous close-ups, grimac-
ing in a way to rival King Kong himself.

Griffith considered himself to be a poet, a dramatist and, only some-

In Griffith's *Broken Blossoms* (1919) Richard Barthelmess plays the lead as a traditional stage Chinaman.

A scene from *Broken Blossoms*, with real, nontheatrical Chinese

what reluctantly, a film director. For this project he also became a composer and is credited as the author of the love theme of the film, a piece he titled "White Blossom." Composing the music for the other portions of the film was entrusted to none other than Louis Gottschalk. As a music composer, Griffith thus placed himself in prestigious company.

Lillian Gish's performance as the slow-witted, much abused Limehouse district waif is one of the most praised in all her career. It was also the most parodied. ZaSu Pitts made a whole career imitating the uncertain, desperate gestures that were so touching as Lillian Gish had done them. And as late as 1928 Marion Davies in *The Patsy* does Lillian as the broken blossom so hilariously that for those who have seen it, it becomes difficult if not impossible to watch the original Gish version without amusement.

Griffith's acknowledged masterpiece, *The Birth of a Nation*, presents an extraordinary paradox. It is both outrageous and irresistible. Until the arrival of *Gone With the Wind* in 1939, *The Birth of a Nation* was far and away the box-office champion of all American films and the most famous. It was the first movie I have any recollection of seeing (although it had to have been a revival showing since the film and I went public the same year). Burdened with aesthetic and technical flaws, the picture nevertheless towers far above dozens of superior films in its exceptional effectiveness. Ancient work that it is, and in many respects already old-fashioned in 1915, its emotional power is undiminished whenever it is shown. The passing of many years and the alleged increased sophistication of viewers have not lessened its overpowering attack on watchers' uncontrollable responses.

A dramatic example—a dedicated woman seeking to improve the social climate in Rochester, New York, asked us at Eastman House to arrange a series of film showings that would reflect bigotry. She specified films with antiblack or at least stereotypical content and anti-Semitic movies. Her idea was to bring the congregations of an all-black church and a synagogue together in a series of discussion meetings to be catalyzed by watching such invidious films together. I told her that finding films with insulting black stereotypes was all too easy, but that anti-Semitic films were rare. Even under the Nazi period, I knew of only two, *The Eternal Jew* and *Jew Suess*, and neither one was in the Eastman House archive. But, of course, such a program should begin with a screening of *The Birth of a Nation*.

When the showing was over, the woman sponsoring the project was shaking. "When I came in here tonight," she said in a voice trembling with emotion, "I was an enemy of all censorship and felt that I would be ready to put my life on the line against any threat to freedom of speech or expression." Her voice suddenly grew strong, and she almost shouted: "But *that* film should *never* be shown *anywhere* to *anyone!!*"

The rabbi was pale under his beard. "There I was, sitting in the front row," he marveled, "and to my utter disbelief, I found myself inwardly cheering on the Ku Klux Klan, urging them with all my being to get there on time—nearly falling out of my seat with excitement!"

The blacks in the audience had not one word to say. Not that they were always so reticent about *The Birth of a Nation*. When Eastman House had first scheduled the film for a showing to its Dryden Theatre Film Society, I was visited in my office by a delegation of black ministers and leaders of several black community-action groups. They informed me that the NAACP was firmly on record as opposed to any public exhibition of the film. I asked them if any of them had ever seen the film. Not one had. The spokesman of the group then advised me that if I persisted in the plan to show the film, the chances were very good that

Klansmen were the saviors of the defeated South in *The Birth of a Nation* (1915).

I might not survive the protests of their more activist groups. We did go ahead with the scheduled showing, and there was no sign of any protesters.

Showings of *The Birth of a Nation* in the first years of its existence were rarely unattended by protests. Even though the film was enthusiastically praised by President Woodrow Wilson, its exhibition in the northern states often brought about so much violent protest that finally the film was banned by statute in the state of Ohio.

Long before the film was made, a touring drama based on Thomas Dixon's novel *The Clansmen*, source of Griffith's scenario, had already provoked riots by protesting blacks and sympathetic white liberals, all outraged by the vicious anti-Negro hatred that inflamed both the novel and the play. It should have come as no surprise to Griffith that his film would run into comparable trouble. In its early plans to circulate the films most important to the history of cinema, the Museum of Modern Art of course included *The Birth of a Nation*. But that institution ran into such angry opposition that it decided to withdraw the film from circulation.

There was another hazard to the life of the film at the Museum of Modern Art. The picture quite obviously was sloppily edited by its creator. (The Cameron boy, for instance, in combat for the Confederacy, is clearly seen to die on two different occasions.) Griffith was, in later years, quite aware that most of his films left much to be desired in their cutting. When one of his productions was being exhibited at the Museum of Modern Art (where, of course, he was revered as a kind of cinema saint) he would slip into the projection room and proceed to revise his original editing of the film. He continued this practice so resolutely that finally, saint or no saint, the museum folks were obliged to bar him from the projection room.

Griffith also was burdened by another unfortunate leftover from the crudities of nineteenth-century popular theatre—the conviction that scenes of terror or intense excitement absolutely required comic relief. Most directors skillful at staging effective melodrama were hopelessly inept in their attempts to create comedy. Perhaps the compulsion in American theatre to include comic relief may be traced to a misinterpretation of the drunken porter scene in *Macbeth*. Whatever the reason for it, Griffith marred much of his finest work with the injection of unfunny comedy scenes. *Way Down East*, in many ways Griffith's best film, is still disfigured by the unbearable antics of the rube comedians.

There seems little doubt that Griffith, powerfully influenced by his devotion to traditions of the theatre, consciously strove to elevate the motion picture to a position of comparable prestige. In 1919 he rented the George M. Cohan Theatre in New York to present a spring screen repertoire season (advertised as the first in the history of the world). Griffith's season opened on May 13, 1919, with *Broken Blossoms*, and *The Fall of Babylon* and *The Mother and the Law* were scheduled to follow. It is interesting that three years after the release of *Intolerance*, Griffith himself saw the wisdom of separating those two films from the hash of *Intolerance*.

But it is hard to understand, given the apparent sincerity of his concern, that as late as 1922 Griffith inflicted film history with one of the worst motion pictures ever created: *One Exciting Night.* This is an incredible disaster, rarely, if ever, mentioned by Griffith admirers. Replete with blackface whites romping about as funny and frightened blacks, the film is an embarrassing abomination made by the "greatest" director of silent films.

A comparable distortion exists in the assessment of Erich von Stroheim's films. In *Blind Husbands* he set a pattern that would be extravagantly expanded throughout his career. It took him only a normal seven weeks of shooting to film his own story of lust and betrayal played out in a pre–World War I romantic setting, supposedly the Austrian Dolomites. The sex triangle involved an Austrian officer, played, of course, by Stroheim himself. In the cast was the heavy-bearded English actor Gibson Gowland, whom seven years later Stroheim would cast as McTeague. Working for Universal Pictures, at that time not considered one of the top American producing companies, Stroheim pleased his bosses by putting their company on the map with a sexy and sensational film that caused more comment than earlier Universal productions had generated. Stroheim took a long twelve weeks to complete his second movie, *The Devil's Passkey*, and while *Blind Husbands* was released in an economical eight reels, this second effort ran to an almost unheard-of twelve.

It was with his third effort that Stroheim got the bit between his teeth. *Foolish Wives* took him a staggering eleven months and twenty-one reels to complete. And again, Stroheim filmed himself as an aristocrat—Count Wladislas Karamzin—and spent thousands of dollars over and above what Universal had considered an unusually liberal budget.

Stroheim fancied himself a creative writer, and indeed he actually published a novel, *Paprika*. In its awkward pseudosophistication, the novel betrays the same comic-book creative impulses of a moderately educated refugee. His turgid twenty-one reels of *Foolish Wives* were cut

Erich von Stroheim's fantasy image of himself—
playing the lead in his own *Foolish Wives* (1922).

to fourteen for release. That made a relatively monstrously long movie at a time when the average picture was about seven or eight reels. But in many places where the film was exhibited, the censors had managed to cut as much as 50 percent of the film, bringing its length down to normal running time in most locations.

By 1922, with the release of *Foolish Wives*, Erich von Stroheim had firmly established himself as one of the stormiest petrels of Hollywood. Not only had he happily become "the man you love to hate" as an actor, but he was notorious among the film establishment as an extravagant, temperamental director reluctantly tolerated only because he could be depended upon to garner undreamed of amounts of publicity for the studio that harbored him. Never mind that his films were generally rejected by the public and most of the reviewers—that very rejection has been cited by his fans as proof that the director was ahead of his time.

A large portion of the torrent of publicity surrounding Stroheim and his films was due to the fantastic fictions that he invented for himself. He posed as a former officer in the Austrian army, with his self-affixed "von." Stroheim had never been an officer in any army. He had been a poor Jewish lad who served as a private in Franz Josef's army, and, like every private, he ate his heart out over the cruel social gulf between a private soldier and a career officer (a career, incidentally, forever closed to a Jew in the intensely anti-Semitic Austrian army). How he had longingly studied the arrogance of the monocled officer class, privileged poseurs who could make an elegant production out of just pulling on their long dress-uniform gloves with deliberate slowness. The very removal, polishing and replacing of a monocle could be an act of contemptuous superiority.

Stroheim's invented biographies delivered to interviewers varied with each interview, but each was a typical Stroheim movie script. In one, he confidently claimed that as an Austrian officer he had performed heroically in the Bosnia-Herzegovina campaign. (American journalists had never heard of either location.) He had had to leave Austria, he confessed, because he had been romantically involved with a general's wife.

In an interview published in *Photoplay* magazine (December 1919) Stroheim volunteered specific information. His full name and rank, it was noted, was Count Erich Oswald Hans Carl Maria Stroheim von Nordenwall. His mother, he claimed, was not only a baroness, but was lady-in-waiting to none other than Empress Elizabeth of Austria. His father was a count and colonel in the Sixth Dragoons. "As is the custom," observed the interviewer, "Erich went in for the military." There, in 1908, mounted on horseback, battling in Bosnia, he received a severe sword wound. Recovering, he was made a palace guard. "And then something went wrong" (the general's wife?). He was banished to foreign soil for five years.

Probably nowhere in the world would these wild biographies be accepted as readily as in Hollywood. That community had a special love for skillful phonies. One of the stars' favorite restaurants in Hollywood was run by a false Romanoff. For years everyone knew Mike Romanoff was a fake, but it didn't seem to matter. He was accepted in the role in which he'd cast himself. Stroheim came to this country in 1909, did a hitch in the U.S. Army—as a private, of course—then managed a whole series of lowly jobs: as a stable hand, a dishwasher and finally a Hollywood extra.

In that capacity he caught the attention of John Emerson, who was directing Wallace Reid and Dorothy Gish in *Old Heidelberg* in 1915. Like the other American film directors, Emerson knew nothing about the niceties of dress for the costuming of European royalty. Stroheim was not shy about pointing out errors in the placement of medals and insignia on the uniform jacket of Prince Karl Heinrich. Impressed by Stroheim's assurance, Emerson used him as a technical adviser for all military matters and protocol in the film. Then he was promoted to an important role in the picture—Lutz, the prince's valet.

Stroheim quickly saw where his opportunity lay. He became the super-Teutonic actor and adviser. The time was perfect for him to occupy this special niche. World War I had been raging for a bloody year, and Prussianism was occupying the headlines day after day. In the United States much of the large German-American population was thrilled with pride and admiration for the military exploits of the German army. Others were appalled at the ruthless invasion of Belgium and the burgeoning atrocity stories. For either group, Stroheim became the very embodiment of a German militarist. He was visible, and he was being written about. Whether hated or admired, he was growing ever larger in the public eye, and thus he found himself singularly employable as an actor. When he was in the cast of Griffith's *Intolerance*, the value of using impressive crowds of extras on overwhelmingly gigantic sets was not lost on the ambitious newcomer. The sumptuous settings and milling hordes that burdened Stroheim's first three works when he began to direct his own films were a kind of tribute to his boss on *Intolerance*.

Stroheim's most famous work and the one on which his reputation rests as the great, mistreated genius of ruthless realism is, of course, *Greed*, delayed for many months and finally released in 1925. These days *Greed* is usually presented with disclaimers—it is but a small part of the whole film, it is far from Stroheim's intention. Viewers are forewarned that the great uncompromising genius was betrayed by his studio—his work was taken out of his hands and edited by studio hacks.

If one finds the remaining version of *Greed* fascinating (and many do!), that fascination is largely due to the writing of Frank Norris. Norris, an American original, was a fine author to whose work academia has paid far too little attention. *Greed* was based on Norris' 1899 novel, *McTeague*; it was, in fact, far more than based on *McTeague*.* Few Amer-

---

* *McTeague* had been filmed before Stroheim attempted it. As *Life's Whirlpool*, it was released January 10, 1916. Barry O'Neill directed it, with Fania Marinoff and Holbrook Blinn as the principals.

ican novelists wrote with such scrupulously visual descriptions. For example, here is the passage in which McTeague, an unlicensed dentist, gets the official news that he must give up his practice:

> McTeague had been making fillings when the letter arrived. He was in his "Parlors," pottering over his moveable rack. . . . He heard the postman's step in the hall and saw the envelopes begin to shuttle themselves through the slit of his letter drop. Then came the fat oblong envelope with its official seal that dropped flatwise to the floor with a sodden, dull impact.

McTeague reads the bad news, then goes to the kitchen to inform his wife, Trina.

> She was in the center of the room, wiping off with a damp sponge, the oil-cloth table cover on which they had breakfasted. . . . "What is it, Mac dear?" said Trina. McTeague shut the door with his heel and handed her the letter. Trina read it through. Then suddenly her small hand gripped tightly upon the sponge, so that the water started from it and dripped in a little pattering deluge upon the bricks.

This intense observation by Norris is maintained throughout his novel. Seldom did a moviemaker, in adapting a novel, have anything so close to an actual shooting script as the details provided by Norris in *McTeague*. What Stroheim did was to film that novel, page after page, filming every sentence as it was written in the book. Little wonder that this film as Stroheim first cut it ran to forty-five reels—a running time of nine hours!

Much is made of the "realism" of *Greed*. Yes, it was real. McTeague's dental office was an actual dentist's parlor. Stroheim insisted that Universal buy the building it was in in San Francisco, tear down the wall to expose the dentist's operating room, and there it was—reality itself. His unfortunate actors, Jean Hersholt and Gibson Gowland, had to play out their final scenes in Death Valley in 161-degree heat. From one sequence to the next you can see these suffering actors getting burned darker and darker by the blistering sun, while their director sat under a great beach umbrella being vigorously fanned by members of the sweltering crew.

Realism to Stroheim meant inflicting his studio with preposterous expenses, the results of which are not even visible on the screen. He decreed that on the underwear of every soldier in one of his Ruritanian armies there be embroidered the coat of arms of the royal house served

Gibson Gowland and Jean Hersholt broil in Death Valley for Stroheim's *Greed* (1925).

by the soldiers. Nowhere in the film did any one of those embroidered underpants show up. But Stroheim sought to justify this vast expense by claiming that just knowing he was wearing the coat of arms next to his skin, the extra would *feel* his role of being a royalist soldier.

At one point Stroheim's pursuit of realism got him into real trouble. In one of his continental movies, for a scene in a grand casino, he couldn't have his players handling stage money—it just wouldn't *feel* right to them. The bills had to be real. He hired a counterfeiter to print French francs so accurately that the movie currency began to show up in banks, having been exchanged for genuine United States greenbacks. On July 14, 1920 (Bastille Day!), Stroheim appeared in federal court charged with counterfeiting. Just how Stroheim beat that rap has not been recorded—another one of the great Hollywood cover-ups. But the movie people have always been kind and caring to any con artist among their own. After all, when David Begelman, the head of Columbia's stu-

dio, admitted to both forgery and embezzlement in 1977, the company
adopted as its year's marketing slogan "Forging ahead with Columbia."

Is this prevalent attitude a kind of recognition of the fact that the
industry is involved in a business of illusion and make-believe? So that
any make-believer is readily forgiven—even admired?

It was in his acting roles that Stroheim was able to make all his
dreams come true. In *As You Desire Me* he was able to kiss Garbo brutally and passionately. His role as the German air force officer in Jean
Renoir's *La Grande Illusion* enabled him to act out the finest ever refine-
ment of what an aristocratic officer ought to be. Best of all, on his
deathbed in Paris, where he lived out his last days, the French government presented him with the rosette of a chevalier in the Légion d'Hon-
neur. He had lived to see his whole fantasy become real at last.

But the realism touted in his films is nonexistent. In *Greed* how real
is the fright wig that Gibson Gowland as McTeague must struggle
under? How real is Chester Conklin, the comic-strip German, parading
along the railroad tracks, tiny American flags fluttering in his hatband
while he's followed by a flock of caricatured Katzenjammer Kids—right

Garbo and Stroheim begin a brutal love scene in *As You Desire Me* (1932).

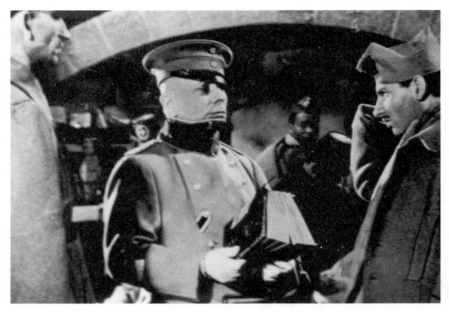

Stroheim's ideal role: the German fortress commander in Renoir's *La Grande Illusion* (1937)

out of the funny papers? So insistent have the pundits been about the superior qualities of Stroheim and Griffith that theirs are the films that have been first preserved, first circulated in the museums and universities, while other directors of those early years have been mostly ignored. For a genuine sense of the history of silent cinema, look at the Thanhouser films of George Nicholls, *The Cry of the Children*, Ince's *The Gangsters and the Girl* and the Asta Nielsen films from Germany directed by Urban Gad, which include *Poor Jenny*, *The Black Dream* and *The Girl Without a Country*. But to praise *Greed*, which appeared in the same year as Chaplin's *The Gold Rush*, King Vidor's *The Big Parade*, Harold Lloyd's *The Freshman*, Clarence Brown's *Smouldering Fires* and Sergei Eisenstein's *Potemkin*—and a whole year later than F. W. Murnau's *The Last Laugh*—does really seem to be a kind of madness.

The other major hazard that the silent film has to overcome as it is exhibited to present-day viewers is incorrect projection speed, which is almost invariably far too slow. The misconception is that there exists a correct standard "silent speed" of sixteen frames per second—another myth that seriously militates against a proper speed adjustment in the increasing transfer of silent films to videotapes. Champions of the false silent speed grow quite heated over the projection of any silent film on a fixed-speed sound projector that runs at twenty-four frames per second.

The historic fact is that more silent films were *intended* to be shown at speeds that were much closer to the sound projector's eleven and two-thirds minutes per reel than the legendary silent speed of sixteen frames per second, which drags the film along at sixteen minutes and forty seconds a reel!

In many, many cases, major silent productions were released with instructions that they be projected at speeds *faster* than current sound speed.

Even beginning film students must realize that most silent films were produced by hand-cranked cameras. Each operator prided himself on his own cadence, believing that regardless of the tempo or the excitement of what he filmed, his hand turned the crank at an unvarying rate with all the precision of a machine.

Precise or not, each cameraman's cadence was different from the other's. Moreover, Ince's scripts of 1912 to 1914 often carried specific instructions to the cameraman to "Crank faster here." How many frames per second was "faster"?

Amateur projectionists confidently believe they are showing *Intolerance* or *Robin Hood* at the speed of sixteen frames per second by switching their projectors to the silent-speed position. Actually, most 16mm projectors having a silent-speed switch are built to run at eighteen frames per second in that position, because at sixteen frames, flicker is quite noticeable.

Showing a 35mm nitrate print as slow as sixteen frames per second on a modern high-powered projector that is geared to run at a variable speed is an invitation to fire. For projectors with an automatic fire shutter, in order to run the film at sixteen frames, operators have been known to wire the fire shutter open so that it *can't* function.

In presenting a silent film to a group of spectators, the program director or the professor should be sure of his purpose. Does he wish (as he often claims) to show the film as it was seen originally? Or does he wish to present the film as its maker intended it to be seen, if that intention is available to his preparation?

If he is seriously reconstructing the conditions of a silent-era showing, he should realize that Douglas Fairbanks' *Robin Hood*, for example, might have been shown in two and a half hours during the slack periods of the day or in a little less than two hours during the evening, to squeeze in an extra show.

If he wants to show *Robin Hood* at the speed originally specified in

1922, he will run it at twelve minutes per reel, which is very close to sound speed. The film will then last two hours and eight minutes.

If it is decided to show *Robin Hood* at the arbitrary sixteen frames per second, the film will last exactly three hours! And this is the way poor *Robin Hood* is usually shown to film society audiences, painfully limping through the forests at a rate that gets him through his adventures a full fifty-two minutes later than Mr. Fairbanks intended.

But running *Robin Hood* at sound speed only misses the original, correct running time by seven minutes.

How does one know at what speed silent films were intended to be run, since they were all obviously filmed at various rates? Silent films were usually released with musical cue sheets supplied in many cases by the producing company. As early as 1916, Triangle published special instructions to the projectionist. Here are some samples: "The best effects in 'The Captive God' will be had by timing the film to run from thirteen to thirteen and a half minutes to the reel. The two big battle scenes . . . should be speeded up considerably. Following the sub-title 'The Alarm,' shoot it through fast."

For *Stranded:* "Time the feature to run fourteen minutes to the reel. Only two places in the five reels call for speed. When the little girl falls from the trapeze there is great excitement resulting. Speed it here."

In *The Half-Breed* with Douglas Fairbanks, Triangle's *Projection Hints* call for several specific scenes where "considerable more speed will help." In the last reel it admonishes "shoot the big fire scenes very fast. The only place where the picture may be slowed down at all is in the church scene."

Thus it should be remembered that it was taken for granted that early films would not be shown at a constant speed at all. The situation was summed up by F. R. Richardson in the projection department of the *Moving Picture World*, December 2, 1911: "Speed is of very very great importance and a comprehension of this fact is absolutely necessary to do really fine projection. The operator 'renders' a film, if he is a real operator, exactly as does the musician render a piece of music, in that, within limits, the action of a scene being portrayed depends entirely on his judgement. Watch the scene closely and by variation of speed bring out everything there is in it. No set rule applies. Only the application of brains to the matter of speed can properly render a film. I have often changed speed half a dozen times on one film of 1000 feet."

Unfortunately, the creative operator that Mr. Richardson called for was more often a workman under strict orders from his boss, the theatre manager, to give him a fast or a slow show depending on activity at the box office.

Filmmakers were aware of the tendency to speed up their pictures in projection. They sought to offset the resulting frantic action by having cameramen shoot faster and faster. Thus many films toward the end of the silent period were actually produced with the studio cameras operating faster than sound speed. When such films are projected at sixteen frames per second by misguided film societies, the distortion can be enormous.

Examination of thousands of cue sheets for silent films has failed to turn up a single one that indicates that a given film should be projected at sixteen and a half minutes per reel, or sixteen frames per second.

In the wonderful days of speechless cinema there was no problem about young people learning to read. We were seeing movies two or three times a week, and we *had* to know what Tom Mix and Doug Fairbanks were saying. We didn't learn to read very much in school. It was the subtitles in silent movies that taught us—fast. And the vocabulary wasn't limited to the silly doings of Bob, Jane and Rover.

For those who have seen the silent film, the only real Robin Hood is Douglas Fairbanks (1922).

In 1922 I was six, and in *Robin Hood* I had to read Guy of Gisbourne calling Doug Fairbanks a "sycophant." None of us was at all sure what the word meant, but it looked awfully bad and seemed more than enough to justify Robin Hood's cracking the bad guy's spine around a pole—just as he'd threatened to do after being called so dastardly a name.

When we reenacted *Robin Hood* all summer long with our home-made bows and arrows and battled one another with lathes hammered into heavy swords, as we snarled "Sycophant!" at our opponents, we may have mispronounced it, but we had been able to read it without academic assistance. By 1925 we were reading such words as "brontosaurus" and "pterodactyl"—but, of course, only in the movies.

It was an ideally shadowy life, and in retrospect I realize I learned infinitely more from the movies than they were able to teach me in school. Granted, the school of cinema provided some inaccuracies in the information afforded, but then what the schools were teaching in the twenties (especially in physics) in later years proved to be just about as erroneous as the history and science emerging from the screenplays of the time.

No one who is now younger than seventy went to the movies regularly during the predialogue period. That eliminates just about every professor presuming to teach the history of motion pictures. It also means that few, if any, of them have ever seen a silent film presented exactly as it was intended to be shown by the artists who made it. Would a serious musicologist try to teach Bach, Wagner or Beethoven using only Edison cylinder recordings played on an acoustic windup phonograph? It is a comparable misrepresentation to project a poorly timed, seventh-generation, 16mm dupe of an important film, run at an erroneous speed that slows down the athleticism of Doug Fairbanks to such a point that his action isn't much different from the comic hesitations of a Harry Langdon.

The predialogue, so-called silent film truly still awaits recognition as the genuine basis and foundation of all in cinema that exists as a form of art.

There are great shocks to be endured in all teaching, but in my own pedagogical career, the greatest one came when I first began to encounter students who had never in their lives seen one silent film. When these deprived moderns saw their first predialogue movie in class, some of them complained, "They're crazy. They keep stopping and starting again with all that writing in between."

Richard Barthelmess, with the last ounce of his determination, gets the mail through in *Tol'able David* (1921).

It was a valid complaint. "Subtitles," as they were called, were always an aesthetic weakness of the medium. Worst were the titles that gave away what was about to happen. Second worst were the editorial titles that told us what to think about what we were seeing. One of the saddest examples of the latter is Henry King's otherwise fabulous movie *Tol'able David*, with its memorable tour-de-force performance of Richard Barthelmess. Despite fantastic and magnificently filmed action in the fight between David and a Goliath of a murderous monster hillbilly, played by Ernest Torrence in his film debut, the utterly dispensable titles insist on informing the viewer over and over how tremendously heroic David is being.

In one curious film of 1920, *The Chamber Mystery*, the innovative director, one Abraham S. Schomer, attempted to solve the dialogue-title problem by actually superimposing comic-strip style dialogue balloons right over the pictures, with the usual stems showing from whose lips those words were coming. Neither that technique nor that director survived that one abortive movie.

Of course simple dialogue titles were the most justifiable, although

In *The Chamber Mystery* (1920) the director tried comic-strip-style dialogue balloons. It didn't work.

it took Georg Pabst and Josef von Sternberg to start using them correctly. The standard system was to have a character in the film seen speaking, cut in the dialogue title, then cut back to the end of the same action shot, showing the player finishing the sentence. Pabst, and sometimes Sternberg, showed the actor speaking, cut in the dialogue title, then cut immediately to a reaction shot of the person being addressed.

It took a long time in the early days of the talkies for some directors to learn to do this in editing their dialogue.

Some unforgettable movie titles have stuck with me as enduringly as a Shakespearean couplet. The name of the film is gone from memory, but one favorite comment of Bill Hart's came about after he'd gotten the drop on a whole saloonful of bad chaps. With his two six-shooters trained on them, he ordered the mob to go to the window and throw their pieces out. One bad guy pretended to toss his pistol, hid it in his vest and tried to get off a shot at Bill. But our hero dropped him before he could get the trigger pulled. "He cheated and fumbled" read the title. "Either is bad, but both is in-ex-cusable."

Another I can't forget is in Garbo's first version of *Anna Karenina*, which MGM called *Love*. Anna is embracing her little son (played by

Philippe De Lacey), and John Gilbert as Vronsky looks on, petulantly observing,

> You love him more than you love me.

Garbo's answer:

> There is no more or less in love. I love you both infinitely.

Was that Tolstoy or the title writer? If only the latter, it is certainly worthy of Tolstoy.

Of course there were turgid titles too that served as dismaying examples of how not to write. D. W. Griffith came up with some memorably lush syntax in his frequent editorial observations. For example, in *The Birth of a Nation* the culmination of the harrowing scene with Mae Marsh as the Little Sister, frantically fleeing from a pursuing "black renegade" played by Walter Long, and finally jumping to her death from a high rock, brings this title:

> For her who had learned the stern lesson of honor we should not grieve that she found sweeter the gates of death.

To be sure, Griffith was not alone in his Victorian phraseology. Even the Westerns were often encumbered with extravagant comments far from the crisp and gritty language of Clarence Mulford in his Hopalong Cassidy novels, or the more spartan prose of Zane Grey, the Louis L'Amour of those days. *Hell's Hinges*, one of the very best Westerns of 1916, confronted viewers with titles like this:

> The broken flight into the desert while evil and madness join hands in the triumph of victory.

But the so-called dialogues of the talkies have some dandy clichés echoing down through the corridors of time. Was there ever a scene of emergency childbirth in which the doctor didn't say, "Get me some hot water—lots of it"? Even in John Ford's *Stagecoach* Dr. Thomas Mitchell, about to do a delivery in a grim desert outpost, rolls up his sleeves and calls for that indispensable basin of hot water—to be conjured up on the moment from what rapid source no one knows.

Water long remained the movies' wonder drug. The heroine

Murnau's *The Last Laugh* (1924), with Emil Jannings, whose acting was so eloquent no titles were needed

faints—"Get a glass of water." In *Dinner at Eight* Lionel Barrymore has a heart attack, and the doctor, Edmund Lowe, orders, "Get me a glass of water." Bebe Daniels breaks her ankle in *42nd Street*—the house doctor's first aid is "Get me a glass of water." Come to think of it, you never see the doctor give the water to the ailing person—he must just want it for himself.

Another old reliable—when the script calls for a character to appear on the scene without any motivation whatsoever, the player always comes on the set with the line, "They told me I'd find you here." Who "they" are is never revealed.

There were some brave attempts to create silent films so eloquent in their pantomime that they needed no intertitles whatsoever—no dialogue, no explanatory titles, just pure, uninterrupted images. What a boon to international distribution—no language barrier anywhere! Most famous of the titleless films is Murnau's *Der Letzte Mann*, released in this country as *The Last Laugh*—with one explanatory caption inserted. Just in 1990, Dorothea Gebauer, a German archivist and film historian, discovered an original script of Murnau's film *with* titles throughout. Now the problem for research is to determine whether or not that memorable masterpiece was ever released in Germany with those titles, or did the trailblazing notion of cutting out all titles occur before the film went public?

In any case, two other fine German films did reach the screen without titles: Artur Robison's *Warning Shadows* and Leopold Jessner's *Backstairs*, with Henny Porten and Fritz Kortner in another alarming portrayal. Even Hollywood tried it at least once in 1921 with a Charles Ray vehicle, *The Old Swimmin' Hole*, unsuccessfully directed by Joseph De Grasse.

Backstairs (1921), with Henny Porten, was another German film that dispensed with titles.

Students watching silent films today may be made to squirm not only by the absence of dialogue, but also by the lack of color. But, again, it's a case of early films being misrepresented by present-day copies. In the first twenty-five years of cinema, most films were printed on toned positive stock, or they were hand tinted. Especially in France, the companies Pathé and Gaumont hired scores of women to sit at Moviolas applying four different colors painstakingly with paintbrushes to each frame of a 35mm positive print. Each woman would do only one of the four colors; the reel would be passed on from the woman doing the blues, to the reds, and the greens and the yellows.

But with 35mm film there are sixteen frames to each foot. A single reel is about a thousand feet. That meant some 16,000 tiny 35mm frames to be hand painted! And at least one eight-reel feature, Augusto Genina's *Cyrano de Bergerac*, was hand colored, with 128,000 individual 35mm frames to be hand colored—each single frame, of course, different from all the others in the disposition of its images.

Throughout the twenties, the majority of films from all countries, even if they were not hand tinted, would be printed on variously toned positive film stock. The basic tint was usually a warm amber. Evening scenes were printed on light-blue stock, nights were dark blue. There were moonlight gradients, rosy dawns and flaming sunsets, verdant greens and golden desertscapes. Not until sound tracks appeared on films did the movies take on the black and white now generally and incorrectly associated with early film. Original 35mm prints of the pioneering movies were all tinted. *The Great Train Robbery* had multiple tints, and so did *The Cabinet of Dr. Caligari* and *The Birth of a Nation*.

Silent features, before they went to the theatres, were assembled not in Hollywood or New York, where the pictures had been produced, but rather in the film exchanges of the towns in which they were to be shown. The major companies—MGM, Paramount, Universal and Fox—all had regional offices in the large cities. Each office, or exchange, employed dozens of women whose job it was to assemble positive prints from the rolls they would receive from the studio. Those rolls would be separated according to the tints: amber, blue, red, green and sepia rolls would come into the exchange, and the girls, using cutting continuities they would get for each different feature, would splice the film according to the script they received.

Every film that was projected in a theatre then would be filled with scores of splices—splices that could not be tolerated once sound tracks became part of the release prints. Overleaf is page 8 of a nineteen-page shot-by-shot tinting continuity sent out by the Fox Film Corporation along with their 1925 Tom Mix feature, *The Best Bad Man*. The numbers refer to the separate shots in the film. The S. T. number lists a subtitle. Note that on page 8 alone, three different tints are called for: yellow, blue and amber.

Page from the Fox Film Corporation's tinting continuity for the Tom Mix film *The Best Bad Man* (1925)

279	Yellow	Int. Tom & Mix fade
280	Blue	Ext. Mix on horse-F. in
281	"	Ext. Swain on, Mix enters
S. T. 70	"	Mr. Swain
282	"	Ext. Cu. Mix & Swain
283	"	Ext. Cu. Mix
284	"	Ext. Cu. Mix, Swain
S. T. 71	"	I want
285	"	Ext. Cu. Mix & Swain
286	"	Ext. S. Cu. Mix, Swain & Peggy
287	"	Ext. Cu. Mix
288	"	Ext. Cu. Peggy & Swain
289	"	Ext. Cu. Mix
S. T. 72	"	On condition
290	"	Ext. Cu. Peggy & Swain
291	"	Ext. Cu. Peggy
292	"	Ext. Cu. Mix
S. T. 73	"	Miss Peggy
293	"	Ext. Cu. Mix
294	"	Ext. Cu. Peggy F.O.
S. T. 74	"	With the
295	"	Ext. office F. in L. S. Mix
296	"	Ext. office Cu. Mix
297	"	Ext. Mix by fence
298	"	Ext. S. Cu. Mix by fence
299	"	Int. Cu. Molly in bed
300	"	Ext. Mix by fence
301	"	Int. Cu. Molly in bed
302	"	Ext. Mix in, Tom enters
303	"	Ext. Cu. Mix & Tom
304	"	Ext. Mix enter to tree
305	"	Ext. Mix on roof
306	Amber	Int. men in room
307	Blue	Ext. Mix on roof

308	Amber	Int. off Cu. Dan & Demlop
S. T. 75	″	When we
309	″	Int. Cu. money
310	Blue	Ext. Cu. Mix on roof
311	″	Ext. Tom playing
312	″	Ext. Cu. Tom playing
313	″	Ext. Molly enters
S. T. 76	″	On Jingle
314	″	Ext. Cu. Tom playing
315	″	Ext. Cu. Molly
316	″	Ext. Molly Cu. Tom
317	″	Ext. Molly on
318	″	Ext. Cu. Tom
319	″	Ext. Molly to F.G.
320	″	Ext. Cu. Mix on roof
321	Amber	Int. Cu. Dan & Frank
S. T. 77	″	Then we

CHAPTER 3

A Reversed Tapestry

D uring World War I, every German soldier wore a belt that proclaimed "Gott mit Uns" on its buckle. By November of 1918, they finally realized that God wasn't. The young manhood of Germany (and of France, and of England) was drowning in a tide of blood that had been running for four years. After the Armistice, defeated German troops returned home to find yet another battle raging in their city streets. The Communist organization the Spartacists had instigated a revolution. The Freikorps, determined to wipe them out, battled the Spartacists with the same weapons they had been using to kill American, British and French troops. Women and children were starving as the economy collapsed, and the worst inflation in history turned daily living into an exercise of insanity.

Greedy foreigners, their bags packed with good currency, came to Germany and bought the cities. In the mad years of "peace" that followed, Berliners and Viennese, statesmen, artists and disillusioned citizens scrambled to move in other directions—any direction other than those that had led them into chaos. The politically minded grouped into 115 different parties—many of them savage—one of them destined to inflame the whole world in less than a dozen years. Artists, despising the old established icons of the art world, aligned themselves with the isms: expressionism, futurism, dadaism, cubism.

The extravagances of some of these artists left the world with far more admirable souvenirs than did the extremists of politics from left to right. For film, by far the most valuable gem formed in that postwar crucible was *The Cabinet of Dr. Caligari*, filmed in 1919 and given its premiere showing in Berlin in January of 1920.

Werner Krauss was the sinister hypnotist in *The Cabinet of Dr. Caligari* (1920), with its dizzying scenery.

The pen falters (and so does the typewriter) in attempting further commentary on *Caligari*. No other film in the entire history of cinema has prompted as much writing and discussion. No other film has been shown so often every single year since its production.

In 1930, discussing *Caligari* in *The Film Till Now*, Paul Rotha wrote:

> It is destined to go down to posterity as one of the most momentous advances achieved by any one film in the history of the development of the cinema. "The Cabinet of Dr. Caligari" and "Battleship Potemkin" are pre-eminent.

It is noteworthy that the preeminence *Caligari* has enjoyed is not due to technological wonders. The stylized performances would win no awards (although Werner Krauss as the sinister doctor should have won some special citation).

The camera work is less than pedestrian. The camera is operated throughout at eye level. Although some reviewers exclaimed over the exciting camera angles, there were none. There was no groundbreaking camera mobility. Only twice was a scene even briefly panned.

Other writers praised the lighting providing startling shadows and highlights. The lighting was flat; what shadows there were, were all painted, save for the shadow of Cesare as he murders one of the students.

After admitting that the film is exceptional, many historians attempted to diminish the work's importance by insisting that it represented a dead end in film art—that it exerted absolutely no influence on films to come.

What myopia! *Caligari* influenced *every* film to come. *Caligari* served dramatic notice that film was a *graphic* art rather than a theatrical form or a branch of photography. Rotha was right to link *Caligari* with *Potemkin*. With both of these masterpieces, film found its areas of extension beyond its kindred arts. The makers of *Caligari* dared to dispense with most of the tools of filmmaking known by 1920. Each frame of the film can be excised, enlarged and framed as a fascinating expressionist design. The content of the great story and the behavior of the players,

Lil Dagover is taking leave of her student friends, Friedrich Feher and Hans Heinz von Twardowski, on a mad *Caligari* street corner.

Henry Stahlhut's poster for the 1937 Greenbrier Hotel
showing of *Caligari*

together with the design, all reveal to engrossed viewers the reversed
tapestry of a madman's mind.

    Caligari was in commercial circulation throughout the 1920s and
well into the 1930s. In 1933 I was able to rent a 35mm nitrate print from
a distributor in Manhattan. In 1935 it was the headliner of the first films
exhibited and circulated by the Museum of Modern Art Film Library. It
was the first film acquired by the legendary Henri Langlois for his private cache, which became the nucleus of the fabulous film collection of
the Cinémathèque Française in Paris. Henri's own 35mm tinted nitrate
print is today one of the few remaining original versions of *Caligari* with
all the titles askew and angled to match the sets in the film. From the

very beginning of film societies and the Little Theatre of the Cinema movement in the United States, *Caligari* was always favorite fare, and its showing was absolutely de rigueur for pioneering film programs in art museums. I myself introduced *Caligari* to members of the Cleveland Museum of Art. It served as the opener of the first film series presented at Western Reserve University in the mid-1930s. There was even a posh showing of *Caligari* in the auditorium of the Greenbrier Hotel, with live accompaniment supplied by Meyer Davis and selected members of his famous society orchestra. The posters for that session were done for me by artist Henry Stahlhut—grand images reproduced in this book. If they come to the attention of their maker, whom I've been unable to trace all these years, I earnestly hope he'll get in touch, as he was never adequately thanked for creating these works, which I treasure only slightly less than I do a copy of the film itself.

Fantastic as the scenery is for *Caligari*, the story is scarcely less so. It is not far from some of the most lurid tales of E. T. A. Hoffmann, and I feel sure that Carl Mayer and Hans Janowitz, the authors, must have had a Hoffmannesque impulse in devising so diabolical a tale. The film begins with two men sitting in a rather scruffy-looking garden. Anything but scruffy-looking is lovely Lil Dagover, in her film debut, who comes almost floating past them. One of the men tells the other that she is his betrothed and that they have just lived through a terrible experience, which he proceeds to describe in a flashback. As that story unfolds, the scenery seems to have been painted by a drunken artist: it is a nightmare of wild angles, distortions in perspective, cluttered by menacing black darts of ambiguous lines like the webs of crazed spiders. We are introduced to Dr. Caligari, a wandering showman who wants to exhibit a somnambulist at the village fair. Werner Krauss as the doctor, in a rusty stovepipe hat and a dusty dark-gray cloak, manages to look as inhuman as the vertiginous designs of the streets, the buildings, the tents and the rooms he enters. His act at the fair is to awaken his sleepwalker, memorably played by Conrad Veidt at his most skeletal, and have his hypnotized captive predict the future. The predictions are often of imminent death, and the doctor has his enslaved creature go out and kill to ensure that the foreseen murders are fulfilled.

When Cesare the somnambulist is sent to kill the girl played by Lil Dagover, the monster cannot harm her, but, like King Kong and Fay Wray, tries to take her with him. That attempt is his undoing. A chase, with the doctor as quarry, winds up in an insane asylum. In a nightmarish denouement, Caligari turns out to be the head of the asylum. We leave him straitjacketed and return to the narrator in the garden. The two men decide to go inside; it's getting cool. We find they have both gone inside a madhouse. For the sake of those folks who unaccountably have still not seen the film, I shall not reveal the gloriously fantastic ending—you do have a cinematic thrill still to look forward to!

When I showed that rented print of *Caligari* and ran it for Frank Wiesenberger, a splendid musician and gifted pianist, the projectionist came out of the booth and implored me to get some other movie. To him *Caligari* was the worst film he'd ever seen, and he had strenuous objections to running it for a paying audience. He needn't have worried. There were no more than twelve in the audience—my family and a few of their disapproving friends. The score provided by Mr. Wiesenberger was superb—the best I have ever heard with *Caligari*. It included Rachmaninoff's Prelude in G, a Dvořák *Slavonic Dance* (Mr. Wiesenberger was the son of a Czech composer) and, most hauntingly, "Less Than the Dust" and "Till I Wake," two of the more sombre Indian love lyrics. Ten years before, Erno Rapee, arranging the score for the U.S. premiere of *Caligari* in New York, had worked a bit of Prokofiev into his arrangement. It was the first time any Prokofiev had been played publicly in the United States.

That session had me eternally hooked. My problem now was somehow to get a copy of the film to have forever. That proved to be not so simple. First I had to transfer my film projects to college—Western Reserve University. While there I started the first film showings at the Cleveland Museum of Art and launched several series on campus. In 1935 most colleges and universities had no film courses, and, save for in California, neither had films made their way into the halls of academe nor were there campus film societies.

The print of *Caligari* I had rented in 1933 had gone the ultimate way of all decomposing nitrate, and any other copies of *Caligari* that may have survived had gone far underground. The first half of that decade was an evil period for silent films. The excitement of talkies was still high. Few people were willing to look at a silent movie, and even fewer had any notion whatsoever about preserving any of them. It seemed reasonable that there might be prints left of it in its country of origin. But how was a sophomore in college to get to Germany to find out? By getting a scholarship to the University of Heidelberg.

As a drama major in Germany, I soon discovered that the professors of the Third Reich took an extremely narrow look at the history of German theatre. It was Schiller, Schiller, Schiller, one of the very few dramatists of the past whose work was approved by the Nazi ideologues.

Happily, the university library (one of the world's best) placed no limit on the number of books an enrolled student could borrow at one time, nor did they even place a time limit on using them. My coal stove–heated student's garret soon held the complete works of Arthur Schnitzler and Hugo von Hofmannsthal. No need to attend class and hear again how Schiller anticipated the glorious world of National Socialism. Instead, class time was spent going to German movies. In a four-month period I managed to see forty-one current films.

One day I saw an ad for 9.5mm films for sale. *The Cabinet of Dr. Caligari!* The print was offered for sale in Düsseldorf. Taking up all the money I had for the second semester, I headed for home—with a stopover in Düsseldorf. At last *Caligari* was in my hands—albeit a drastically shrunken version, reduced from 35mm to 9.5.

Once released from college, I spent three somewhat misguided years trying to make films rather than collecting and showing the work of others. It was back to Germany to film the beginnings of World War II in Danzig. The history books are wrong—as usual. The invasion of Poland began, not on September 1, 1939, as we are invariably advised, but rather on August 14, 1939. I know. I was there, and much of my film was collected by the Gestapo, and for a frightening while, its maker was collected with it.

Safely back home, I became head of a documentary film and photography project for the New Deal government until the U.S. Army clapped a uniform on me, and there I was in the same Astoria Studio where Gloria Swanson had starred in her Manhattan-made hit *Manhandled.* Most of us film people were there as buck-ass privates. George Cukor (who had directed Garbo in *Camille*) pulled KP with the rest of us. Film collector Charlie Turner was one of the gods—he was a sergeant on the permanent staff at the Signal Corps Center in the Astoria Studios. Collector and later director David Bradley and photographer Brett Weston passed through those hallowed halls in uniform. But at last World War II was atomized, and I could expect to be freed. The collecting could be resumed!

CHAPTER 4

The Long and Short of It

I n one particular area film scholarship has fallen into a deplorable
semantic trap. The publishers of *The American Film Institute Catalogue* have arbitrarily differentiated between films of four reels or
fewer and those of any greater length. A film of three and three-fourths
reels is a short, while any film in excess of four reels is a feature. This
neat classification has all the logic and rationality of that ancient determination regarding the number of angels that have room to cavort on
the head of a pin. The concept of some basic difference between a short
and a feature film has delayed both the preservation and the study of
those films that first established the most significant elements of cinema—the characteristics that justified considering the medium as a form
of art.

Film students have waited for years for the American Film Institute
to publish its invaluable catalogue of American films made in the historically crucial years of 1911 through 1920. This essential compilation was
published in 1990, and with it, one can begin to estimate, with some
approach to accuracy, the ratio of American films that were made during
that period to those that have survived.

Of course, that ratio cannot be exact. Many titles eluded the com-
pilers at the American Film Institute. Private collectors are wary
of revealing their holdings, and many of them cherish pictures known
to exist only to their circle of closest friends. Their paranoia is understandable. Possession of copyrighted films by an individual who has
not purchased rental rights from the corporation that made and copyrighted the films has been considered illegal, and collections of such
films have been subject to seizure by the FBI. The FBI has not been

shy about swooping down on private film collections and carrying them off. Roddy McDowall, one of the few Hollywood actors who cares enough about film to have amassed a large and important personal archive of prints, was given a rough time defending his treasure from the Feds.

I myself was once guilty of setting into motion a maliciously inspired FBI seizure. A major Chicago 16mm film library was going out of business and offering for sale its large rental collection. Representing Eastman House, I went to Chicago to make our offer for the collection. For some mysterious reason, there exists a big-city contempt for the inhabitants of such out-of-the-way places as upstate New York, Rochester, or midwestern cities: Cleveland, Indianapolis, South Bend, Milwaukee or Toledo. The Chicago people were rudely insulting to this envoy from what might as well have been Dawson City. They scoffed at my offer and showed me unceremoniously to the door.

Suspecting that they had only rental rights to the films they were trying to sell outright for a preposterously high amount, I alerted the FBI. Their whole library of films was promptly seized by the FBI, and the prints were returned to the various producers. The arrogant Chicago people wound up with $0.00. One of the largest of those producers, expressing gratitude to Eastman House for "protecting their legal interest" in the films, turned over to Eastman House all of their prints that had been confiscated. The others just destroyed their films.

But, alas, the most significant titles missing from the AFI 1911–1920 catalogue are those that, simply by their length, do not measure up to the minimum so arbitrarily established by the editors. From 1911 through 1915, American films of one, two or three reels were overwhelmingly in the majority of American releases. The information gap in the catalogue for those vital years is serious indeed. Unlisted are all the Chaplins made for Keystone, Essanay and Mutual. All the key Griffith Biographs are not there, although most of them have been thoroughly discussed by the Griffith specialists. But most unfortunate has been the inattention to the dramas of companies other than Biograph, including the Western dramas of William S. Hart, Tom Mix and Broncho Billy Anderson, the distinguished Thanhouser dramas directed with such admirable style and sincerity by Carl Gregory and George Nicholls, along with the first tantalizing dramas made by John Collins at Edison, all great films that didn't quite make the absurd four-thousand-foot limit. No matter in what semantic category these one-, two- and three-reel films may be placed, they cry for more attention—they need to be catalogued, and most of all they demand to be seen. Films casually designated as "shorts" have been brushed aside as being of lesser importance than the so-called feature films.

Each film scholar has a special area of predominant interest to his studies and is liable to overlook work that lies outside that area. There is now a tendency to focus on films that reflect a concern for social values. With early film audiences in this country made up predominantly of immigrants and workers with highly limited cultural backgrounds, the producers tended to slant their story lines very much in the direction of the laboring class.

Others have found that the "art of entertainment" is the most valid clue to the history of film. Such investigators can trace the cinema's growing potency for first attracting the unsophisticated, then engrossing those seekers of extratheatrical dramatic creativity and, finally, enlisting and capturing the devotion of intellectuals.

Here are some urgent recommendations in all three categories: the film of genuine social concern, the classic thriller intended for simple entertainment and perhaps America's earliest avant-garde piece. They are Thanhouser's *Cry of the Children* of 1912, Ince's *The Gangsters and the Girl* of 1914 and Vitagraph's *The Yellow Girl*, which appeared in 1916. I submit that each of these "shorts" is as innovative as any one of the feature films that appear in the AFI 1911–1920 catalogue.

The earliest of the three, Thanhouser's *The Cry of the Children*, immediately associated itself with some high-level names in the world of respectability—audacious for a nickelodeon production to dare in 1912. First, the film purported to be based on the poem of the same title by no less than Elizabeth Barrett Browning. Some of the titles throughout the film are directly quoted from that poem. Second, in Thanhouser ads for the film, it was alleged that two presidents of the United States, in their quest for social reform, had cited the film by name as showing the evils of child labor. Named were Theodore Roosevelt and Woodrow Wilson, the latter quoted from one of his campaign speeches. If Wilson had indeed seen *The Cry of the Children*, he must have been one of the most prestigious of the early academic film fans. In the elaborate program of *The Birth of a Nation* the then president is quoted with words of the warmest praise for Griffith's controversial epic.

The content of the film is so strongly anticapitalistic that, viewed a few years later than 1912, it might well have fallen victim to the fears of

Bolshevism that haunted the American establishment starting in 1918. By the time *The Cry of the Children* appeared in the spring of 1912, this nation was ready for cinematic outrage. Just the year before, the infamous Triangle Shirtwaist Company fire had killed 146 sweatshop workers —most of them underage girls. The year 1912 was off to a bad start. In January, 25,000 workers struck the American Woolen Company in Lawrence, Massachusetts. By February, many of the striking workers, young children among them, began to starve. The IWW (Industrial Workers of the World) tried to transport the children to other towns to be fed. Enemies of the strikers called it kidnapping, and on February 4, as a group of the refugees was boarding a train bound for Philadelphia, they were charged by the police, who mercilessly clubbed children and their parents alike.

Fiction does not dare to reproduce outrageous reality if it is to maintain credibility. And so *The Cry of the Children*, undertaken just one month after the brutal attack of February 4, told a relatively subdued story. But it did not shrink from placing Carl Gregory's camera right inside an actual mill for all to see the sickening spectacle of children toiling at the whirring, high-speed looms. The scenes that immediately grip the viewer are the documentary shots inside the plant. In these exceptional images one sees nonacting youngsters actually working alongside the adults at the obviously dangerous machines. The shots are worthy of the famous photographs of Hine, whose pictures of child workers did much to alert a slowly outraged public to the shameful fact of industrial abuse of very young children.

The mill-worker family lives in an unheated shanty without water. One of the chores of stay-at-home little Alice is to get buckets of water from a nearby stream. On one such outing Alice is noticed by the wealthy mill owner's wife, who happens to be driving by. She is taken with the sunny personality of the little girl and, childless and bored, offers to adopt Alice. Alice is beguiled by a visit to the palatial home of her would-be benefactress. Her family is frightened by the prospect of losing her to the elegant lady, but much relieved when at last Alice declines the offer.

The mill workers, finding conditions in the mill and their own poverty intolerable, go on strike. The strike continues with no concessions from the owner. The workers' families begin to starve and the beaten workers return to the mill with nothing gained but more misery. The owner and his dinner-jacketed friends are shown celebrating the victory in his mansion, attended, of course, by liveried servants.

Driven over the edge of survival, the family has barely enough strength to return to work. For the mother, a collapse makes it impossible for her to continue working. Shielded Alice must go to the mill in her mother's place. The sequence showing her apprenticeship at one of the whirling looms is truly appalling. Losing her health and her gaiety working the tortuous hours in the plant, Alice returns to the mill owner's wife, now quite willing to be adopted. But there is no movie happy ending to this film. Alice is no longer the appealing, joyous child that she had been before joining the workers. The owner's wife has a poodle pet. She heartlessly turns the little girl away. Unable to cope with her strenuous job, Alice dies at her machine.

Turbulent 1912 brought forth other brief films noirs dealing with prevalent social injustices. Edison, for example, had already made *Children Who Labor*. But there was much about *The Cry of the Children* that placed it far ahead of the competition, according to the enthusiastic reviews it prompted. The cast is superb, acting with far more restraint than was usual in films of 1912 (and in those much later as well). There is an outstanding, understated portrayal of suffering and concern by Ethel Wright as the mother. James Cruze, far more renowned as the director of *The Covered Wagon* than as an actor, plays the father with a restrained dignity rare in early films.

Only the behavior of Marie Eline (the Thanhouser Kid) is damagingly dated. Marie was an immensely popular child star. In the many popularity polls conducted by the fan magazines, the Kid far outdistanced the leading players of the Thanhouser Company—a fact that could not have been lost on the director. No other way to explain his allowing the Kid's performance to proceed completely out of harmony with the low-key realistic acting of all the others. Marie Eline was undoubtedly coached by some exponent of the worst traditions of the melodramatic theatre. She rolls her eyes, addresses the camera lens more often than she does the other players and brings a hippity-hopping energy to her role that becomes positively obnoxious. But even in 1912 it seems that a director could not quarrel effectively with superstardom.

There is still another element in its production that should make the work of particular interest to the historian of developing film techniques. After a funeral scene in a graveyard where the martyred child is laid to rest, there comes a rapid-fire double-exposed recapitulation sequence, flashing the highlights of the preceding actions. This kind of recap flashback became a cliché of countless films later on—especially favored in documentaries. The cameraman, Carl Gregory, later became a kind of dean of special effects. It was Carl Gregory, with Dr. J. Sibley Watson, who put together what was probably the earliest optical printer in Rochester, New York, in order to produce the Watson-Webber avant-garde *The Fall of the House of Usher* in 1927.

Thomas Harper Ince began his film career with D. W. Griffith but early on left the Biograph Company to do his own directing for KB Films (Kessel & Baumann). Ince deserves to be remembered for much more than being the victim of one of Hollywood's most legendary unsolved murders. Ince was undoubtedly the best organized and most meticulous of all American filmmakers. The shooting script he devised as soon as he left acting to direct became the model of the industry. Basically it has not changed, save for the addition of dialogue. The Ince films were cut with a precision that was unrivaled except by the films of Mack Sennett.

In 1914 Ince produced *The Gangsters and the Girl* and obviously took more than a routine interest in its making—he even appears in the film as a police detective. The leads are Charles Ray and Elizabeth Burbridge. Ray, also a police detective, is ordered to go undercover and attempt to join a gang of too-successful burglars. Arthur Jarrett, a handsome and rugged actor, plays the leader of the gang. His girlfriend, Molly, not one of the criminals, is falsely accused of a crime and sentenced to jail. En route to the pen, she is rescued by a daring auto pursuit of the police car. Ray, as Detective Stone, succeeds in joining the gang and becomes interested in the leader's girl, who is in hiding with them. The not-too-bright detective has left his badge in his jacket, and Molly, tidying things up, discovers the badge. She has fallen in love with Stone and now faces an awful decision. Should she expose him as a cop and see him killed by her boyfriend? Or should she keep her knowledge to herself and see her boyfriend jailed or killed by the detective?

The girl's mental struggle is shown through a brilliant innovation. On the left side of the screen she stands in frozen anguish. Acted out on the right, in diminished perspective, are two different results of her imagined response to her discovery. In one scenario she sees the detective killed by the gang leader. In the second, her lover is the loser. These are flash-forwards in imagined time, and neither reveals the actual denouement. In 1950 Alf Sjöberg used the same device in his master-piece, *Miss Julie*. Julie describes to the valet the events with her father as she foresees them, and we see these imagined scenes take place. Shortly thereafter, we see what actually does happen, action quite different from the scenes depicted in the flash-forward.

Apart from this pioneering exercise, Ince's gangster film anticipates much that is still happening in all the multitudinous cop-and-robber episodes on TV: the ubiquitous car chases through city streets, the haz-ardous position of the undercover lawman and shoot-outs on skyscraper roofs. Varied camera placements and tight cutting keep the film moving at a brisk pace TV directors rarely achieve. The acting of the principals is exemplary: no mugging, no melodramatic posturing. One or two of the gangsters may look a little too deliberately sinister, but this seems to be the prerogative of mobsters—even in contemporary films.

Our third recommendation is Edgar Keller's 1916 Vitagraph, *The Yellow Girl*. In discussing any phase of film history, one should never use the word "first"—if, that is, the writer wishes to preserve any degree of credibility. Were it not for this self-imposed discipline, I would be tempted to describe *The Yellow Girl* as the first American avant-garde film.

Although the famous watershed Armory Show had not yet taken place, and the art world of the United States was not yet shaken, it was, at the very least, made uneasy by the creative upheavals taking place in Europe. Futurist painting was often ridiculed by traditionalists review-ing the earliest examples exhibited in this country. But film reviewers, unprejudiced in discussing a medium still quite free from tradition, were generally much friendlier to experimentation. The fan magazines gave both *Caligari* and *Potemkin* favorable reviews when they first appeared in this country. And *The Yellow Girl* rated this mention in the November 1916 issue of *Motion Picture* magazine:

> This is a novelty picture. It smacks of the Futurist school and is artistic and beautiful. Every interior and exterior scene was laid out with brush and stencil by an artist, and the artist might have been Aubrey Beardsley. A very pleasing, high-class piece of work.

Well, the artist, Edgar Keller, was no Aubrey Beardsley, nor did the decor of the film have anything to do with the futurist school. Keller was

what one used to call a commercial artist. He was often called upon to
design and decorate the covers of popular sheet music. The sets of *The
Yellow Girl* are characterized by a profusion of arcs, curves and curlicues.
The costumes of the players tend to match the backgrounds in a sort of
inebriated art nouveau. The style is lush and lavish but rather defies

The earliest American avant-garde: *The Yellow Girl* (1916)

intelligible description other than to admit that it is definitely arty.
There is beauty in the film—it is enacted by Florence Vidor and
Corinne Griffith, two of filmdom's most exquisite beauties. As for
Aubrey Beardsley, his art had to await Alla Nazimova's 1922 *Salome*, with
Natasha Rambova's costumes and sets designed deliberately to evoke
Beardsley's special mixture of decorative decadence.

Alla Nazimova in the 1922 *Salome*

CHAPTER 5

Rescuing Peter Pan from the Phantom of the Eastman Theatre

When Herbert Brenon's *Peter Pan* came to the Allen Theatre in Cleveland, Ohio, the last week of 1924, it became my favorite movie. For years I longed with desperate nostalgia to see it again. It would be a quarter of a century before so intense a pleasure was granted—and then under unimaginably odd circumstances. Like the Lost Boys that made up Peter's band, the film itself became one of the lost ones. It could not be found either by the Museum of Modern Art or the Cinémathèque Française. (It would not even be looked for by the British Film Archive.) Nor had it been gathered in by any of the most determined of the private film collectors throughout the world. It was one of the most important of missing American films.

Why important? Brenon occupies no hallowed niche in anyone's index of great directors. Not even the French critics revived his prestige. And Betty Bronson, though idolized by Bill Everson, is not one of the major stars of the silent period.

The greatness of *Peter Pan* resides in its magic, the roots of which stretch back three decades and across the ocean. The beauty of *Peter Pan* derives directly from Georges Méliès and, like his films, and like *Caligari* too, demonstrates anew that film is not part of photography—that its goal need not be banal realism. Over and over again filmmakers are confused by the great paradox of cinema. Often one's creativity is blunted when working in a medium that potentially knows no limitation in the realm of fantasy, but that nevertheless insists on rendering its images with a stubborn photographic fidelity that shouts "reality" to its beholders. In the formative years of cinema, filmmakers had little success in repeated efforts to capture images beyond actuality.

In this country only Mack Sennett was succeeding notably with the creation of a genuinely surrealist cinema. Of course he would have stared with hostile incomprehension at anyone suggesting to him that his madly illogical, riotous chases through bath- and bedrooms and over rooftops were anything but slapstick comedy. Or that he and his cutters had completely anticipated Russian constructive editing. Years before the 1925 *Potemkin* there was Sennett's wondrously exhilarating *Teddy at the Throttle*. For the villain, Wally Beery, to tie the heroine, Gloria Swanson, to the railroad tracks was in itself an innovation. In the old melodramas, it was the hero who was tied to the tracks to be saved in the very last moment by the heroine. (I know: as a long-ago actor, I was tied there myself in Agustin Daly's *Under the Gaslight*.) But as the menacing express locomotive comes hurtling down the rails toward struggling Gloria, Keystone Teddy, the screen's first wonder dog, is racing to the rescue along with Bobby Vernon, mounted on a bicycle, hanging on to the noble dog's tail. Trying to cross a trestle is too much for the bike, which is derailed, an event that stops the hero, but not the dog, who plunges from the bridge at least fifty feet into water below. All this hec-

Bobby Vernon, Keystone Teddy and Gloria Swanson in *Teddy at the Throttle* (1917)

tic action is intercut with five- or six-frame shots of the locomotive wheels, the smokestack, the passengers, Gloria's face, gloating close-ups of the villain expecting momentarily the demise of Gloria. The dog takes a note from desperate Gloria to the cab of the onrushing locomotive. The engineer is able to brake his engine so close to Gloria that the skidding wheels break the chains that bind her to the track. Russia's Eisenstein never bettered this sequence.

In the 1920s Hollywood was beset by a burning need to import creativity. Goaded by the prestige and critical acclaim being won by the post–World War I Germans with their *Golems* and *Caligaris*, films hailed for the artistry of their "grey magic," the more ambitious American producers hired more and more Europeans, hoping to provide us with a touch of Continental film art. Authors and artists associated with art nouveau in design and fantasy in letters were brought to Hollywood. Among them were Maurice Maeterlinck, Paul Iribé, Maurice Tourneur, Herbert Blaché and Erté. Even the trendy world of the dance was beckoned, and Theodore Kosloff, of the Russian ballet, and the American pioneer of dance, Ted Shawn, were lured to film with intent to diminish the general banality of our movies. But most of these efforts to class up the product met with critical scorn and, often enough, with box-office disaster.

Of the major producers in the 1920s, it was the heads of Paramount—Zukor, Lasky and DeMille—who were the most concerned with corraling big names in art and literature. Noting that Sarah Bernhardt had been paid thirty thousand dollars for one afternoon's work filming *Camille*, Adolph Zukor imported her subsequent feature, *Queen Elizabeth*, in 1912. Jesse Lasky had produced Broadway musicals and was himself a musician. DeMille, from a family of New York play brokers, was thoroughly nurtured in theatre and was keenly aware of the contributions of design to theatrical effect. Thus it was under the banner of Paramount that Enrico Caruso and Anna Pavlowa were brought to silent films, and at Paramount DeMille starred Geraldine Farrar and used Iribé for many of his sets; Kosloff both acted and directed large ensembles for DeMille. Ted Shawn could be seen tempting Gloria Swanson in a typically DeMille, erotic flashback decorating *Don't Change Your Husband*.

But the biggest literary game hunted by Paramount was Sir James Barrie, whose *Peter Pan* had dominated the theatre of fantasy since Peter's first stage flights in 1904. In this country Maude Adams captured the role for her own and kept Peter aloft in countless revivals right through 1913. Miss Adams proved as coyly resistant to film offers as did

Sir James himself. Film producers, attracted by the vast popularity of the story as well as the opportunity of film to exploit the aerial action prescribed by the script more spectacularly than stage mechanics could, hounded both Barrie and Adams for two decades.

Before World War I had ended, Jesse Lasky himself was in London on behalf of Paramount, importuning Sir James with not altogether inconsequential diplomatic skills. Ultimately, the author yielded—but not without making some characteristically whimsical demands. Barrie was to be given full right of approval of any players selected to enact any of the roles he had devised, particularly any to be entrusted with the challenge of Peter—by now a theatrical plum as traditionally ripe as Juliet or Camille, especially alluring to actresses who saw themselves forever young. Although Barrie had the final say on casting, he had neglected to protect the title itself. It turned out that he was lucky that it stayed *Peter Pan*. One of the most enduring of the many legendary quips involving American film tycoons' linguistic limitations is the alleged response by Paramount's home office to Lasky's triumphant cable advising that Sir James Barrie had agreed that *The Admirable Crichton* would become the first of the Barrie works to be filmed. The Paramount executives, according to the legend, objected that any film about an admiral would call for sea battles, much too costly to produce in 1918.

Whether the non-Goldwyn Goldwynism really was iterated or not, it was true enough that the word "admirable" was sufficiently foreign to Hollywood parlance to cause Paramount to change the title of its new property to *Male and Female*. With this alteration, all Hollywood felt semantically secure. One wonders how the great British master of whimsy reacted to this American violence done to his drama even before the cameras rolled. If he was stunned by the new title, he must surely have been staggered by the DeMillean additions to his plot when he beheld Gloria Swanson, all decked out in peacock feathers, being fed to the hungry lions of Ishtar in one of C.B.'s most lavish flashbacks to savage goings-on in Babylon.

Although *Male and Female* was a huge success with the public, it would be six more years before Paramount was ready to announce plans to tackle the Big Barrie: *Peter Pan*. When the word went out in 1924, there began a frenzy of testing and hunting that was not matched until Selznick started his epochal search for a Scarlett O'Hara. Every ingenue under contract to Paramount was tested and retested. Mary Pickford let it be known that she was longing to fly as Peter. But Barrie had the final

Maude Adams as Peter
Pan; she played the role
continuously from
1905 to 1907.

word, and his overworked word was "no." Paramount's top star, Gloria
Swanson, hurried off to London to see Sir James face-to-face. The word
was still "no."

When Maude Adams became the first Peter Pan of the American
theatre in 1905, she played it for three straight years. In the middle of
that run, Betty Bronson was born in New Jersey. As is the case with
almost every female theatre celebrity, it was the mother who had determined on star status for her daughter right from birth. Betty's mother
had her studying ballet with the Russian dancer and ballet master
Fokine. While still a teenager Betty had done extra work in dozens of
movies. She was one of the many on the Paramount lot who was tested
in the role of Peter Pan.

The tests were all being sent to Sir James Barrie. When he saw the
Betty Bronson test he saw the face of a little, unsophisticated girl in a
lighter-than-air dancer's body. He cabled Betty Bronson, not the studio,
that he had picked her to be the movie's Peter Pan.

The news created a sensation. *Photoplay* magazine headlined: "Un-
known Girl Chosen for Greatest Role. Young Dancer Selected over
Stars to Play Peter Pan." Betty was just seventeen. She cabled back to
Barrie: "I feel like a new Cinderella."

Betty Bronson won the coveted role for the first film version of *Peter Pan* (1924). Fokine's ballet training helped her to really seem to fly.

For a film to attain the resounding success enjoyed by *Peter Pan*, there must be a combination of factors that include many accidental ingredients along with those carefully planned. After the fact, analysis can never determine which factors entered by chance or what portions of the recipe were attributable to foresight, taste and cinematic experience. DeMille, having done the first Barrie with great success, might have been handed *Peter Pan* had he not been near the climax of a long quarrel with Paramount that saw him temporarily leaving the company he had helped to found ten years before. The film was entrusted to Herbert Brenon, who had unspectacularly but skillfully operated as one of the more intelligent of pioneer directors. Behind the scenes, Brenon had played a major part in persuading James Barrie to risk his work in films. As an Irishman, Brenon could be counted on to deal with that curious mix of pirates, fairies and Indians without any urge to turn all the doings into pseudo-science or to reveal in the last reel that it had all been a dream. The choice of Esther Ralston to play Mrs. Darling was a fine one. No other actress in Hollywood as young or as beautiful as Miss Ralston could have been coaxed into playing a mother of three. And Ernest Torrence as the "not altogether unheroic" Captain Hook after his triumph as the dust-encrusted desert scout of *The Covered Wagon* was brilliant casting.

Esther Ralston was
an idealized,
lovely Mrs. Darling
in *Peter Pan*.

But best of all was the magic. At last the paradox that drove Méliès back to his painted sets was resolved. The Darling children, taught to fly by Peter, fluttered about their bedroom in the best flights ever managed in film—levitation never improved upon in our days of super–special effects. When they zoomed out the upstairs window and soared off over Kensington Gardens, the whole audience gasped.

The beautiful pirate ship was real, its good oak planking revealed in textured detail through Jimmy Wong Howe's faithful cameras. All the more wonder when the ship was airborne, dripping seawater from its keel and parting the clouds as gloriously as Howard Hughes' raiding zeppelin in *Hell's Angels*.

Tinker Bell was a miniaturized Virginia Brown Faire, fighting the bedroom air currents as she strove to open the dresser drawer that held Peter's lost shadow. Who could forget her languishing in her tiny bedroom in Peter's underground hideout as the audience was implored to clap its belief in fairies as the only possible way to restore her flickering light? Surely Brenon and company had solved the magic riddle. Not with ghostly transparencies but with real and solid images breaking new trails through stars and star wars to come.

Best of all about *Peter Pan* was Betty Bronson. It's one thing to fly around a bedroom, alighting delicately on a mantelpiece, but quite another to do it with Fokine-trained grace and with a seventeen-year-old, unactressy face. Everything about the film was exceptional.

But into what Never Land had all the prints of *Peter Pan* disappeared after so notable a success? After a copy of *Caligari* was safe in my cabinet, *Peter Pan* stayed at the top of my want list for the next twenty years.

I had almost given up hope when an astonishing rumor of *Peter Pan's* existence originated from the most unlikely source in the world. It came from Vachel Lindsay Blair, nephew of the poet and boyhood fellow suburbanite in Shaker Heights. We had last met in 1936, both recently back from separate countries in Europe. We reclined on the grassy banks of one of the Shaker lakes, exchanging tales of our exploits, his in Spain, mine in Germany. A few years later, World War II saw us both in uniform, serving in different parts of the world.

When the war was over and the long-dreamed-of day of discharge was approaching, I was flown, still in uniform, to Rochester, New York, for an interview at the Eastman Kodak Company. The job they wanted to offer me was as writer-director-cameraman for Kodak's Informational Films Division. When I walked into those offices in the Kodak Tower, out of one of the cubicles came Vachel Blair. We were both utterly stunned. I had no idea that Vachel was working in Rochester (or even that he had survived the war!). He had no warning that I would be coming in for an interview. It was one of those inexpressibly delightful surprises, and it was our first meeting since 1936 in Shaker Heights. As soon as the army finally relinquished me, I began to work at Kodak, and Vachel and I were able to continue worrying about films and life's injustices.

Lunching one noon in the executive dining room, Vachel mentioned casually that he'd been at a party where they'd shown a silent film (he knew I preferred them without dialogue). Even after three years, three months and twenty-three days in the cavalry, the Signal Corps and Intelligence, I was still a dedicated film collector and ever on the alert to news of a silent. With appropriate eagerness I asked, "*What* silent?"

"*Peter Pan*. The Captain Hook was really great. The trick work was—"

Dropping knife and fork: "You saw *Peter Pan? Peter Pan*, with Betty Bronson? You mean *Oliver Twist* with Jackie Coogan, don't you? Or the Russian *Peter the Great*? It couldn't have been *Peter Pan!*"

"That's what it was, buddy. With Ernest Torrence and a very young Anna May Wong in the cast."

"*Where* did you see *Peter Pan?*" My lunch would be left on its plate.

"At a private party in a fellow's hideaway in the Eastman Theatre. If you improve your sloppy table manners, I may be able to arrange another showing for you. *Oliver Twist!*" He snorted.

The next week, still doubting that I was really closing in on number one on my Ten-Most-Wanted List, I was introduced to a short, chubby sound engineer called Chum Morris. Chum was one of those constant smilers. He explained his connection with the theatre; he was the expert on loan from Stromberg-Carlson who did the recording work for the Eastman Philharmonic.

The Eastman Theatre, in Rochester, New York, though not an international tourist attraction like the Paris Opera, has roughly the same dimensions—if you don't count all those subcellars, black lakes and sinister passages alleged by Gaston Leroux, author of *The Phantom of the Opera*, to honeycomb the lower depths of the Opera. The Eastman seats well over three thousand in exceptional luxury. The auditorium is completely carpeted—not just down the aisles, but beneath and all around the seats as well. Concertgoers' feet in the Eastman never encounter anything but marble or deep-pile carpeting. A gigantic chandelier hangs threateningly from the ceiling—and once it did indeed fall to the seats below, mercifully at a time when there was no audience beneath it.

Most Rochesterians are unaware that George Eastman had not built his magnificent palatial theatre with its Maxfield Parrish murals simply to indulge them in one of metropolitan America's favorite snobberies: attending symphony concerts. For George Eastman, the music was a secondary consideration. In 1922 he intended the Eastman Theatre as a showcase for the best motion pictures, accompanied by full orchestra and preceded by stage spectacles. The stage prologues were directed by Rouben Mamoulian, imported from London for that purpose. A decade later, Mamoulian would be in Hollywood directing Gary Cooper in *City Streets* and Greta Garbo in *Queen Christina*. Martha Graham was among those dancers cavorting in the Mamoulian Eastman Theatre prologues. Apart from the vast principal auditorium, the Eastman Theatre complex includes Kilbourne Hall, a smaller theatre where Fritz Lang's *Siegfried* was given its American premiere, accompanied by a live Wagnerian score. The entire building is filled with rehearsal rooms, studios, classrooms, a ballet room and offices. It was Eastman's intention to provide training for young musicians in the special art of providing music for films.

As I followed Chum Morris through a maze of twisting corridors, he proudly told me of his discoveries. "Where we're going is to the old screening room for student organists. This is where they used to show them films and let them practice playing for them. I guess it had been closed up and forgotten ever since talkies came in. It's a comfortable cozy place, and I fixed it up with my own things to make it livable. It's much nicer than my room at the Y." He opened the door with a key, and we stepped into a cozy, cerise room, all velvety with sofas, easy chairs, lamps and a glowing Oriental rug bringing all that comfort together. "That phone is connected with my room at the Y, my official residence, though this is where I really live."

"Where are the films?"

He led me out of the room and across the hallway. There was a heavy metal door, looking as husky as a bank vault. There was an enormous padlock hanging through the hasp. Big as it was, it had been smashed, and the door was slightly ajar. "Who the hell ever blasted that lock open—and just left it hanging there?" I asked. Chum's only answer was a giggle. He pulled the creaking door open, and familiar fumes of nitrate and phosgene rushed out at us. There was decomposing nitrate of cellulose within some of those scores and scores of film cans ranged on the vault shelves.

"My God!" breathed the film collector.

Chum's eyes were gleaming with proprietary pleasure. "The film companies sent all these prints in the 1920s for teachers to use training student organists to play with the movies. My room over there was their classroom. Behind it is the projection room. Everyone here has forgotten all about these rooms and these films. So I have parties and show them to my friends. These old movies are so campy you have to scream. The guys all wear lipstick—the women have black around their eyes and the film is colored—amber, pink, green, blue. They're really funny. There are hundreds of reels in here. I still have a lot to show that I haven't seen. What would you like to see?"

Engineer that he was, Chum had both the old Simplex projectors oiled and groomed to purring efficiency. He laced up the 1924 original print of *Peter Pan* as I settled myself into one of his secret pad's armchairs. The projection room was separate from the screening room, and the ports were glassed in. Behind decorator's curtains that opened smoothly, an old-style silver screen was revealed at the end of the room. All that was missing was the Allen Theatre's full orchestra of the Christmas-week run. The picture sparkled on the screen with its amber toning and the blue virage for nighttime in Kensington Gardens. I was ecstatic.

That forgotten vault was filled with still more treasure. After the *Peter Pan* screening, my trembling and hasty inventory revealed prints of Lubitsch's two great Pola Negri spectacles, *Carmen* and *Madame DuBarry*. John Barrymore's *Dr. Jekyll and Mr. Hyde*, another one near the top of my

Lubitsch's *Carmen*
(1920), with
Pola Negri and
Harry Liedtke

Emil Jannings and
Pola Negri in
Ernst Lubitsch's
Madame DuBarry
(1919)

Mr. Hyde relishes the murder of his prospective father-in-law: John Barrymore and Brandon Hurst in *Dr. Jekyll and Mr. Hyde* (1920).

want list, was there, and Chum obligingly screened it to my almost unendurable joy.

There were also prints of Emil Jannings as Henry VIII in *Anne Boleyn*, George Arliss' first version of both *Disraeli* and *The Man Who Played God*, Chaplin's *A Dog's Life* and several dozen programmers, for students had to learn to play for ordinary pictures as well as for the big ones. I felt like Ali Baba in the treasure cave. But I recognized that it would take almost forty thieves to carry out the operation that instantly came to mind.

"Chum, sit down and listen hard," I said. "We've got to figure something out. You think this stuff is funny. I think it's about as hilarious as the treasure stashed away in King Tut's tomb. This is mother-lode material in movie history, and it's at greater hazard than you can possibly imagine."

"Seems pretty safe to me. I've been using these films here for two years; no one seems to care or notice."

"Come on, Chum. I know you're an electronics technician. That's some kind of scientist, isn't it? So you must know *something* about chemistry. You can smell that smell in the vault, can't you? It means some of your films are stinky rotten. Haven't you come across any of them that have gone gooey?"

"Well, yes, one or two cans I've opened have film that's wet and sticky."

"All right. Know what that smell is? Part of it is phosgene gas. If you've read anything about the First World War, you know it's not healthy stuff. Know what those films are made of?"

"Celluloid, of course."

"Nitric and sulfuric acids, ether and alcohol; that adds up to what we used to call guncotton—an explosive. Nitrate-of-cellulose film will burn in a blinding flash. It will burn under water because it supplies its own oxygen. Since it is guncotton, it can explode. Spontaneous combustion can set it off. If one single can in your vault goes off, it will set off all the rest, and the explosion and fire could take not only your whole theatre, but the entire city block along with it."

Chum wasn't just pale; his forehead was sweat beaded. "Wait a minute, Card! These aren't *my* films! I didn't put them in here!"

"No, but you seem to be the only one who knows they're here. If the boys find out there's a whole vault of old, old nitrate film in the middle of the Eastman Theatre, where two or three thousand people gather every night in the week, all the safety experts in town will be swarming all over here."

"Who's going to tell them?"

"For God's sake, Chum, I already heard about your little film soirees in the executive dining room. Sooner or later the word will get around. Then one day they'll move in with the fire trucks and grab all these wonderful films, rush them out to the Park and dump them all in the silver-reclamation tanks."

"How come you're so certain of hysteria? No matter what you say about guncotton and all that crap, you can't convince me that films are more dangerous than gasoline. Does anyone run around hysterically because most everyone in the suburbs sleeps every night over ten or fifteen gallons of gas right under their beds in attached garages?"

"A lot of people are uptight about movie film because of a real bum rap nitrate took in Cleveland back in 1929. Ever hear of the Cleveland Clinic disaster?"

"I did at that. My dad lost a cousin in that fire. Now that you mention it, I remember it was blamed on burning X-ray films that were sup-

posed to have exploded, wasn't it? Why do you call it a bum rap for
nitrate film? That's what the X-ray film was, wasn't it?"

"Dr. George Crile was a name next to God's in Ohio. Clevelanders
figured the Crile Clinic was on a par with the Mayo operation. The
X-ray films were all on nitrate stock—their fumes when they burned
were blamed for the one hundred twenty-four deaths and the more than
forty other patients who were critically affected. It was a bum rap
because those fumes couldn't have killed patients all over the building.
I've been in seven nitrate-booth fires myself, and I'd be dead seven times
over if fumes of burning nitrate were as deadly as they claimed. What
puzzled me for years was that some of the rescuers working over the
victims outside the building, giving them artificial resuscitation, were
sickened by the fumes just coming out of the victims' lungs. Not even
phosgene will do that!"

"So what do you think it was?"

"Twenty years later I noticed a tiny item in the newspaper. To the
effect that Dr. George Crile's brother had just been awarded a special
medal by the War Department. For his pioneering efforts in developing
a poison war gas."

"That's a sick idea, Card. And it has nothing to do with the situation
here. What do you think we should do?"

"One way or another, we've got to get these films out of here before
the fire department gets wind of them. Who knows who the other guys
at the lunch table might talk to after Blair told us about your parties! I
have a buddy who collects 35mm film; I know he has hundreds of reels
of advertising stuff he's not much interested in. Let's get a count of the
actual number of reels of the stuff that ought to be saved."

We got right at it. *Peter Pan* was on eleven reels; *Dr. Jekyll and Mr.
Hyde*, seven; *Carmen*, six; *Anna Boleyn*, ten; *Passion* (*Madame DuBarry*),
eleven; *Disraeli*, nine; *The Man Who Played God*, eight; *A Dog's Life*,
four; *Primitive Lover*, seven.

"OK, Chum, that's seventy-three reels we've got to move out. All
the rest we'll leave for you to play with. I'll get in touch with my buddy
Johnny Allen. He's sure to go along with it. When we settle on a time,
I'll get back to you."

"What do you think you're going to do with seventy-three reels?"

"Get them copied on 16mm. It'll take us years, but remember,
Chum, half of those titles are *unique*. If we don't do it, they'll be lost
forever!"

Although Chum Morris looked a little dazed, he voiced no objections. Since Vachel Blair had broken the whole thing to begin with and was a cofounder of the Rochester Film Society, I knew him to be sympathetic to the need for saving the films. I felt he had to be in on the plot. But the key person was Johnny Allen, Sr.

On my job interview with Kodak, the man who was to become my great boss, Ken Edwards, head of Informational Films, used the existence of John Allen as part of his pitch to bring me to Rochester. He told me that John was, or had been, one of the country's most active film collectors. Professionally, John was a still photographer. But he had a passion for owning motion picture film. He had nitrate film stashed all over his home, under beds, in the closets, in the basement, the attic and the garage. Just the year before I'd come to Rochester, John's wife had delivered an ultimatum: "Either the films go or I go. Make up your mind." John then became the first major donor to the Library of Congress film collection. But his donation didn't move fast enough for John's first wife. She left him before all the film had gone to Washington.

Vachel and I arranged a hasty meeting with John Allen and Chum Morris. "John," I urged, "we need seventy-three reels of scrap 35mm film in twenty shipping cases. We'll need three limos or station wagons brought to one of the theatre's side doors on Swan Street after midnight. Chum, you be inside waiting for us and open the door at the time we arrange. Then we'll all have to scramble to lug in those twenty cases of scrap. We'll replace the reels of ten features in the vault with the scrap and rustle one hundred reels of the original prints back down to the cars. If Kodak ever cleans out that vault and destroys the films, it'll be mostly scrap that's lost."

"What do you expect to do with the originals?" asked John, a collector's gleam in his eyes. John had remarried, and his new wife took a much more civilized view of old nitrate. "Where will you store it?"

"In my garage. I'll put another plaster on the house, and little by little, have the films copied on 16mm—then put the originals back in the vault."

"That would take you thirty years," John said.

"Well worth it. Don't you realize, this is certainly the only print of *Peter Pan* in all the world we're talking about?"

"When will you be ready?" asked Chum.

"I'll have to rummage around a bit to line up a hundred reels of scrap—on reels," John admitted with some sorrow. "The three cars I can manage any time. How about the day after tomorrow? Two-thirty a.m.? Shall we synchronize our watches, men?" That was John Allen. Accommodating, and a man of action and few questions.

In retrospect, it does seem morally a little strange that, in all our councils regarding this caper, not once did any of us question the ethics of what we were about to do. Two factors may possibly help explain, if not justify, our attitude. First of all, a great war of liberation had just been completed. For the Allies, the term "liberation" came to be extended beyond a purely political sense. All manner of goods and properties were "liberated." I have seen important paintings—paintings by El Greco, Rembrandt and Renoir—hanging proudly in the homes of highly respected citizens, paintings that had been liberated from German homes, museums and strange hiding places while the war was ending for Germany.

Other than that lingering postwar semantic softness, there was the film fanatic's obsession, best expressed by Willard Van Dyke when he headed the Museum of Modern Art Film Library. He was describing the intense dedication of a veteran member of his curatorial staff. "She would sell her own grandmother," he insisted, "to save a film she considered important." Quite frankly, I am not too certain about how safe my grandmother might have been vis-à-vis *Peter Pan.*

In any case, morality aside, at precisely 2:30 a.m.—the hour at which sober citizens are said to sleep most soundly—three long black cars rolled to the curb of Swan Street, to the stage door of the Eastman Theatre. We waited for it to open. And waited. It never did.

By 3:30 a.m. I was frantically calling Chum Morris on his private line. When he answered, he didn't sound as though he were still smiling. "I've been trying to reach you all night! You're not going to believe what happened."

I was silently ready not to believe.

"They're planning to have a gala celebration of the twenty-fifth anniversary of the Eastman Theatre. The conductor of the Philharmonic, Guy Fraser Harrison, remembered the films. They came to the vault today and made an inventory of everything in it. They're going to show *Disraeli* at the gala. With the full orchestra in the pit. The Kodak people are coming today to check the films and take out all the reels that have begun to go. That's the end of it."

I had never known so bleak a moment. It was only 3:30 a.m. There was nothing I could do. There was no one I could see before nine o'clock. Six hours of agonizing frustration.

Since the death of George Eastman, the theatre had become part of the University of Rochester's Eastman School of Music. All the public functions involving the theatre were controlled by a kind of tsar—the head of a group of Rochester VIPs called the Civic Music Association. Arthur M. See was the autocratic boss of all that went on inside the Eastman Theatre.

I was in his office when it opened that morning. I was figuratively, but almost literally, on my knees to Mr. See. I warned him that Kodak would cheerfully melt the silver off the whole collection of nitrate film at the slightest whiff of decomposition. Mr. See was a man obviously uncomfortable with hyperbole, and as I tried, with surely too much desperation, to tell him how rare most of those prints were, and, in some cases, how absolutely unique in their survival, he grew more and more impatient with me.

As a last resort I tried revealing to him a well-kept secret, officially known to not more than five top Kodak executives, all of whom would have been quite dismayed to learn that the nosy Mr. Card had snooped out knowledge of it months ago. That secret was that in a year's time, the former residence of George Eastman, then the domicile of See's own boss, the president of the university, would become a museum of photography and motion pictures—an institution that would be hunting all over the world for films like those in his own vault, about to be melted away by Kodak. At this, he looked at me with alarmed skepticism. I begged him. "Call Iris Barry at the Museum of Modern Art! Ask her about these films and their importance."

That much he was willing to do. To their eternal credit, the good folks at the Museum of Modern Art urged him to send them the films. They agreed to care for them against the day when there might really be a museum at Eastman House.

All the nitrate prints that were not decomposing were sent to the museum in New York. Except for *Disraeli*, which had been chosen for showing at the twenty-fifth anniversary of the Eastman Theatre in 1947, with music furnished by the entire Philharmonic.

In a happy epilogue to this drama, in 1951, when there really was an Eastman House film collection and a Dryden Theatre to show nitrate films, the museum sent the films all back to Rochester in my care. There, the whole Eastman Theatre collection was copied on safety film, while the original prints are to this day still available for screening in the Dryden Theatre.

It was an exceptionally rare and satisfying return engagement: on the evening of January 13, 1973, there was celebrated in the Eastman Theatre an event called the Golden Twenties Gala in Honor of George Eastman and the Fiftieth Anniversary of the Eastman Theatre and the Rochester Philharmonic Orchestra. *Peter Pan* was back on the screen of the Eastman Theatre, with full orchestral accompaniment.

CHAPTER 6

A Tsardom of Shadows

O ne of the most important of all early film books is not listed in any bibliography that I have ever seen. It is Boleslav Matuzewski's *La Photographie Animée* (Paris: Imprimerie Noizette, 1898). It may be the most rare of all published works on motion pictures.

The book exists because Tsar Nicholas II became the world's most highly placed movie buff of the nineteenth century. His coronation in 1896 was the earliest investiture ever to be recorded by a motion picture camera. The enterprising Lumière brothers, having invented their Cinématographe just the year before, sent their man Francis Doublier to Russia to film Nicholas' assumption of the throne.

As the first king ever to be captured on film, Nicholas was enchanted with this device that offered him a lively immortality. He hoped to keep the magical machine all to himself, but in the spring of 1898, two years after his coronation, the Cinématographe made its public debut in St. Petersburg. The sensational event took place on May 16, 1898, when films were shown between acts of *Alfred-Pasha in Paris*, a trivial operetta that possesses no other distinction than having embraced the premiere showing of motion pictures in Russia.

The next Russian showing of the Lumière films took place in Nizhni Novgorod. Covering that event for the *Odessa News* was a young journalist, Maxim Gorki, who reported:

Yesterday I was in a tsardom of shadows. You can't imagine how strange it was there. There were no sounds and no colors. There, everything—the earth, the country, the people, the water, the air—everything is painted in a grey monotone: in a grey sky there are grey rays of sun; on grey faces there are grey eyes; the leaves of the trees are as grey as ashes. . . . This isn't life—it's a shadow of life. This isn't movement—it's a soundless shadow of movement.*

Evidently the film Gorki watched had been poorly developed—a not-unexpected fading of the image, what with the film's travels from Paris to Russia. Later on, Gorki was less critical. In fact, he became fascinated with film and was one of the first to become totally aware of its devastating possibilities as a political weapon. He expressed his enthusiasm to none other than Lenin himself, who announced that film was "the most important of all the arts for us."

Since the movies as a medium slipped from his personal grasp, Nicholas did the next best thing. He became a moviemaker himself. He established the post of royal court cinematographer. The position went to the pioneer Polish cameraman, Boleslav Matuzewski. Matuzewski, when he was not filming the royal family, found a great deal to occupy his camera. He shot military training films, recorded unusual operating techniques in the imperial hospitals, and, of course, he covered all the events that the court considered of historical import.

As his film records grew in number, Matuzewski realized that he was capturing a unique treasure trove of the very source materials of history. Excited by this notion, he wrote his book about all that he had been doing and the significance of motion picture documents for education and information. Then he went to Paris with a brave and daring idea. He knew that other cameramen were beginning to record news events and scientific and instructional films in Paris, Berlin, New York and Chicago. To an enraptured French press, Matuzewski announced that he had been authorized by the tsar to establish in Paris the first of an international chain of motion picture archives. Historians of the future would have the privilege of consulting filmed documents of all the world events from the year 1898 on into infinity and the television and videotape era—thanks to the depots of film archives throughout the world.

The project was greeted with enormous enthusiasm by the French press. But the chain of depositories never came into being. Notwithstanding its imperial champion in Russia, film had just not made it yet into the kind of respectability that would induce endowments. The

---

* N. A. Lebedev, *Ocherk Istorii Kino SSSR*, translated by Barry Paris.

great chance was lost to have an unbroken motion picture record of the formative years of cinema and a complete film archive of the fascinating period when the nineteenth century gave way to the twentieth. And even Matuzewski's own Russian archive was scattered like the White Russians themselves during the chaotic days of the Revolution. Both Poland and Russia now claim Matuzewski as a major film pioneer. But his position as a crusader for the saving of existing films has never been acknowledged.

Had it not been for the letter of the copyright laws in the United States that specifically mandated paper copies, many decades would have gone by before any attempt was made to save motion picture films in this country. The wording of the law of copyright in the United States specified submitting work on paper in order to have a creation protected. Thomas Edison was a stickler for the legal protection of his projects—especially those he'd "adapted" from other inventors. As the law made no mention of submitting film for copyrighting, the Library of Congress, as the governmental granter of copyrights, insisted that filmmakers print positive images of their negatives on rolls of paper. With Edison's films, the paper prints were made directly from unedited film negatives. Eighty years later, misguided film historians, transferring those paper rolls to film again, excitedly proclaimed that the Edison films showed an audacious way of filming. Edison's chief cameraman, Edwin Porter, shot all the exteriors at the same time, then all the interiors. For his release prints, of course, he edited his shots in the negative to obtain consecutive action. But the unedited paper rolls group all the exteriors together, followed by the interiors. Thinking this was Porter's deliberate release-print editing, the historians put together a film (narrated by Blanche Sweet) claiming a discovered technique in their reconstruction of *The Life of an American Fireman*. Oddly, it never occurred to these discoverers that Porter had simply printed the paper rolls the way the negatives had been shot: all the interiors one after the other, the exteriors done at another time and the scenes intercut later.

Matuzewski had not been the only one to publish a call for some kind of film archive. Burns Mantle, film critic and reviewer for *Photoplay* magazine, reviewed Tourneur's picture *The Last of the Mohicans* in 1921. He wrote: "If we had a National Cinematographic library, as we should have, into the archives of which each year were placed the best pictures and finest examples of the cinematographic art achieved during that year . . . I certainly should include 'The Last of the Mohicans.'"

Not until the mid-1930s did the pleas of Matuzewski and the hopes of Burns Mantle materialize. There had been specialized film archives usually maintained by the military establishment of the major powers, after all the generals and the war-games officers eagerly reviewed what motion picture records they had of actual battles and armaments in use. The Germans even preserved such flights of fancy as Urban's *Battle in the Clouds* of 1909—a Vernean melodrama that showed the bombing of Britain by dirigibles, the gasbags being attacked by defending combat planes and the ultimate weapon—a guided missile.

At last three nations had the foresight to combine in their mutual interest in preserving, exhibiting and circulating films they considered important to the history of the medium that more and more savants were daring to call a form of art. It was Britain, Germany and France that became the charter members of the International Federation of Film Archives, soon to operate under the rubric FIAF (Fédération Internationale des Archives de Film). The organization unified the projects of the Reichsfilmarchiv in Germany, the British Film Archive and the Cinémathèque Française in Paris. The members of FIAF restored and exhibited many of the early films they were able to acquire. The newly established Museum of Modern Art in New York set up a film library in May of 1935. For its first curator, it brought the British film critic Iris Barry from London. Shortly thereafter, the film library joined FIAF.

Iris Barry considered the Museum of Modern Art Film Library to be a colonial outpost of the British Film Archive. She approached her responsibility as a film curator not as an historian, but with the attitude of the film critic that she had been. Imagine a film archive headed by a film critic like *Esquire*'s John Simon, saving only those films considered worthy by its curator! Iris Barry's taste was only slightly more catholic than one might expect from a critic with little regard for the history of cinema.

Yet Iris Barry's selections for preservation were crucial. In 1935 all 35mm negative stock was on nitrate film—that material doomed to disaster or to certain disintegration. Films throughout the entire world were printed on nitrate of cellulose, and thousands of titles had already been lost through fires, decomposition or deliberate destruction in silver-recovery vats. The motion picture industry itself was paying no attention whatsoever to preserving its own films. Original negatives were held in its vaults only as legal proof of ownership. If Paramount was to sell its rights in a film to MGM, the legal papers concerning that sale, along with the original negatives of the film being sold, would be moved from the Paramount vaults to those of MGM. Each major producer usually kept a 35mm library positive on hand for his own directors and producers to consult in the event of a remake. But as soon as his vault men reported the tiniest whiff of decomposition, the entire film, negative or library positive would be discarded. Unhappily, subtitles, spliced into the film, were the last bits added to a print, and they were done in a hurry because there were constant changes being made to the text. And as it was with the hurriedly printed newsreel, the labs just didn't take the time needed to wash all the hyposulfate out of those films. Remaining hypo inevitably caused rapid disintegration of the film. So often the decomposition detected by the vault man would be confined to only a few titles that could have readily been spliced out, thus saving all the rest of the film. But that was not done; one mark of decay in one part of a one-thousand-foot reel would condemn the whole film—even the perfectly healthy other nine or ten reels of a feature. In this way, thousands and thousands of American films were lost forever.

Thus it was that any film chosen by Iris Barry for the Museum of Modern Art Film Library had the best possible chance of survival. Her rejection of any film for preservation was tantamount to condemning it to death.

But even the placement of a sole-surviving copy of a given film in the museum's collection (or in any other collection) was not certain insurance for its continued existence. In a carefully concealed series of fires in the museum's vaults, a tragic number of irreplaceable films were lost. Among them were Theda Bara's *Cleopatra* and *Salome*—films that as of this writing are still not known to exist.

Disastrous nitrate fires have happened to every major archive handling old 35mm film. The Cinémathèque Française lost von Stroheim's *Wedding of the Prince*—the second and crucial part of *The Wedding March*—and *A Social Celebrity*, with Louise Brooks. No copies of either have since been located. Film archives in France suffer under a series of Lewis Carrollian enactments: it is unlawful to *have* nitrate film, to store or project nitrate film, and it is illegal to transport nitrate film anywhere—not even to a dump or an incinerator. In this country, the Museum of Modern Art and the George Eastman House are two of the very few places one may still see projected, original, 35mm nitrate films.

As a Briton, Iris Barry disliked many American films, and through unfamiliarity with regional aspects of life in the United States, she

Was the Egyptian queen a
vamp? As embodied
by Theda Bara, Mark
Antony hadn't a chance, in
Cleopatra (1917).

Add John the Baptist to
the victims of Theda Bara
in *Salome* (1918).

Iris Barry with
Ove Brusendorff, director
of the Danish Film
Museum, Copenhagen

found many to be utterly unintelligible. "There's less to this film than meets the eye" was the neat put-down Iris originated.

In a Museum of Modern Art bulletin of 1941,* Iris wrote a piece on selection problems: "Take the case of Will Rogers' 'The Headless Horseman', first feature film on panchromatic stock. . . . It would be difficult to view without boredom."

All right, Iris, we'll take that case. Thousands of Americans have viewed it without boredom. Many of us to this very day are able to enjoy in it the almost unique attention given to the early Hudson River background. Not only was the film beautifully photographed on the new panchromatic film, but the picture was shot on location using as many as possible of the buildings still standing from Ichabod Crane's time. Perhaps Will Rogers was not the ideal embodiment of Washington Irving's Ichabod, but how delightful it was in the movie when the grotesque schoolmaster took his charges on a tour of the seventeenth-century graveyard and read to them the tombstone inscription: "Here lies the body of John Mound; lost at sea and never found."

* *The Bulletin of the Museum of Modern Art* 5, no. 8 (June–July 1941).

There was also an exceedingly important element in the film that completely escaped the notice of a former Londoner. This is an episode in *The Headless Horseman* that did not come from Washington Irving's *Legend of Sleepy Hollow;* a group of folks, instigated by Ichabod Crane's rival for the affections of Katrina Van Tassel, have seized the hapless teacher and are about to tar and feather him. Tarring and feathering was a colonial-period form of punishment that, along with ducking stools, has usually been presented as a somewhat comic activity. Neither was very funny. They were both cruel and savage tortures. The tar-and-feather routine was usually inflicted by vigilante mobs and involved stripping the victim and coating him with boiling, liquid tar before the feathers were added. It amounted to execution by burns, which, if not immediately fatal, permitted the dying person to be "ridden out of town on a rail," the object of vicious derision. In the film Ichabod is saved from this ghastly treatment only by the heroic efforts of a young black boy—about ten or twelve years of age. This handsome hero, with never one frame of cuteness, with no white teeth flashing or eyes rolling, is shown to ride like Paul Revere to Crane's rescue, summoning the good burghers of the town to save him from the tar bath, which is shown ominously bubbling and boiling over the sides of the cauldron.

Such noncaricaturized use of a black character is without parallel in American movies before Monta Bell's *Man, Woman, and Sin.* Strange that neither of these films was mentioned by Peter Noble in his monograph for *Sight and Sound* ("The Negro in American Films"). For many years the British enjoyed castigating Americans for their cultural mistreatment of blacks—through the years before the wholesale immigration of Indians to the British Isles.

In the 1930s American intellectuals were having their great flirtation with Marxism, and for them a Soviet-Russian movie, however stupid, was a splendid example of "the people's art." Pre-1933 German films were considered important, too. (This was before Siegfried Kracauer, in his *From Caligari to Hitler,* tried to show that the important German silents all foreshadowed the coming of Nazism.)

The first film series circulated by the Museum of Modern Art Film Library included some strange choices. Shorts and excerpts from several films were included, but shown completely were these features under the following program headings: "The Development of the Narrative," *Queen Elizabeth* (1911), French, with Sarah Bernhardt.

SERIES I: THE RISE OF THE AMERICAN FILM

	A Fool There Was (1914) the celebrated Theda Bara vamp movie
D. W. Griffith	*Intolerance* (1916)
The German Influence	Murnau's *Sunrise* (1927)
The Talkies	*All Quiet on the Western Front* (1930)
The End of the Silent Era	*The Last Command* (1928), von Sternberg with Emil Jannings

SERIES II: SOME MEMORABLE AMERICAN FILMS

The "Western" Film	*The Covered Wagon* (1923)
Comedies	*The Freshman* (1925), Harold Lloyd's masterpiece
The Film and Contemporary Life	*Cavalcade* (1933) [This Noel Coward hit certainly had nothing to do with contemporary American life!]
Mystery and Violence	*Underworld* (1927), von Sternberg
Screen Personalities	*Monsieur Beaucaire* (1924), Rudolph Valentino

From 1935 to 1950 the Museum of Modern Art made ruts in film history so deep that obliteration has seemed impossible. Theirs were the films that were circulated to American museums and schools. Whatever was written about early films was based on seeing these, the only movies available to study in the United States. Of course, the foreign archivists were busy exchanging films with one another. The curators of the British Film Archive and the FIAF archives of Copenhagen, Rome, Turin, Lausanne and Tokyo were able to appreciate and treasure the jewels of the Cinémathèque Française. But a certain reverse chauvinism prevailed. In London, British films were slighted, and, again thanks to Iris, there was little respect for English films other than those of Alfred Hitchcock and Anthony Asquith. The art of cinema continued to be exemplified by the films of Russia, Germany, France and Sweden.

Rudolf Arnheim's *Film** (1933) and Paul Rotha's *The Film Till Now*

* *Film als Kunst.*

(1930) were perhaps the most influential works read in English that helped create a slowly dawning awareness that there could be serious appreciation of motion pictures as art.

Iris Barry had published *Let's Go to the Movies* (1926) while she was still a London critic, but during her tenure as film curator at the Museum of Modern Art she did not venture a book, which might have established her criteria. Perhaps she was far too busy. Charting the hazardous course of America's first film archive was more than a full-time job. The Hollywood establishment was suspicious and paranoid about any institution's having physical possession of its product, even more wary of having some corporation other than its own circulating its films for money. The last to tentatively participate was MGM, and after a few years it withdrew all its films from the museum, as it saw more and more of its properties appearing for sale on the black market.

The museum had on its board a number of heavyweights that Hollywood could not easily ignore. Along with Nelson Rockefeller, Jock Whitney and William Paley were big guns that folks in the film world, their home offices in New York, had to deal with frequently.

One disastrous nitrate fire, publicly unreported, all but wiped out the museum's entire 35mm collection, and Iris Barry was forced to go to European archives to replace most of the museum's basic holdings. But the unique prints, like the Theda Baras, were irreplaceable. Such accidents were not reassuring to the American film industry, nor was the increasingly frequent appearance of the museum's films on the growing black market.

Dick Griffith, then Iris Barry's assistant, tells of going into her office, where he could usually expect to find her in a frenzy of activity, but now she just stood looking out the window, staring down onto West Fifty-third Street. Amazed, he asked, "What are you doing, Iris?" "I'm waiting for the next disaster to happen," she answered.

Instead of writing her own book, Iris decided to godmother a French history that she thought well of. It was Maurice Bardeche and Robert Brasillach's *The History of Motion Pictures*, published in New York in 1938 by the Museum of Modern Art, translated and heavily annotated by Iris Barry—annotated so heavily that many of her footnotes completely negated the observations of the authors. (Immediately after World War II, Brasillach was even more severely negated. The French executed him as a collaborationist.)

The nearest work to an official Museum of Modern Art film history came from Iris Barry's other assistant, Arthur Knight. But his *Liveliest*

Art (1957) was really an elaborate catalogue of the museum's collection. Significantly, it was published by the H. W. Wilson Company, a specialist in catalogues and reference works. The author never strayed very far in his "history" from those examples held by the Museum of Modern Art Film Library.

The result was the establishment of a highly limited pantheon of "significant" films. Until 1950, when Eastman House began its film collection, there was no other in the United States that offered an alternative to the museum's. Although the Library of Congress was groaning with prints submitted to establish ownership and copyright, it could neither circulate nor exhibit those legal documents.

After 1912, the library had modified its requirements so that it would accept prints on film rather than on paper. It was soon realized that with upward of three hundred features being submitted in a year, the library would speedily run out of storage space. The first solution was to accept frames clipped from a film work to be submitted, along with a script, in order to copyright a feature or a short.

When it was objected that a script and a few frames hardly constituted an adequate record of an important film, another concession was made. A library committee was formed to select a limited number of films each year that the committee considered most worthy of preservation—in their complete form. They could then each year request, from a producer seeking to copyright his work, not just the deposit of an envelope of clips, but the submission of the entire film. Obviously the situation was not conducive to research. But then in the 1930s, other than in California, no universities were conducting film courses. The few writers who hoped to discuss film history had to go to the major producers. If the writer possessed sufficient prestige or effective connection to persuade Paramount, MGM, Fox or Universal to pull its library positives out of the vault and admit the would-be author to its private screening rooms, the writer just might be able to look at a few subjects other than the "classics" available at the Museum of Modern Art.

There were few writers who troubled. Terry Ramsaye, involved in trade-journal publishing, did his two-volume *A Million and One Nights* in 1926, long considered the bible of the industry and not to be challenged.

Benjamin B. Hampton in 1931 did a much less opinionated *History of the Movies.* Gilbert Seldes[*] and Lewis Jacobs[†] wrote widely read film books in the 1930s, but for the most part, they wrote about too many

[*] Gilbert Seldes, *The Movies Come from America* (1937).
[†] Lewis Jacobs, *The Rise of the American Film* (New York, 1939).

films they'd never seen, providing widely accepted misinformation they never bothered to correct in several reprintings. Surmise and speculation, carelessly blended with fact, have passed from writer to writer, from country to country. The real madness of the situation can be appreciated by imagining critical evaluations of music based only on titles printed in record catalogues. Or the serious discussion of a whole school of painting by a writer who predicates his conclusions on some museum's catalogue descriptions without having troubled to look at the artist's work.

Yet film writers have not thought it Gilbertian to classify a film on the basis of its title alone. They have coolly compared the merits of various pioneers' contributions with nothing more to go on than catalogue synopses of their unexamined work. Authors have been known to describe the content of an unseen film in their published work without giving the reader the slightest hint that the information is utter supposition.

Publishing irresponsibility reached a nadir in the second edition of Lewis Jacobs' *The Rise of the American Film*. By that time, there were enough crotchety film buffs who had written to Jacobs protesting the wildest of his errors. But not a single one of them was corrected. In the second and all subsequent editions, there remains a hopeless tangle concerning Griffith's films *The Battle* (1911) and *The Battle at Elderbush Gulch* (1913). Jacobs' book reproduces Griffith's famous ad in the *New York Dramatic Mirror* of December 3, 1913. That curious proclamation of Griffith's "priorities" clearly states that *The Battle of* [sic] *Elderbush Gulch* was a multiple-reel feature that had not yet been released, and it lists *The Battle* as a separate production. Mr. Jacobs apparently hasn't read his own copy, for he misinforms the reader that *The Battle* is the shortened title under which *The Battle of Elderberry* [sic] *Gulch* was released.

As a ghastly example of how four different historians, copying one another's misinformation instead of *looking at the film* they presume to discuss, have succeeded in muddying up the record of one very important film, here are two fat mistakes and their offspring:

ERROR 1: Lewis Jacobs in *The Rise of the American Film* calls *The Battle at Elderbush Gulch*, "*The Battle of Elderberry Gulch.*"

ERROR 2: Jacobs says that *The Battle* is the shortened title under which *The Battle of Elderberry Gulch* was released.

ERROR 3: Seymour Stern in *An Index to the Creative Work of David Wark Griffith* in a *Special Supplement to Sight and Sound* (April 1944) lists *The Battle of Elderbush Gulch* and states: "Also known as

'The Battle at Elderbush Gulch' also erroneously as 'The Battle of (at) Elderberry Gulch.' A lengthier and more ambitious one of the Civil War genre-and-battle films, anticipating 'The Birth Of A Nation.' "

ERROR 4: Peter Noble in *The Cinema and the Negro, Special Supplement to Sight and Sound* (March 1948) lists *The Battle at Elderbush Gulch* and notes "This was, to quote Seymour Stern, 'a lengthier and more ambitious one of the Civil War battle-and-genre films, anticipating "The Birth Of A Nation." ' "

Unfortunately for the pertinence of Mr. Noble's index, there was not a single black in the Griffith film. Unfortunately for the accuracy of the whole mess of comments, the film had *nothing* to do with the Civil War! It is the story of a group of Western settlers embroiled with Indians. Perhaps it seems unduly pedantic to discuss each error that veils this particular film. But it serves as an illustration of the vicissitudes of a single mistake and how that error can be taken up by other misinformed writers.

Peter Noble was the editor of *The British Film Yearbook* and the author of *The Art of Cinema, The Negro in Films* and *Hollywood Scapegoat: The Story of Erich von Stroheim.* He was one of those British writers who found a wide readership and made a career of castigating Americans for their mistreatment of blacks and such creative geniuses as Stroheim. He includes *The Battle at Elderbush Gulch* in his index *The Cinema and the Negro* merely on the basis of Stern's mistaken contention that the film had to do with the Civil War and the assumption that any Griffith film on the Civil War *had* to malign the Negro. Of course, Noble did not list in his index *The Headless Horseman* or any other American film that presented a favorable image of a Negro. Also he quite inaccurately includes in his index as a British film (and hence less discriminatory than American movies) Paul Robeson's second film, *Borderline,* which was by no means British. It was a Swiss film made by Kenneth MacPherson. Here we have three different writers classifying an important film that none of them had ever seen.

Given the illusory nature of the medium, just seeing a picture once is not really enough to write about it confidently. In *The Liveliest Art,* Arthur Knight undertakes to describe the emotional power of the close-up. Quite rightly, he states:

> The close-up does more than merely emphasize what is important in a scene: it eliminates everything else. It forces the audience to see what

the director wants it to see—and only that. It concentrates attention on the significant detail, whether it be an object, an actor, or a portion of an actor. Griffith discovered that the close-up of a hand, an arm, the eyes or lips could often be far more expressive on the screen than the most highly trained actor projecting an emotion in theatrical terms. Unforgettable is the scene of the Little Colonel's homecoming in "The Birth Of A Nation" (1915). Only the arms of the mother and sister are seen as they tenderly enfold him and draw him in toward his family.

Unforgettable indeed, but Arthur Knight did forget that the scene he described so vividly was not shot in close-ups at all. The whole sequence was in a medium-long shot. Mother and sister were both invisible just inside the door. Only their arms could be seen as they drew Henry Walthall inside. But it was a *theatrical* scene, one that could have been produced exactly that way on the stage with the same effectiveness.

If we are to teach film history and film aesthetics and if we are going to write about films, they better be watched carefully, and, ideally, each had better be seen more than once. The emotional impact of a movie, especially a good one, can easily lead the observer down the primrose path of inaccuracy.

Mae Marsh and Henry B. Walthall in the memorable Southern Ermine scene from *The Birth of a Nation* (1915)

CHAPTER 7

The Rochester Rival:
"An Archive of Trivia"

In 1905, George Eastman, the snapshot tycoon, occupied palatial quarters on East Avenue, the elm-shaded multimillionaire row of Rochester, New York. But his castlelike mansion was a forbidding stronghold. Bachelor Eastman lived with his mother. Their home lacked only a moat and portcullis to make it appear that Mrs. Eastman was an ensorcelled queen secluded behind grey walls.

Eastman's solution for her rescue from surroundings so gloomy was to build a bright new palace, set far back from the avenue on ten acres of dazzling gardens, fountains, trellised walkways and even a mini-herd of cattle to graze picturesquely over a carefully tended, modified meadow. Supplied with milk, cream, cheese and even water, all fresh and pure from their own estate, Eastman and his mother lived in their baronial surroundings, now blessed by sunlight and beauty. In the sitting rooms were oil paintings envied by the local art museum. There was a Tintoretto, a Rembrandt, a Van Dyck, a Romney, and for a while *The Blue Boy* hung on Eastman's wall until he decided he didn't much like it. A mighty theatre organ, manipulated by a private organist, turned the breakfasts that George Eastman took in a leafy solarium into daily inspiriting musicales.

In his will, Eastman specified that his home should provide living quarters for the presidents of the University of Rochester until such time as the university might come up with some more useful role for the home. Eastman's suicide ("My work is finished. Why wait?") occurred in 1932, and two different university presidents dwelled in Eastmanian luxury until, in 1948, the powerful Eastman Kodak Company (which thought

The George Eastman House, built in 1905, opened as a museum of photography in 1949.

nothing of bullying the University of Rochester) decided to move President Alan Valentine across the street and make other use of the George Eastman House.

There was an official and an unofficial reason for the decision. The official reason was that Kodak had purchased the world's greatest photographic collection from the widow of Gabriel Cromer in Paris and needed a place to put it. Cromer, with the single-minded obsession of a great collector, had gathered in all existing incunabula significant to the development of photography, as well as the French contributions to motion pictures. The collection included Daguerre materials and cameras, the Wedgwood experimental apparatus, original work of Julia Margaret Cameron and Nicephore Nièpce, the pioneer artist-photographers—even original posters by Toulouse-Lautrec, advertising early camera shops. It was a prodigious collection, and throughout his life Cromer never doubted that the French government, as a matter of national priority, France having been the birthplace of photography itself, would eagerly care for his surviving wife and its own cultural heritage as well. Alas, after Cromer's death, the French government chose to ignore both the Widow Cromer and the Cromer collection. Dr. Walter Clark, formerly of the British Museum, was one of the top scientists in Kodak's research laboratory. He realized the enormous importance and value of the Cromer collection and urged the company to acquire it and provide a museum to house it. It was assumed that Walter Clark would become the first director of such a museum.

But assumptions often take highly unexpected turns when decisions lie in corporate hands. The Eastman Kodak Company was controlled by executives who looked out over the whole city of Rochester from the windows of their Kodak Tower offices. For years the tower was the tallest building in the city and, of course, the most prestigious.

Kodak, unlike universities and most museums, did not replace its chief executive officer from time to time by sending out a search committee. Traditionally, the company filled its top positions from its own ranks. And power was both symbolically and literally ranked from floor to floor, the offices on high being the most lavishly arranged and furnished and enjoying the most spectacular views.

There was one joker in the stacking of that deck. On the top floor, the best office was occupied not by the president or even by a senior vice president. Not even by the chairman of the board. It was held by one General Oscar Nathaniel Solbert. And his company rank was ambiguous; he was designated as an assistant to the vice president.

General Solbert had a résumé far more formidable than any of the other executives, with only one exception: Major General Ted Curtis, head of the Motion Picture Division. Ted Curtis had been a combat flyer in World War I and a senior staff officer in the Air Corps through World War II. Oscar Solbert was outranked by Curtis, being simply a brigadier general. But the factors that rated him the best office in the tower included having been a friend of George Eastman himself, a wondrously stubborn contender in the battle of life, a social lion among lesser cats and a climber who never relaxed for one waking second in his life. To the end of his life in the 1970s, his enduring enthusiasms were unquenchable.

Oscar was one of five children born in a hamlet far to the north in Sweden. In 1893 his family arrived in the United States and settled in Worcester, Massachusetts. Oscar didn't stay settled very long. He managed an appointment to West Point, and in 1910 he graduated sixth in his class. Four years later he was back at West Point as an instructor. In his class on the art of war, one of his cadet pupils was Dwight D. Eisenhower.

In 1917, when the United States entered the war, we simply had no intelligence in place. As it would also be in World War II, "neutral" Sweden was the happy hunting ground of espionage agents—or rather, the capital of the agents' spymasters. A pioneer in military intelligence,

Oscar became military attaché to Denmark and Norway with special personal links to the royal family of Sweden, whose members he cultivated like a hungry relation.

Five years after the war ended, Oscar Solbert became military attaché in London, where he also became a hunting buddy of the future king of England, then the Prince of Wales. Under the Coolidge presidency, this well-connected immigrant from Sweden became the military aide in the White House. It was from this lofty position that he went to Kodak and then took time out to become chief of special services in the European theatre during World War II. One of Oscar's newsworthy coups was to put up the king and queen of Sweden in George Eastman's home while the boss was off hunting big game in Africa with Osa and Martin Johnson.

This was not a man who could be easily dislodged from the best office in the Kodak Tower. Nevertheless, in those days stupidity did not reign at Kodak. They found an irresistible way to lure the general from his aerie. The brilliant solution was to place the Cromer collection in the George Eastman House, to make Oscar Solbert the museum's first director, allowing him to make his home in the very rooms where the king and queen of Sweden had been houseguests. Dr. Walter Clark, who had persuaded Kodak to rescue the Cromer collection from France, was passed over in favor of General Solbert, who cheerfully vacated the coveted Kodak Tower office.

Beaumont Newhall, who had been the Museum of Modern Art's curator of photography, was brought from New York to become the curator of the George Eastman House of Photography. I managed to get there the same year, 1948, but not without a carefully crafted plot that involved dangling as bait my personal film collection.

By 1948 my collection had grown to some eight hundred titles. Gathered around my treasured *Cabinet of Dr. Caligari* were some other jewels. There was John Collins' impressive *The Cossack Whip*, starring his wife, Viola Dana, and *Maciste in Hell*, an Italian spectacle that is really more than spectacular. There were rarities like the 1917 *Log of the U-35*, a German U-boat commander's filmed log of his sinkings of Allied shipping, and *Unmasked* of the same year, a melodrama directed by Francis Ford, who later urged his brother John to come to Hollywood, where he became one of the ace American directors. *Unmasked* starred Francis Ford himself opposite Grace Cunard, one of the serial-specialist heroines of Hollywood movies during the teens.

Lent to Eastman House, my collection would become the nucleus of

Viola Dana in *The Cossack Whip* (1916). Trained as a dancer, Viola was impressive as a dancing spy.

its own famous archive, but first I had to get myself on the staff. I had not been invited to join it. There was a long-standing tradition that no one ever willingly resigned from the lifetime featherbed offered by the Eastman Kodak Company. General Solbert was a notorious pinch-penny. His idea was that I should continue at Kodak, letting them pay me, while he used my films and enthusiasm for free at Eastman House. But for three years I'd been driving past Eastman House on my way to the Kodak office, and every time I passed that beckoning mansion, I longed to be there, as some yearn for the fields of Paradise. I not only threatened to leave Kodak, I lined up a job with filmmakers in Chicago and rented a house in nearby Evanston. This convinced the general. He then offered me a job at Eastman House. But at less pay.

I became officially the assistant to the curator, Beaumont Newhall. My first assignment was to make three films—one on the making of daguerreotypes. The other was to be on the wet-collodion process, and the third on the British inventor Henry Fox Talbot, who worked with paper negatives.

Ultimately, I would become vice director, then director, of the

The Dryden Theatre of George Eastman House, which opened in 1951

The theatre seated 550 and was usually filled to capacity for every film program, preceded by a brief commentary by James Card.

Department of Film and, finally, acting director, while the search committee found someone who knew and cared nothing about motion pictures to be director after Beaumont Newhall left our happy home.

The whole year of 1948 was hectic for the three of us, getting the place ready for a scheduled opening in November of 1949. But once the preparations and the festivities were over, I could turn my full attention to building a film collection. The Cromer collection, although rich in cinematographic incunabula, unfortunately included no films. There was the apparatus of Georges Demeny, Bouly's pre-Lumière Cinématographe and all the zoetropes, Praxinoscopes and every other kind of scope one could hope for. There were multiple examples of the Gaumont sound and color cameras and projectors, along with the sound discs of 1909, but, alas, not a single one of the films they had produced and projected.

And my own films needed a place to be shown. In 1946, while I was still at Kodak, Vachel Blair and I had started the first film society of Rochester, with meetings in the art gallery. But if Eastman House were to have an important film collection, it needed a theatre.

George Eastman's only living relation at that time was his niece, Ellen Andrus Dryden, wife of Chicago rubber baron George B. Dryden. The Drydens were persuaded to build us a theatre attached to Eastman

The film vault at Eastman House

House. In 1951 it was opened to the public with a showing of Jean Renoir's *Nana*, one of the prized films in my collection.

The Dryden Theatre Film Society was established with three thousand ardent members. Since the theatre seated only 550, each film showing was repeated three times. With this kind of numerical and monetary success, the project of collecting films was off to an auspicious start. First on the agenda was to get the precious Eastman Theatre nitrate prints back from the Museum of Modern Art. Back they finally came, after much diplomatic importuning. Good thing too; the museum had not copied a single one of them. We immediately began making dupe negatives.

We had two great advantages to offset the enormous obstacle in beginning a film archive. The biggest obstacle was the conviction in 1951 that all films worth preserving were already in the Museum of Modern Art collection. If a film was worthy, why wasn't it at the prestigious MoMA? In most quarters there was little enthusiasm for going after any other titles. But I was certain that Iris Barry had missed many of the best ones, such as King Vidor's *The Crowd*, von Sternberg's *The Docks of New York*, DeMille's 1915 *The Cheat* and some of the essential experiments like von Sternberg's *The Salvation Hunters*, which the museum had lost. Our greatest strength was Kodak's vice-president in charge of motion pictures, Major General Edward Peck Curtis, known to the whole film world as Ted Curtis. For years he had been the company's chief liaison in Hollywood. An altogether charming man's man, adored by women, a handsome combat flyer in World War I, he was respected by every producer, executive and film star in pictures. He played golf with Jack Warner, Barney Balaban and Spyros Skouras. He was a buddy of David Selznick and Fay Wray. If Eastman House wanted a specific film, Ted Curtis, then back in Rochester, had only to pick up the phone, call Jack Warner or Barney Balaban and ask, "Boys, can you help them out at Eastman House? They'd like to borrow your negatives of *The Docks of New York*. We'll make them a print at Kodak Park and send your negatives right back." In three days the original negatives would be in our hands.

The folks at the Museum of Modern Art did not cheer the titles we added to the list of films saved. They felt that every film we selected for the collection was a kind of reproof of their taste—an attitude that was essentially correct. Iris Barry's longtime assistant, Dick Griffith, took to referring to the Eastman House collection, with a contemptuous sniff, as that "archive of trivia." He complained that Jim Card and his counterpart in Paris, Henri Langlois, were not really film historians, but merely film buffs. Perhaps he was right, but hundreds of great films that exist today would not be available but for our buffdom. And when the Museum of Modern Art began borrowing and exhibiting our "trivia" in 1952, we knew they finally recognized that our catholic approach had been quite right.

By 1952 the members of FIAF began to get rumors that the upstart archive at Eastman House had collected many of their most longed-for American silents. In the very first batch we had printed from the original negatives entrusted to us were *The Docks of New York*, *The Crowd*, *Ben-Hur* and *Beggars of Life*, the last not because anyone thought it a great film, but simply because of my infatuation with its star, Louise Brooks, an emotional devotion that had begun at the age of fourteen.

Every film archive in the world aspired to become a member of FIAF. Dictated by two of the remaining founding archives, the British Film Archive and the Cinémathèque Française, along with the Museum of Modern Art Film Library, which had been recruited to replace the Reichsfilmarchiv (lost to FIAF in World War II), membership required some groveling on the part of hopeful archives. In 1952 Beaumont Newhall was in Paris on the lookout for great photographs by Henri

Beggars of Life (1928), with Louise Brooks, was one of the first films to be preserved at Eastman House.

Cartier-Bresson and Eugène Atget. He was invited to attend the sessions of FIAF's yearly congress, that year being held in Paris. They begged Beaumont to have Eastman House join, so powerful had the spreading word become of the vast treasures we were gathering through the easy pipeline to the Hollywood vaults. Like many or most international organizations during the height of the cold war period, FIAF was strongly politicized. The Soviet Union was not yet a member, although most of the membership fervently hoped it would soon join—all those great Russian and Ukrainian films were known to have been preserved by a government that never forgot Lenin's solemn dictum: "Cinema must and shall become the foremost weapon of the proletariat." The Soviet film archives were therefore considered by the government as a kind of arsenal. For years FIAF continued in office as their president one Jerzy Toeplitz, a Polish Communist, to make it easier for the Russians to join FIAF. By profession, Toeplitz was a lawyer and a professor in a film school in Lodz. He was a slick parliamentarian who knew all the tricks to keeping a formal meeting going the way he wanted it to proceed. He was also an unctuous Continental type who always introduced himself to personages of the Western world as a "liberal Communist." In 1952 that was a contradiction in terms. In spite of his pose, Toeplitz was no Gorbachev. In fact, I found him to be the most detestably devious, untruthful and hypocritical individual I have ever met in my entire sixty-five years of international acquaintances.

Our director, General Solbert, having been involved in military intelligence since 1917, had his cold war concerns, too. Empowering me to accept or decline the FIAF invitation that had been extended to Beaumont Newhall, in 1953 he sent me on a long tour of the European archives and film studios, with an itinerary that included London, Stockholm, Copenhagen, Oslo, Nice, Paris, Munich, Berlin, Zurich, Milan, Barcelona, Saragossa and Madrid, charged to hunt films all the way and to meddle in the political structure of FIAF. At that time I had not yet met Henri Langlois, the legendary founder and head of the Cinémathèque Française. We had corresponded at length and had also exchanged films on a collector-to-collector basis. Henri was then suspected widely of exerting an inimical, perhaps even Soviet-oriented, control of FIAF. Henri was blamed for the uncontested tenure of the Communist Toeplitz as president. My assignment was a role I relished as an amateur meddler in the murky area of international skulduggery. As a result, some Europeans viewed me as a clumsy McCarthy operator or, even worse, as an incompetent CIA agent.

Henri Langlois, the founder of
the Cinémathèque Française

My first stop was London to meet Ernest Lindgren, head of the British Film Archive. Lindgren was party to the suspicions about a Langlois-Toeplitz conspiracy, and we decided that together we would try to undo it at the forthcoming 1953 FIAF Congress, to be held in Vence. This plot eventually took a wholly unexpected turn, as such subversive intentions usually do. Langlois and I, recognizing that we were totally kindred spirits, became best friends. Lindgren turned out to be one of the bad guys, conspiring with Toeplitz to unseat Langlois, a feat they almost accomplished in Stockholm in 1959, in a dreadful ploy that split the unity of FIAF seriously.

Vence is a medieval town in the mountainous region of France just northwest of Nice. It is an area of heart-wrenching beauty both in its landscapes and its ancient buildings. Nearby is St. Paul de Vence, a required tourist stop since Matisse decorated the local chapel.

Learning that I would be bringing a print of King Vidor's great work *The Crowd* to the FIAF Congress, Langlois eagerly arranged for the first showing in Europe since its original release in 1928. Not even King Vidor himself had seen a complete version of his masterpiece since its initial run.

The promised screening of *The Crowd* was anticipated as a major European event. Langlois had picked the location, an ancient restaurant, the Colombe d'Or, in St. Paul de Vence. Several centuries ago that hallowed inn with its massive grey stones and vaulted ceilings had been a monastery. How the word was spread that *The Crowd* was to be shown there was a total mystery, but on the designated afternoon an extraordinary gathering of legendary folks showed up in St. Paul de Vence. Tall, gaunt and long-bearded Gordon Craig was there: he who was famous as a designer of memorable stage sets; he who was the father of the first child of mythic Isadora Duncan and the son of the equally legendary Ellen Terry. Also on hand was Marc Chagall, whose greatest fame lay still ahead of him. And, ironically, present was Iris Barry, who had deliberately scorned *The Crowd* when she put together the film library for the Museum of Modern Art. Then retired from her curatorship, Iris was living a deliberately isolated life in nearby Faience in a centuries-old farmhouse, as the unwed wife of a young French sailor. There were two Rothschilds present, as was Mary Meerson, dragon lady of the Cinémathèque Française. Mary Meerson had been a Russian beauty much sought out as a model by eminent French painters and sculptors in the 1920s. In the 1930s she had been married to Lazare Meerson, the fabulous designer of movie sets for *Sous les Toits de Paris* and *La Kermesse Héroïque*. Henri, as a teenager, had fallen in love with images of the gorgeous Mary Meerson about the same time that I had been enraptured by Louise Brooks. Now, in 1953, Mary had become a huge, strong-voiced, dominating woman who acted as something of a Jewish Mamele to Henri Langlois. Lotte Eisner, Langlois' brilliant gofer, was in the audience, as was Nelly Kaplan, an American girl, new to the international group. But she would bring fresh recognition to Abel Gance, and then become a filmmaker herself, working in France. At the FIAF Congress, along with myself, she was suspected by the paranoiac French of being a McCarthy spy.

All the way from Rochester I had clasped the 16mm print of *The Crowd* (then one of only two in existence) to my side as though I were carrying the Giaconda. Looking at that audience, which had collectively generated several tons of newsprint over the years, I realized that a Vidor work had never before been exhibited before a comparable group. Certainly not in a screening room as architecturally intriguing as the monks' ancient refectory of the Colombe d'Or.

Someone had provided a 16mm projector that wasn't too much newer than the film. I threaded the precious print doubtfully. The showing began—the viewers were breathless. When the early scene came on

Left to right: Nelly Kaplan, Lotte Eisner and Ove Brusendorff, director of the Danish Film Museum, at the film archives convention in Vence, 1953

with the young boy climbing a menacing stairway to learn of his father's death, Iris shouted out, paraphrasing the famous Nazi storm trooper's comment, "When I see art, then I reach for my revolver!"

Shortly thereafter, one of the Rothschilds came angrily over to me at the projector. "You're running the film too fast! Silent film must be run at sixteen frames a second. You're ruining it!" This outrageous complaint was like having a bank clerk accuse Albert Einstein of having made a mathematical error.

The best projection speed for silent films of *The Crowd*'s time was twenty-four frames per second, or sound speed—the closest one could come to the original rates of showing silents of 1928. But the voice of a Rothschild cannot be ignored in Europe. Of its own accord, the projector began to slow down. It ran slower and slower to the groans of the watchers. There was a flash of flame, and the projector went up in smoke.

This was the first time that I became acquainted with Henri Langlois' Buddha smile. Unpredictable, he could be lashed into a fury if he had to listen to someone mangling French, a language he somehow regarded as sacred. But in the face of disasters more grave, his cool could

Above and below: Eleanor Boardman and James Murray in King Vidor's *The Crowd* (1928)

sometimes be taken for outright pleasure. Now he strolled about, pleasantly reassuring everyone that someone was already on the way down to Vence to get another projector.

While waiting for the projector from Vence, we lost Gordon Craig. When the projector arrived, it turned out to be even older than the smouldering one. Its maximum capacity was for 400-foot reels. *The Crowd* was mounted on 1,600-foot reels. "Pas de problème," smiled Langlois. While I watched, shuddering, he placed the charred projector alongside the antique that had been designed to project home movies, not Hollywood features. He replaced the 1,600-foot reels on the dead projector, looped the film audaciously over to the fresh machine, then back to the original with the 1,600-foot take-up. It was a Rube Goldberg solution, and, miraculously, the little projector started up, feeding off the other. But neither had been designed for the 1902 vintage electrical system installed in the Colombe d'Or. It was direct current, and the flame that destroyed the second projector was even bigger.

Langlois was unruffled. "We will all go down to Cannes and run the film in the theatre there," he announced. Most of the audience obediently trooped down to Cannes, but on the way, we lost Chagall and Iris Barry.

CHAPTER 8

To the Stars!

From the seventeenth century on, the history of the theatre is written with the names of great players: Garrick, Kemble, Henry Irving, Bernhardt, Ellen Terry, Eleonora Duse, Edwin Booth, Maude Adams, Modjeska, the Barrymores. Yet behind every single performance that burnished the immortal fame of those great players, there was a director. What became of their names?

Film historians are in grave error with their almost exclusive concentration on film directors. They have even invented the auteur theory to support their myopia—a theory that ignores the creative authority of producer, studio head, supervisor and superstar. Even Alfred Hitchcock had to trim his sails on the insistence of David O. Selznick. Perhaps historians are afraid to acknowledge the stars for fear of being taken for fans.

Granted that in recent decades significant portions of the audience may be in the theatre because the film was directed by Ingmar Bergman or Luis Buñuel. But the silent films that lured multimillions to see them did not attract fortunes to the box office through the name of any director. Who went to see *Ben-Hur* because Fred Niblo directed it? Who cared in 1925 that *The Big Parade* had been made by King Vidor? Who knew that *Flesh and the Devil* was a Clarence Brown production? The multitudes flocked to see Ramon Novarro, John Gilbert, Greta Garbo. Who cared that *The Son of the Sheik* was directed by George Fitzmaurice? Rudolph Valentino would have drawn them to see the film if it had been directed by Ben Turpin.

One of the more delightful fringe benefits of working as a film historian for a well-known museum was the opportunity for personal acquaintance with the players and directors who had created many of the films I found so infatuating. Some of those acquaintanceships over the years actually developed into friendships.

The better I came to know some of the directors and the more legendary stars, the more puzzling it became to adjust to a dual relationship. For the actresses particularly, their screen personae seemed so remote from, sometimes even at odds with, their flesh-and-blood selves that the diversity could be bewildering. If their screen personalities inspired irrational admiration, how did one deal with them as people? Enormously popular stars, although perfectly aware that fandom is directly connected with their monetary strength with the studio, are usually bored and annoyed with fulsome devotion when it confronts them directly. It is then a nuisance, too often in public, an embarrassing obstacle to freedom of movement and even to their freedom of behavior. John Barrymore likened fan mail to having a hippopotamus come clumping into one's living room and stand there dripping muddy river water all over one's carpets.

Film artists' attitudes toward a historian-curator were quite different of course from their response to their own directors, studio bosses or journalists and interviewers. They were pleased that a curator was occupied in saving their work for posterity; there was little question of his passing judgment on their art other than the fact of feeling it important enough to be saved. But they also felt that his approval did not constitute the kind of fandom that would want either their autographs or portions of their clothing. As a result of this relaxed and unsuspicious feeling, many of the most notoriously "temperamental" film people were able to reward an unaggressive historian with the kind of uninhibited camaraderie usually reserved for one's close friends.

While very much enjoying and appreciating these rare relationships, I nevertheless pondered endlessly the qualities that seemed to separate both directors and stars from these real human beings and the gods, goddesses and directorial geniuses they were known to be professionally.

When Louise Brooks began to write, it amused me to observe that the schism began to perplex her, too. She was even mystified by her own screen image. She professed to have had no idea of what she was doing before the camera and even less of a notion as to what effect her performance might be achieving.

Writing in *Image* about her work with Georg Pabst, she confessed, "The first day of shooting on 'Box of Pandora' a big fat translation of the script was given me to read which, after less than ten minutes I dropped

Clara Bow in *Hula* (1927)

on the floor beside my chair and happily never saw again. But if I made that picture with only the dullest notion of what it was about, on my second picture with Mr. Pabst, 'Diary of a Lost Girl,' I had no idea at all of its plot or meaning till I saw it twenty-seven years later at Eastman House."

Weigh this confession against an anecdote Clarence Badger relates describing the acutely conscious technique of Clara Bow as he directed her in *It*:

> Clara Bow was a pleasure to direct. She would melt into the character she was portraying so cleverly, just as though it was, in reality, the story of her own life being picturized. Shrewd minded too, always having in mind the box office and her audience when before the camera. For instance, when filming her in one particular close-up shot for "It," which called for expression of that great moment when love first enters a young girl's heart, Clara, following my directions, gazed at her sweetheart with an expression of lingering, calf-like longing on her pretty face; perfectly all right if she had stopped there. But she did not. Continuing on, the camera still grinding away, her doll-like tantalizing eyes suddenly became inflamed with unwholesome passion. Then the young

rascal suddenly changed her expression again, this time to one of virtu-
ous appeal. I stopped the camera. "And what was that all about, Clara?"
I demanded.

"Well," she came back, "if you knew your onions like you're supposed to, you'd know that first expression was for the love-sick dames
in the audience, and that the second expression, that passionate stuff,
was for the boys and their papas, and that that third expression—well,
Mr. Badger, just about the time all the old women in the audience
had become shocked and scandalized by that passionate part, they'd
suddenly see that third expression, become absorbed in it, and change
their minds about me having naughty ideas and go home thinking how
pure and innocent I was; and having got me mixed up with the character
I'm playing, they'd come again when my next picture showed up."

In Louise Brooks' unpublished book, "Thirteen Women in Films,"
she mused further on the Jekyll-and-Hyde duality that has haunted me
since meeting film people in person. This time she offered a positive
opinion: "An actress in the beginning of her career is chosen for a part
because her looks and personality are as near as the director can get to
those of the character she is to play. If this turns out satisfactorily for the
public, the producer, and the actress, then she will go on to succeed in
this kind of part. And leading a double life will not confuse her because
she will see the vision she projects on the screen and know the person
she is in private to be separate yet harmonious."

Maybe, perhaps, Louise. But my own doubts are not resolved.
Louise's foregoing remarks were apropos of her chapter on the acting of
Joan Crawford. "Thirteen Women in Films" was to have been a Brooks-
Card coauthored work. The plan was to have each of us write a chapter
on a dozen actresses whose work interested Louise; the thirteenth was
Louise herself, who would write herself into each of her chapters as one
who knew personally the actress under her often savage scrutiny. I had
met Joan Crawford and had admired her as an actress and was fond of
her as a person. The Brooks estimate of her acting was merciless, con-
cluding that the essential trouble was that "the vision she projects on the
screen" was far from being separate though harmonious with the person
she was in private. When Louise finished her chapter on Crawford, she
handed me her manuscript with the challenge, "Here, put her back
together again."

I had already gone on record as a champion of Joan Crawford.
Although she had played leads opposite Harry Langdon, Lon Chaney,
Ramon Novarro, William Haines and John Gilbert, Joan Crawford

Joan Crawford, 1939

did not achieve the official status of an MGM star until after her great hit as Diana in *Our Dancing Daughters*. The title was conferred upon her most belatedly by MGM in June of 1929 as *Our Modern Maidens* was being made ready for release. This tardiness is curious when one considers that she had played the lead in no fewer than sixteen MGM features and had accumulated several buildings full of fan mail, along with an ardent following that would not desert her for the rest of her life.

That first official hit film, so popular and so much a personal triumph for Joan Crawford that her studio could no longer ignore her power, was *Our Dancing Daughters*, with John Mack Brown, Anita Page and Dorothy Sebastian giving solid support to the direction of Harry Beaumont. For the social historian, *Our Dancing Daughters* is an important film. It is a morality play of the latter twenties—a visually eloquent dramatization, for popular understanding, of the era's basic clash between a puritanical heritage and the postwar, youthful urge toward a new attitude to sexual freedom and the hedonistic enjoyment of all possible privileges of a prosperous segment of society.

For the art historian, the film is no less valuable. Cedric Gibbons, set designer for MGM, became the most widely observed exponent of art deco. His settings for many MGM films and particularly his designs for *Our Dancing Daughters* became the definitive art deco styles for all sections of the United States, eager to adopt any and all versions of what was widely perceived to be modern design.

Joan Crawford's career had been lacking a certain focus. In her role in this film, her vivid, totally committed involvement achieved the acknowledged stardom she deserved. No other actress of the time could have remotely combined the sense of Amazonian, sexual aggressiveness with complete probity of character in the way that Crawford, with her sincere portrayal of 1920s decency, was able to present.

In *Our Dancing Daughters* there is only one character in the cast who has any means of support either visible or mentioned. These young members of the yacht-club set lead lives that on the surface appear to be ideally ambiguous. They are neither students nor career seekers. This breed of youth flourished at a peculiar time in our history, and it is hard to believe that they actually existed—yet they very definitely did. Years later they might have been called the jet set. But this was a time when all flying was done behind propellers. The year was 1928. Lindbergh's feat was a year old. Although it was not a time of inflation, money, it appeared, was no longer a problem: it was taken for

In 1928 in *Our Dancing Daughters* the Cedric Gibbons design introduced art deco to millions of Americans.

granted that everyone was either reasonably or magnificently wealthy.

Survivors of that era of optimistic presumption may have memories somewhat hazy; those who missed it may be skeptical. On November 3, the jewelry firm Black, Starr and Frost took a two-page ad in the *New Yorker*. They were offering for sale one pearl necklace—price $685,000.

Money was not a fashionable worry. But there was something troubling folks in 1928. Strangely enough, it seemed to be—morality. The American sons and daughters of the Puritans had thrown away the bundling boards and turned Victorian samplers to the wall. In the mid-1920s they ran up the banner of a new slogan: "Eat, drink and be nasty."

Very much in the news was Judge Ben B. Lindsay. Alarmed by the increasing divorce rate, Judge Lindsay advocated companionate marriage and started one of the major controversies of the 1920s. Naturally the young people thought the judge's plan of tryout marital relations would constitute a bright new world.

And then there was Bertrand Russell, the British mathematician who laid aside his logarithms long enough to publish some most unscholarly views on sexual relationships. High school students, hereto-

Crawford with Johnny Mack Brown, wealthy jazz-era playmates in *Our Dancing Daughters*

fore unfamiliar with the work of this respected philosopher, read his observations with eager attention and often with disastrous results.

Then along came *Liberty* magazine, sounding an alarm to parents in a series of articles called "The Amateur Competition." It was suggested that professional hookers were being displaced by the amateur generosities of high school and college girls. The *Liberty* series caused gasping conversation at countless PTA bridge parties for months. Anxious mothers looked at their streamlined daughters with new concern and wondered rather desperately to what catastrophes those mad days might lead their smoking, necking, slangy, devil-may-care dancing daughters.

The movie *Our Dancing Daughters* captured accurately the fact of youthful, confused integrity as opposed to the helplessness of parents in guiding their children through uncharted areas of doubt. As a good fable should, this picture shows case histories of the generally basic character types—all faced with similar stresses. The three principal young ladies, as portrayed by Anita Page, Dorothy Sebastian and Joan Crawford, are such elementary types that any young girl who saw the movie could readily fit every one of her own acquaintances—and perhaps even herself—into the situations and thus be forewarned and instructed.

Our Dancing Daughters was just such an instructional film—a parable of morality—graphically pointing out the perils that lay even in the paths of those golden youth with never a care about where their next yacht ride was coming from.

If there is a little oversimplification in the story, it is not present in the acting of Joan Crawford. The nuances of her eloquent face surely deserve all the praises that have kept alive the memories of great actresses. Joan Crawford acted too soon; if only the movies in the twenties had been more respected, she might have been acknowledged as the formidable actress she was. Scott Fitzgerald himself singled out Joan Crawford as the one film actress who most completely embodied the flapper.

For a year before I met Joan Crawford, she had beguiled me with an intense and intimate correspondence. I was far from alone in her pen-palism. Publicist and agent John Springer is a former Rochesterian. His brother and dentist assured regular visits to the old hometown by John, who usually arranged, once his brother had taken care of him, to stop in on Eastman House for equally regular visits. Together we enjoyed sharing screenings of old films and talks about old actresses. I mentioned my admiration for Joan Crawford. "Write to Joan," he suggested. "She'll answer you—personally—and not briefly. Acknowledge her answer and she'll respond to that with an even longer letter. She'll never stop. Where she finds time to do these long letters is a mystery, but she'll let you know about everything that happens to her and every thought that comes into her head."

He was right! Here's a typical Crawford letter—this one written October 21, 1953:

> My dear Jim:
>
> Please forgive my not answering your wonderful letter until this very late date. But between preparing for my first Western and trying to clean up all the tag ends of publicity, conference calls, interviews etc on "Torch Song" (prior to the opening dates) it's really kept me running and working about twenty hours a day.
>
> As you can see, I am in Sedona, Arizona on our location for "Johnny Guitar." It's beautiful beyond belief in this country. I thought Canada was about the most beautiful thing I'd ever looked at and Carmel, Monterey—these were my favorites. Of course this is a different kind of beauty—not the kind that makes you gasp or makes you want to cry, but the kind of rugged beauty and you just stand in silence—in awe. And of course with the lights—different every hour on the buttes and mountains—and different coloring each time you look at it.
>
> Our hours are rather rugged—for a 7:00 a.m. shooting call, I have to get up at 3:00. Then we work until 4:30 or 5:00—dinner at 5:30. And I must say that bed looks awfully good around 6:30 because there's studying to be done, removing the makeup, bathing—all the things preparatory to the next day's work.
>
> I love your letter more than I can possibly tell you. And indeed I did mean what I said when I wrote you "I have not accomplished enough yet to write a book." Your letter is one I shall keep forever. Now—is that telling you how much it means to me?

When plans were set for my first trip to Hollywood, I wrote Joan to let her know I was coming. She insisted that I come to see her before calling on anyone else in California. So there I was, trotting up the sidewalk of her Brentwood home, invited to dinner and punctual to the second.

How could I know that punctuality was not one of the Hollywood vices? The short, freckle-faced girl who answered the door had a tall glass of frosty liquid in her hand. She looked at me as though I'd come to read the meter. I looked at her without seeing Joan Crawford at all. Dawn came to her before it awakened me. A dazzling smile as she pulled me indoors. "Jim Card! I called every hotel in LA! Where the hell are you staying? This"—indicating a professorial-looking elder with a glass also in his hand—"is Kyle Crichton. He's here writing my autobiography."

"I hope not," I said, trying to recover from my astonishment at that little woman's being Joan Crawford.

"You mean I haven't done anything great enough yet to have my autobiography?" There was a hint of an edge to her voice.

"I mean it's not time yet. The best is still to come."

With much more than a hint of an edge, Crichton asked me to come with him to the sunroom-library. He took down the current *Who's Who*. "Hmmm—Card—Card—James, is it? I don't seem to find your name here." Joan joined us.

"Can I bring you a drink? What will it be? The others will be coming soon so I'll be going up to put my face on. You'll have what I'm having? Better not. Gin and tonic? OK?"

She left us. "Isn't that gin she has?" I asked the great biographer.

"Her own brand. One-hundred-eighty proof. Wisely, she doesn't share it. Card, look at that goddamned jukebox at the other end of her beautiful swimming pool. I tell you, every cliché about Hollywood is true."

Right on the cliché cue, in bustled Joan's wirehaired fox terrier. "What's his name?" asked Mr. Innocent.

"Daff," lied Mr. Diabolical.

The two other guests arrived. Top guest was Milton Rackmil, then head of Universal Studios. With him was the chief of Universal's Australian offices. His name was Albert Daff. Stupid of me not to have known Joan's famous pet was named Cliquot. Lucky of me not to have essayed any talk to the dog.

Before our hostess had reappeared, we were summoned to the table by Hollywood's favorite Danish rent-a-butler, who hired out to supervise filmdom's formal dinners. The settings for hostess and four male guests were complete Emily Post for state dinners. There were more pieces of silver at each place setting than I'd had to wash on army KP.

With her four guests waiting at the table, the lady of the house made her entrance at the head of a staircase. No doubt about it now. It was Joan Crawford. That mouth, those eyes—they were all in place. Majestically she descended, flowing down the stairway amid clouds of a filmy, elaborate designer's masterpiece. She took her seat, alone at the head of the long refectory table. Along the two sides sat her guests, ranked appropriately—the two film executives on either side and the two literary types next to them.

Through the ritual of the introductory courses, talk was idle and gossipy. Before the main course, Joan turned to Rackmil and said, "Mr. Card doesn't think it's the right time for my autobiography."

Crichton spoke up. "Of course it's the right time. What do you think I've been doing here these last two weeks?"

It was the wrong question. Joan shouted at him furiously, "Drinking up my booze, that's what you've been doing! You've paid no attention to me as a mother—never once watched me with the children! You've just been sponging and not giving a damn about finding out anything about me!" She burst into tears, sobbing hysterically. Rackmil jumped to his feet and tried to comfort her. No one paid much attention to the main course. We decamped into the library, now converted to a projection room.

The film we looked at was her most recent vehicle, *Sudden Fear.* Nestled close to me on the couch, Joan gave a running comment on every single sequence. When the séance was over, she called a taxi driver whom she knew by name and asked him to take me to my hotel. As I left, Crichton came over and hissed into my ear, "You bastard, you've cost me five thousand bucks tonight!" That night I climbed into bed feeling quite confident about tackling Cecil B. DeMille the next morning.

That session with Joan Crawford made even more baffling the riddle I'd been trying to unravel: How much of her *own* identity did a successful film actress allow to show on the screen? Or did the very illusory nature of the medium wreak its special hallucination to create *another* aspect of the actress, observable to film watchers but perhaps not understood or even recognized by the star herself?

The Joan Crawford who had greeted me at her doorway seemed to have no connection whatsoever with *any* of the characters I had ever seen that she had created on the screen. Yet once she had "put on her face," donned a regal dress and grandly descended the staircase to her guests, she was, without any doubt, the Crawford one had seen dozens of times on the screen. And she was that same great star when she wept at the table and stormed at her author.

But the Gloria Swanson that I knew had no relation to any of the Swansons I'd ever seen in a film. Swanson's behavior when she moved anywhere near a stage on which she was expected to appear was that of a no-nonsense director—all business and everything better be right and

Later in her career, Joan Crawford had two faces: her own and her film mask. From *Sudden Fear* (1952).

in its proper place. But as a friend she was warm, generous and brightly animated.

My first meeting with Gloria Swanson was completely out of context. She was in Rochester promoting her line of dresses—Forever Young—and touring the big department stores. Because I was known to be involved with films, I was invited by the store management to attend a luncheon held in her honor. Gloria had started making films in 1915 when she was a Chicago teenager. In two years' time she was a major star and known around the world. When I met her in 1952, Gloria was a smooth, slick-looking, sexy woman who looked about about twenty-eight to thirty-three.

For years and years she had had to put up with meeting white-haired old ladies who tottered up to her saying, "Oh, Miss Swanson, you were my favorite movie star when I was a little girl." I had just sense enough not to tell her I'd been watching her in films ever since I was a little boy. At the luncheon they took our picture together. Gloria is in the act of putting a carnation in my lapel. She is smiling a smile and giving a look that could have ignited whole vaults filled with nitrate film. I'm standing there looking like a dumb ox about to be prepared with a sledgehammer for a steak roast.

Years later, after we'd come to know each other well, Gloria took my

Gloria Swanson and
James Card: first
meeting, 1952

prized print of our first meeting and wrote along her outstretched bare
arm: "To Jim, the one and only." Still much later, in her Fifth Avenue
home, I was looking through her own collection of several hundred
stills. I came across nine other pictures of her in exactly the same pose,
from her department-store-tour period, pinning her trademark carnation on a whole series of dazzled-looking merchandising types. I asked
her if she'd written on her arm for any of the others. She said she
couldn't remember. I took that to mean that she had.

In Chicago, George K. Spoor and his partner, Max Aronson, formed
a pioneering film company that provided a major impetus to the very
early advances of the movies. Spoor developed a projector that was a distinct improvement over existing models. Aronson changed his name to
Anderson and became Broncho Billy Anderson in countless one- and
two-reel Westerns. The company was known as Essanay, and it not only
roped in the very top stars of the pre–World War I era, but it employed
a surprising number of unknowns destined to become some of the greatest. Wallace Beery, acting in drag as a grotesque immigrant maid,
appeared in a series of *Sweedie* comedies. Chaplin left his initial job with
Mack Sennett to join Essanay for some of his most successful early works.
Francis X. Bushman became one of the first movie matinee idols. And
after his triumph as the Little Colonel in *The Birth of a Nation*, Henry B.
Walthall was to be found acting Edgar Allan Poe characters with Essanay.

A movie-struck Chicago teenager took to hanging around outside the Essanay studio. As a proper lady-killer, Bushman had a sharp eye for beauty, and he recognized it in Gloria Swanson, the hanging-around girl. Bushman brought her indoors, and soon there she was, playing bits opposite Charlie Chaplin.

In her autobiography, *Swanson on Swanson*, Gloria gives us a detailed account of how she, as a fastidious teenager, came to marry Wallace Beery. In later years Gloria was sensitive, almost apologetic, about this first marriage of hers. Beery was an enormously talented slob—one of the screen's really great actors—but still a slob. He had a slobby background. He had been a circus roustabout and elephant keeper. Always defensive about her taste in marrying Beery, she used to insist that in those days he was as handsome as Clark Gable! Stills of Beery as Sweedie make that claim very hard to believe. Then when she came to write her autobiography she was much less kind to her first husband; she recounts a terrifying experience of being raped by him on their wedding night.

Gloria and her mother had traveled to California after Beery had left Chicago and was continuing his film acting with great enthusiasm for the West Coast areas. According to some accounts, Gloria did her first California work with Universal in a film that may have been a Richard Travers vehicle called *The Romance of an American Duchess*. This is a mysterious film in that no record of it seems to exist, nor does Gloria make any mention of it in her own book.

But she arrived on Mack Sennett's Keystone lot at a crucial moment in the career of Clarence Badger. He had just been promoted from the scenario department and been given a chance to direct. His first directorial effort did not please the boss, and Badger was put back into the stable of writers.

Then Sennett assigned him to direct two newcomers to the Sennett company: Gloria Swanson and Wallace Beery. Their first film together with the French acrobatic comedian Bobby Vernon was exceptionally successful—so much so that Sennett decided the team consisting of Gloria Swanson, Bobby Vernon and Clarence Badger as director should be continued. The trio made eight two-reel comedies for Mack Sennett, including *The Danger Girl*, *Whose Baby?*, *A Dash of Courage*, *Hearts and Sparks*, *A Social Cub*, *Haystacks and Steeples*, *The Nick-of-Time Baby*, *Teddy at the Throttle*, *The Pullman Bride* and *The Sultan's Wife*. As late as 1957 Clarence Badger, retired and living in Australia, wrote fondly of Swanson. He recalled, "Gloria Swanson was wonderful to work with. Even then, in those, her youthful days, she was most talented, appealing and

Gloria Swanson, Bobby
Vernon and Tom Kennedy in
Sennett's *Haystacks and
Steeples* (1916)

And Swanson and Vernon are
harassed by the law.

Swanson (center) in the 1918 Triangle drama *Secret Code*

charming, definitely possessing screen personality to such an outstanding degree, that it was easy to foresee she would go a long way in pictures."

Gloria was then and remained a delightful comedienne. But others at Triangle saw in her the same potential that Clarence Badger predicted. She was moved from the Sennett lot and in 1918 joined the Triangle players, where she was entrusted with major roles and for the first time was able to work with serious directors who were busy making an altogether different kind of film history. The directors she worked with included Frank Borzage and Albert Parker. She was entrusted with a leading role in her first Triangle drama, *Society for Sale*, directed by Frank Borzage in 1918. Performing leads in multireel features was a far different experience from the rough-and-tumble slapstick two-reelers she had been making for Mack Sennett. There were eight Triangle features starring Gloria Swanson in 1918 and 1919, and by that last year, she had won the attention of critics and had begun to amass a following that would support her every effort for the next fifty-four years!

Gloria was unique among film stars to have begun her career in such broad comedy as that of the Sennett factory and then to have gone on to achieve lasting stardom in dramatic roles of every conceivable type. Of all the Triangle features she made, at the present time only one is known to have survived. Fortunately it is a particularly good one, *Shifting Sands*, directed skillfully by Albert Parker. The film has captured a memorably winsome Gloria Swanson, who is able to portray a downtrodden young artist, railroaded to prison, encouraged by a hitch in the Salvation Army and then becomes a charming wife and mother and a courageous battler for home and husband—a big assignment for a recent graduate of the frantic Sennett school and a triumph for a maturing film actress on her way to enduring stardom.

By 1919 World War I was over, and the United States was going through one of the most profound changes in its history. Women not only were granted the right to vote, but they finally decided to alight from the false pedestal that Victorian mores had decreed they should occupy. Public attitudes toward American women were changing rapidly, and the newly enfranchised ladies were vigorously helping the changes along.

That astute filmmaker Cecil B. DeMille recognized the bandwagon and saw his chance to jump onto it for what would be a lucrative ride. He was ready to exploit the New American Woman, but he needed just the right actress to portray her.

DeMille's choice was Triangle's rapidly ascending star, Gloria Swanson. He promptly hired her away from Triangle and entrusted her with the challenge of bringing to life his own vision of modern womanhood. Thanks to that particular director-star combination, nothing quite like the new Gloria Swanson had ever been seen before, nor is it likely that a comparable manifestation will ever appear again to beguile the millions into admiration and emulation.

DeMille saw that in his films Miss Swanson combined certain elements of her sprightly Sennett style with the daringly gowned, provocatively coiffed, glamorous beauty that the master director surrounded with every sensuous setting and prop that his prolific imagination was able to conjure.

Through DeMille's skillful showmanship, Gloria moved rapidly along the route to becoming the indisputable queen of Hollywood; in turn, Gloria Swanson's fabulous success as a DeMille heroine brought to that flamboyant director much of the fame and fortune that qualified DeMille himself as the most legendarily famous and monstrously successful of all the world's motion picture directors.

Out of a curious loyalty to DeMille, Gloria tried to establish that she was discovered as a major leading lady in the DeMille films, right after her time with Mack Sennett ended. She all but denied her stardom in

Swanson: the Triangle heroine before she worked for DeMille

the Triangle films. Like Marlene Dietrich, who pretended that her film career began with von Sternberg's *The Blue Angel*, in the face of the existence of a half-dozen silent film roles (she was *not* an extra in Pabst's 1925 *The Joyless Street*, by the way), Gloria chose to ignore her successful Triangle career.

Early in 1919 Paramount released the DeMille-Swanson film *Don't Change Your Husband*, a story of the New American Woman who finds her husband unable to keep up with the jazzy pace of postwar America. Filmgoers of 1919 voted overwhelming approval of this audacious drama of the emancipated wife.

Ever hopeful of scenting a trend, Paramount and DeMille contributed a sequel in 1920 with, this time, the husband finding his wife not keeping up. Gloria's delightful transition from frumpy wife to gorgeous femme fatale is one of the elements that made *Why Change Your Wife?* a rare example of a sequel that was able to surpass its model.

When DeMille adapted Sir James Barrie's *The Admirable Crichton* in 1919, changing the title to *Male and Female* was not the only alteration Sir James' work suffered in Hollywood hands. *Male and Female* reflected much more accurately the new emphasis placed on the story than did the original title. Although ostensibly the movie was still concerned with an English family, no one could possibly mistake Gloria Swanson for a Londoner. It became unquestionably an essentially American battle of the sexes between Gloria and Tommy Meighan as the stalwart Crichton. And it also had one of those special DeMille flashbacks into ancient times that would eventually lead him into his more celebrated biblical spectacles. This was the one in which Gloria, bedecked in peacock feathers, is fed to an obviously puzzled lion who can't decide whether the meal offered him is flesh or fowl.

DeMille's most ambitious contribution of 1921 to the photoplay of manners and morals was his adaptation of Schnitzler's *The Affairs of Anatol*. The great Viennese playwright's series of dramatic vignettes did not find the wholehearted response of the American public that his purely domestic essays had evoked. But filmgoers' wariness where Continental stories were offered was generally offset by their chance to see Gloria teamed with the unforgettably charming Wallace Reid, the most popular male star of the period. All in all, DeMille produced seven works with Gloria Swanson before he relinquished her to other directors. Between *The Affairs of Anatol* and *Manhandled* Gloria Swanson had starred in twelve Paramount productions. Among them were memorable hits including *Beyond the Rocks*, with Valentino, and *Zaza*, the last directed by

Swanson held by Wallace Reid in DeMille's *The Affairs of Anatol* (1921). Looking on is Theodore Kosloff, late of the Russian ballet.

In *Beyond the Rocks* (1922), being seduced by Rudolph Valentino

Allan Dwan, a director under whom Gloria would work more happily than with any other except DeMille himself.

The fortuitous combination was at its best in *Manhandled*. By 1924 Gloria Swanson was the foremost American star, adulated by millions of fans, pestered and pursued by relentless fan-club members. In the course of her nineteen films with Paramount that she had made before *Manhandled* she had appeared in every conceivable extravagant costume and avant-garde gown. Gloria determined to shift gears abruptly by playing a gum-chewing department-store salesgirl with a slick and shiny bobbed hairdo that created a sensation. Gloria was mobbed in personal appearances by women who actually tried to feel the back of the head shingle that was a feature of her style-setting bob. *Manhandled* is a breezy, brisk comedy-drama with Gloria in very top form. As the shop girl Tessie, she goes to a party where Ann Pennington and Brooke Johns, then big stars of the Ziegfeld Follies, are guests. At the party Pennington and Johns go into their dance, and others are persuaded to perform as well. Tessie's contributions are an imitation of Beatrice Lillie and also her skillful Chaplin act, which she was to re-create so wonderfully twenty-six years later in *Sunset Boulevard*. Those were not the only imitations she offered in *Manhandled*. In the story, Tessie makes her way up in the world, finally becoming a fake Russian countess, dazzling customers in a swanky tearoom. Pola Negri had begun to challenge Gloria's top-star status, working in the same studio, Paramount. Gloria's Russian countess in the tearoom is a savage and skillful caricature of Pola Negri.

In 1925 there appeared another Allan Dwan–Gloria Swanson vehicle: *Stage Struck*. Again Gloria appears as a downtrodden member of the working class. She is a waitress in a cheap riverside restaurant who dreams of becoming a great actress. The film opens with an elaborate prologue in Technicolor as she dreams of her stage triumphs. Ironically, the dream sequence is both documentary and prophetic of Gloria Swanson's actual career: in 1925 she was indeed one of the most admired and envied of all the glamorous film personalities at a time that marked the peak of Hollywood's renown. And she had come back to Hollywood from France, newly become Marquise de la Falaise de la Coudraye, to one of the biggest newsreel and frantic crowd receptions that little town had ever seen. That triumphal procession through the film capital looked as though it had been coproduced by Cecil B. DeMille and Erich von Stroheim.

Nineteen-twenty-five was the vintage year of the silent dramas, and the highest priestesses, with Gloria Swanson at their head, could not

In *Manhandled* (1924)
Gloria wore a slick, short
bob that did much to
popularize a coiffure that
characterized the
twenties. It was in this
film that Swanson first
did her great Chaplin
imitation (below). With
her are Marie Shelton
and Lilyan Tashman.

know that the very next year would bring a discordant gadget called Vitaphone. The reverberations from that audio device were to change completely the entertainment world that looked so secure, so promising, so spectacularly dedicated to the Hollywood dream of 1925. The dream sequence of *Stage Struck* did indeed come true. But it was a truth that lasted only briefly.

Gloria Swanson was faced with two embattled years of heroic struggles and devastating frustrations. Ironically, it was sound and dialogue, words and music—the talking picture that had destroyed so many whose careers had been built on silence—that rescued Gloria Swanson from the weird, nightmare dead end of von Stroheimism.

In mid-1926, it was the decision of Marquise de la Falaise de la Coudraye to leave Paramount Pictures, where she had made twenty-seven films in eight years. It was time, she decided, to become an independent producer under the imposing banner of United Artists. The artists so united included Charles Chaplin, Mary Pickford, John Barrymore, Douglas Fairbanks and, now, Gloria Swanson.

For her first independent production, Gloria chose a play that was perfect actress bait. In *The Eyes of Youth*, gazing into the crystal ball of a seer, the leading lady sees herself in a whole series of juicy roles: a prima donna, an abandoned woman, an aging Madame X, a virgin sacrificed in an ancient rite. *The Eyes of Youth* had been made in 1919 as a vehicle for Clara Kimball Young, supported by Edmund Lowe, Milton Sills and Rudolph Valentino. To direct the film, Miss Swanson sent for Albert Parker, the Englishman who had guided her so well in the 1918 *Shifting Sands*. Her version of *The Eyes of Youth* was retitled *The Loves of Sunya* and it proved to be an unlucky venture. True, it demonstrated beyond all question an actress's range and versatility, but the admirers of Gloria Swanson did not need to be reminded that she was versatile; they had been delightedly watching her inject comedy nuances into semiserious situations or wring their hearts in unrelieved sequences of drama for years. A picture of episodic little stories that the viewers knew were just possibilities revealed by a crystal ball did not satisfy filmgoers who were already beginning to be unaccountably fascinated with some primitive dialogue recited by Al Jolson.

The cool reception of *The Loves of Sunya* incited Gloria to try something hot—in fact, a real sizzler. The Hays Office, firmly entrenched as overseer of morality in Hollywood film production, was opposed to the possibility of John Colton's play *Rain*, which brought so notable a triumph to Jeanne Eagels on Broadway, ever endangering the puritanical

Frank Morgan and Swanson in the Pola Negri sequence of *Manhandled*

Gloria Swanson as Salome in *Stage Struck* (1925)

Gloria as Sadie Thompson, hard to be convinced by Lionel Barrymore's invidious Davidson, in *Sadie Thompson* (1928).

Raoul Walsh, who directed *Sadie Thompson*, also played the marine who won her heart.

status of the American cinema. In 1928 Gloria Swanson was feeling rebellious over the slighting of *Sunya*. She was inspired to bring *Sadie Thompson* to the screen in spite of the adamant disapproval of Mr. Will Hays and his officers. The Colton play *Rain* was expressly taboo. But no stricture had been placed against the short story "Miss Thompson" by Somerset Maugham, which had been adapted by Colton in writing his hit play. Swanson's announcement that the scenario of her picture was based on Somerset Maugham confused the opposition sufficiently, and a determined Gloria Swanson was able to bring to the screen, with outstanding distinction and success, a Sadie Thompson that every film actress of the day had been eating her heart out to play. Directed by Raoul Walsh, who also played the marine who lost his heart to the ministerially harassed prostitute, Gloria achieved by far her best performance.

Gloria had no crystal ball to warn her that involvement with the Kennedy family would lead to disaster. She had become the inamorata of the very head of the clan, Joseph Kennedy himself. It was his bankroll that was the enabling factor in one of strangest tales in the extravagant lore of Hollywood, the abortive history of *Queen Kelly*. In 1928 Gloria decided, after her successful encounter with Maugham's heroine, that she should embark on a vastly ambitious undertaking with the most notoriously extravagant director then operating in the United States— or elsewhere. Anyone with less courage and confidence than Miss Swanson would have considered a venture with Stroheim doubtful in the extreme. But Gloria seemed willing to gamble the bankroll of Joe Kennedy on her bid for the kind of cinema immortality that the historians of the day seemed to be assuring for any creation of Erich von Stroheim. Stroheim's silent version of *The Merry Widow* had suffered a turbulent history of feuding between temperamental Mae Murray and the director. There were the postdirectorial alterations standard for any Stroheim production. But with all its troubles the film was a box-office champion, and perhaps Miss Swanson felt the possible gains were worth the considerable risks. What she overlooked in gauging the success of *The Merry Widow* was that it was the brilliant presence of John Gilbert as Danilo that turned *The Merry Widow* into a box-office blockbuster. Gloria never considered that for her production to qualify as a potential winner, she needed a John Gilbert as her leading man. Instead she cast a handsome actor, Walter Byron, unknown to filmgoers who, when they got a look at him, were unmoved by his stilted behavior and left cold by his nonexistent personality. Byron was the smallest of the disasters that battered the production. The costs skyrocketed to such an extent that they finally became so formidable as to be noticed with some alarm by Joe Kennedy's financial watchdogs. Moreover, it became more and more apparent that dialogue films were bearing down with gathering momentum on the motion picture industry. Accordingly, it was announced that dialogue sequences would be added to *Queen Kelly*. This moved a writer in the magazine *Closeup* to prophesy in the November 1928 issue: "Gloria's voice will be heard in her next. But as that is a Stroheim, we shall probably all be having three-dimensional color television by the time it is shown." What an accurate prediction! Gloria's voice was indeed heard in her next—but her next turned out to be, happily, not the Stroheim, but *The Trespasser*, directed by Edmund Goulding.

When at last it became apparent that Stroheim was never going to

Erich von Stroheim finally won over his antagonistic leading man, John Gilbert, in the silent *Merry Widow* (1925).

Signe Auen and Gloria Swanson in Stroheim's abortive *Queen Kelly* (1928)

be able to finish *Queen Kelly*, Gloria was vigorously nudged by Joe Kennedy to call a halt to further production. Then a succession of other directors were brought on—not to continue shooting, but merely to try stitching up the existing footage into something vaguely resembling an exhibitable motion picture with a makeshift ending. There was a limited release of the film, and fortunately for Gloria's reputation, very few people ever saw it.

Gloria lost no time licking her wounds. Without further delay she knew she had to answer the challenge of the sound track. Cured of her hypnotic faith in the Stroheim myth, she awakened to cinematic reality by hiring the rising British director Edmund Goulding. Goulding was only a little less versatile than Noel Coward and even more charming—to the ladies who responded to him like cats to catnip. Mr. Goulding had written plays that were successful on Broadway and that became solid movies like *Dancing Mothers*, which had boosted Clara Bow to her special area of fame.

In an astonishing burst of production speed under Goulding's confident and efficient guidance, *The Trespasser* was ready for release in a month. Goulding casually composed a hit song for the film, "Love, Your Magic Spell Is Everywhere." Gloria handled the dialogue as though she had been in the theatre all her life. She sang Goulding's theme song so effectively that it became a best-seller, while the film was a smashing success at the box office. The financial carnage of Stroheim's unbridled excesses was mopped up completely by approving fans lining up to see *The Trespasser* and eager to confirm the happy news that their favorite had broken the sound barrier with unqualified success.

Gloria's next film, *What a Widow!*, brought about a reunion with Allan Dwan, who had directed her in six silent films at Paramount. In this farce Gloria's fans were pleasantly reassured that dialogue was no deterrent to the robust comedy techniques that Miss Swanson had never forgotten since the days she had clowned so memorably for Mack Sennett.

And lest one err in thinking that Gloria's gifts as a comedienne were confined to broad comedy, her 1931 *Indiscreet* contained charming light gaiety piloted expertly by Leo McCarey, who was rapidly developing into a master of the genre. *Indiscreet* is a pleasant souvenir to remind us that even during the Depression, the film people could now and then offer a pleasant hour and a half of escape—if one could spare the thirty-five-cent admission.

The classic deathbed encounter of wife and mistress: Purnell Pratt, Gloria Swanson and Mary Forbes in *The Trespasser* (1929)

In *Perfect Understanding* (1933) Gloria is surprised to find Laurence Olivier in her bedroom.

Gloria Swanson, hyperactive though she was, only made three films abroad. Her first had been the 1925 *Madame Sans-Gêne*, made in France with the pioneer director Léonce Perret, creator of that early master-piece of 1910, *The Child of Paris*. In 1956 she made a film in Rome with none other than Brigitte Bardot, Vittorio De Sica and Alberto Sordi. It was called *Nero's Mistress*, and I have never met anyone who ever saw it! Of much more import to her destiny was the British *Perfect Understanding*, made in 1933. Her leading man was Laurence Olivier. Apart from the interest in seeing an incredibly young Olivier supporting Gloria Swanson, this film, shot partly in Cannes, is a period piece that will intrigue connoisseurs of the Scott Fitzgerald tradition. Its opening is somewhat similar to the spirit of Jean Renoir's *Rules of the Game* which appeared six years later. Also in the cast is Brooklyn-born John Halliday, apparently painfully aware that his Cunard dock British accent with the native Brooklynese showing through is in trying company with the British cast. His uncertainty slows down the picture lamentably. Most of the time he speaks as though he were on a poor transatlantic tele-phone connection. Gloria, on the other hand, playing an American visitor, was never more relaxed, charming and bright. Also in the cast, playing a handsome Riviera playboy, is Michael Farmer, Gloria's husband and father of her daughter Michelle. Michelle, long married to a French film producer, is now an elegant, completely lovely Parisienne and keenly devoted to looking after her mother's still-lingering business affairs.

Back home the next year, Gloria came under the sway of that legendary German producer, Erich Pommer. For him she made the 1934 *Music in the Air*, an Oscar Hammerstein–Jerome Kern movie. Gloria played a diva, a faintly amusing role, not particularly memorable, directed by the German Joe May. But another German involved in this production was to provide a far more significant contribution to her career. One of the screenplay writers was Billy Wilder, a German refugee who sixteen years later would direct one of the best films ever made in the United States when he created *Sunset Boulevard*.

How wonderful, how perfect that Gloria Swanson should star in by far the best film ever made about Hollywood. And what a strange, once-in-a-lifetime regrouping of persons involved in the career of Gloria Swanson: Cecil B. DeMille, acting himself with unforgettable charm; Erich von Stroheim, the uncontrollable genius of *Queen Kelly*, reunited with the star he almost ruined, cast as her devoted servant. In the 1929 *Trespasser*, there had been cast a child actor. His name was William Holden.

On September 22, 1983, the William Doyle Galleries in New York auctioned "Property from the Estate of Gloria Swanson." In the morning, dresses, coats, hats and other clothing and some of the gowns she'd worn in her films were sold. Those items brought more than $100,000—twice the amount the galleries had estimated. The afternoon auction disposed of "Personal Memorabilia," and again the proceeds just about doubled expectations.

A public auction of the personal belongings of a loved one can be far more traumatic than the funeral itself. The "remains" bear no resemblance to the living person. But the clothes she wore, the combs, the hats, the artwork she loved and the creations she made with her own hands and spirit, all these were intimate parts of Gloria. To have them plundered by competitive strangers (albeit admirers) and carried off to hundreds of remote corners of the world meant heart-wrenching sadness for some of us.

For Gloria Swanson, some inner call-board must have told her she would soon be appearing in another theatre. That summer, in 1983, she called me, worried about what to do with her collections. Film scripts, stills—a vast amount of Swanson memorabilia—along with her famous wardrobe, made up an extraordinary treasure trove of movie arcana from 1914 through the 1950s.

Much of her collection had been deposited in the Museum of Modern Art. When John F. Kennedy began his campaign for the presidency, Gloria heard that some of her personal films had been taken from the collection by the Kennedy people. Outraged, she withdrew her entire collection and placed it with the George Eastman House in Rochester.

When I left Eastman House in 1977, she took her collection back again and asked me "Where now?" My suggestion was the Metropolitan. It was eager to have the costumes, but could not accept the rest, and Gloria hoped to keep the materials all together. Much that was not auctioned wound up at the old Astoria Paramount Studio now converted to a museum. This is an appropriate denouement, for although Gloria had reigned as the queen of Hollywood, she had become the quintessential New Yorker, and many of her most popular films had been made during the 1920s in the Astoria Studio.

In many ways, movie stardom began with Gloria Swanson. The magic of a personality requires a special skill to register powerfully in the medium of shadow and illusion. The indefinable ingredients of this magic separate the mere performer from that unique creature, the film goddess—one who provokes admiration, imitation and sometimes the most total and irrational devotion of a multitude of worshipers.

Movie mystique apart, Gloria was a great performer onstage. For three years she toured in *Butterflies Are Free*, winding up with a much-praised Broadway run. Gloria owned the movies and triumphed in the theatre not only because she was a gifted and brilliant actress, but in a large measure because she was a gallant and untiringly courageous woman. Gloria was known to her family—and to some of her friends close enough to count as family—as Glory. My wife, Jeanne, and I lived with her and her last husband, Bill Dufty, for a fabulous time in Florida.

Today many folks concerned about ecology and the elimination of poisons in what we eat, drink and breathe are discovering the pioneering role Gloria played in persuading much of the basic food and drug legislation to emerge from timorous Washington. She was absolutely serious and committed in her battle for organic foods and safeguards against inimical additives, and consequently demanding in her own cuisine. Husband Bill Dufty was the official chef, and wherever they went, he had to lug along footlockers filled with proper foodstuffs. More than once in Florida, Jeanne and I were good-humoredly reprimanded for sneaking out of the house for contraband consumption.

In Orlando Gloria was participating in a two-week program of films I had brought together for a major review of her movie career. Onstage presenting that program, she demonstrated her perfectionist obsession. She dismissed an organist hired to accompany the silent films— bemused by what he saw during rehearsal, he simply forgot to go on playing. She altered and had repainted a staircase on the stage that displeased her; she reset the entire lighting arrangement.

The retrospective showing of her films was to go on for a week. Opening night was a sellout. In the middle of the week, only a few Floridians lingered to watch the early silent films. Gloria ordered that the entire population of a nursing home be brought in to fill the theatre. "Those people will remember me!" she proclaimed. She was right.

In 1974, opening the first Telluride Film Festival in Colorado, she shared honors with Germany's Leni Riefenstahl. There were the expected protest marchers objecting to the presence of the noted maker of *Triumph of the Will*. Gloria vigorously defended her cohonoree. "We're here to look at the film we've made—not to answer for the gossip that attempts to scandalize. I've been controversial all my life. Now we're here to talk about the work we've done—not about what gossips think of our private lives."

In 1957 Gloria was in Rochester to receive the George Award, voted to her by the actresses, actors, directors and cameramen who had worked in Hollywood and New York throughout the period of her career. She was back in the 1960s for a special award. For her seventy-fifth birthday Henri Langlois invited her to the Cinémathèque in Paris for a great homage. For that occasion I made up a two-hour compilation of excerpts, starting with scenes from her Essanays with Chaplin in Chicago. It contained sequences from a score of her great films, including the delightful Chaplin imitation she did in *Sunset Boulevard*.

Instead of trying to put seventy-five candles on a single birthday cake, Langlois scoured the bakeries of Paris and assembled twenty-five little cakes, each with three candles. When festivities were about to start in the film theatre of the Cinémathèque in the Palais de Chaillot, some enemy of the establishment phoned in a bomb threat. A gendarme appeared on the stage and ordered the audience to evacuate the building until the bomb squad could finish its search. What a tribute to Gloria! Not one person in the audience left the theatre. The policeman acknowledged defeat with the classic gendarmian shrug—and the show went on.

In 1978, to inaugurate a tiny repertory cinema I had opened in East Rochester, Gloria appeared, and, after rearranging the lighting and demanding that the PA system be changed—immediately—she graciously and ceremoniously dedicated the theatre. Later she chatted with her fans at the reception and made the evening an event for each individual who talked with her.

On January 14, 1983, she called to thank Jeannie for the Christmas card—a woodcut print my wife had made. Unusual for her, Gloria admitted to having been ill. In March she went to the hospital, and in April, while asleep, she left us. Looking again at the Doyle auction catalogue—filled with lovely photos of Gloria, I see that someone paid $8,000 for the Salome scarf she wore in *Sunset Boulevard* and $4,750 for a Lalique cologne bottle etched with the name Gloria. Someone paid $950 for the certificate nominating Gloria for the Academy Award for her Norma Desmond.

Like Greta Garbo, John Barrymore and Charles Chaplin, Gloria Swanson was never awarded an Oscar for any of her performances, which made up so major a portion of film history. On page 31 of the catalogue I see a corner of the room where we sat laughing at the cigarette in the bust of Bill that she had made. That sculpture went for $175. On the next page, there is a photo of the room where the three of us sat laughing at a TV airing of "The Norman Conquest." There is the painting of Gloria by Richard Banks (estimated at $200 to $300, sold for $2,500) that Gloria was so fond of she asked me to have Kodak make a special color print, actual size, that she could keep in her room when the portrait went on an exhibition.

And I see the head she did of herself, which she was justly proud of when it was exhibited at Hamilton's in London. And there, sure enough, are her three awards from Eastman House: the two George Awards and an exquisite silver bowl by Hans Christensen, presented in 1966. That went for $200 (a steal—the silver alone was worth more!). And, ah, yes, item 46: "the James Card Award, Montreal, 1977." Sold for $150. Sic semper gloria!

Of course the greatest stars of the predialogue days were not all women. It was only in my own later years that it began to seem so. In my own earliest concentration on movies, fascination was almost limited to Douglas Fairbanks, Harold Lloyd, Buster Keaton, Wallace Reid,

Charlie Chaplin and, somewhat to my own surprise in retrospect, John Barrymore.

The contributions of John Barrymore as a film artist to the enrichment of a tradition of American cinema may not be readily apparent to those who don't count themselves among his particular admirers. In a medium not especially noted for the seriousness, dedication or consistency of its creators, Barrymore was even outstanding for his attitudes rapidly changing from almost childish enthusiasm to bored indifference. And ultimately his cosmic ennui gave way to a flamboyantly nihilistic determination to destroy completely any surviving residue of the laurels he had gathered and the honor he had brought to the American theatre as a conqueror of both Shakespeare and Tolstoy, as an actor whose victories have become lasting legends in spite of his campaign to smother them in ridicule.

Followers of his theatrical career sometimes realize that John Barrymore was a rare giant of a player who bridged two centuries of disparate acting styles. Somewhere out of the glow of his great theatrical ancestry he was able to rekindle the fire and flame of Edwin Booth; in memorably intimate moments he was able to anticipate the instinctual-impulse kind of acting that later became accepted as "natural" or "real" style.

In his films—however bad the picture or however erratic his performance in the worst of them—there was never a portrayal without at least a moment worth more than the price of admission. In some, he achieved sequences absolutely ineradicable from memory: the scene in *The Beloved Rogue*, with Villon as King of Fools in traditional clown makeup, learning of his banishment from Paris. Only in his stricken eyes can one see the bitter pain of such punishment, and as he slowly removes the clown makeup, his face becomes ever more grotesque and ever more a mask of the most acute suffering. Then in *Beau Brummel* as he takes the last pinch of snuff on the wrong side of the garden gate that has barred him from his beloved—a shrug and a slight twist of his head let us know this man's entire life would change from that very instant. Who could forget the moment in *Counsellor-at-Law* when all seems to have gone hopelessly awry, his bleak look at the window of his skyscraper office? And in *Dinner at Eight*, the muted cry of the utterly defeated actor just before he arranges his pitifully theatrical suicide?

As a person, John Barrymore seemed to some of his admirers to be a living synthesis of Lord Byron and Dorian Gray—an embodiment in one player of all the mysteries and excitement of gothic romanticism.

And the gothic in Barrymore that leered out of the wings to mock the classic beauty of the famous profile led him gleefully into such excesses as the maniacal Ahab, the mouldering madman that consumed the elegant fastidiousness of George Bryan Brummell, the flame of tortured Villon, the caged and slavering des Grieux, a Don Juan who before our very eyes and without makeup magic turned into a malevolent Gustav von Seyffertitz, a supernatural Svengali and, of course, the progressively more nauseatingly monstrous Mr. Hyde. One forgives Mr. Barrymore the actor for these frenetic digressions, remembering that he was an actor reluctantly and would have preferred to indulge his Gustave Doré nature as an illustrator.

The films of John Barrymore should be confronted much in the way one reviews the work of Greta Garbo: none is a completely great production, but every one is a joy to watch for those who respond to the magnificence of the artist. In *Grand Hotel* when the two work together, they do indeed push the film near greatness. And just as Garbo had *Camille* and *Ninotchka*, Barrymore too was lucky enough to appear in a few films of real integrity and even artistic success—a small list admittedly, but one that surely must be headed by *Counsellor-at-Law*.

Who could discover the real motive behind Barrymore's apparent attempt to destroy his own reputation and prestige in the grossest buffoonery so eagerly exploited by radio and film and theatre in his last tragic days? Was it despair over failing powers, or a deep doubt of the ultimate merit of what he had accomplished in his most serious efforts?

At the time of this writing, the earliest Barrymore film known to exist is the 1915 *Incorrigible Dukane*. He had made four films before it, and like its predecessors, it was a comedy-drama. It presented the actor during his heavily mustached period, when he was very much one of the high-living Greenwich Village young men about town. Not until his twelfth film, *The Test of Honor*, did he attempt a serious role on the screen. Meanwhile, the 1917 *Raffles* preserves the appearance of John Barrymore at the time of one of his most successful stage roles in *Peter Ibbetson*, with brother Lionel. Filmed in New York, exterior backgrounds provide nostalgic records of more than a half century ago as Raffles meets Bunny in front of the Players Club. An English town house is seen to be another Manhattan landmark. Frank Morgan, acting Bunny, would not encounter Barrymore in another film for sixteen years, when they celebrated their *Reunion in Vienna*.

In 1920 Barrymore established himself as America's finest Shakespearean actor in his stage production of *Richard III*. But he still found

John Barrymore as Richard III in
his triumphant stage production
of 1920; (below) Mr. Hyde
menaces Dr. Jekyll's fiancée,
Martha Mansfield (1920).

The brothers
Warner: Jack, Harry
and Sam

time to personally supervise every detail of the filming of *Dr. Jekyll and Mr. Hyde* in Paramount's Astoria Studio. His was the choice of Louis Wolheim (erstwhile Cornell professor of mathematics) to play the sinister-looking keeper of the dive that celebrated the vivid beauty of Nita Naldi. Miss Naldi was personally recruited from the Ziegfeld Follies by an appreciative Barrymore, who nevertheless insisted on calling her "my dumb Duse." Much of the set was decorated with antiques he hunted out of shops and friends' old homes. Portions of the film evoke an atmosphere sometimes more Wildean than Stevenson, perhaps more redolent of Thomas Burke than of the nineteenth century, but always and most completely steeped in the special Barrymore seasoning of Grand Guignol.

The Warner brothers traveled to the East to woo the triumphant portrayer of Hamlet after the history-making 101 nights on Broadway. Not only was Barrymore persuaded to forsake the stage to return to the movies, but charmed by the sunshine and dolce vita of Hollywood, Barrymore ended his New York period. For the rest of his life he was converted to California. The Warners mounted their prize acquisition in a sumptuously produced, Barrymoresque variation on a popular drama by Clyde Fitch, *Beau Brummel.* Handsomely costumed in some of Richard Mansfield's own Brummell wardrobe, John Barrymore performed exquisitely in a film tableau totally without action, utterly without filmic properties.

One of Barrymore's most cherished prizes gained by his service and sometimes servitude to film was his magnificent yacht, *The Mariner.* A passionate sailor, Barrymore served the Warners with an ultimatum: either he would be allowed to play Captain Ahab or he would have nothing to do with any of the romantic matinee-idol roles the Warners were plotting for him. The star did not realize that casting Dolores Costello in a role that Melville never dreamed of in *Moby Dick* would evoke Barrymore's most romantic behavior both on and off the screen. Dolores captured the actor totally and became his third wife and the mother of John Barrymore, Jr.

The skepticism and reluctance of Warner Brothers in permitting Barrymore to indulge in his seafaring project was repaid by the pleasantly surprising box-office success the film earned. Nevertheless, Warner Brothers sought to have its handsome star make up for what it thought to be lost time by involving him with every beauty on the Warner lot as the traditional Don Juan. He pretended to find it extremely vexing but obviously enjoyed himself immensely in his first

Jack Warner brings his guests from Paris to visit the set of *The Sea Beast* (1925): Millard Webb, the director; Jack Warner; Dolores Costello; M. C. F. Bertelli; John Barrymore and Madame Bertelli.

Ahab in hot pursuit of Moby Dick in *The Sea Beast*

John Barrymore at the moment of truth in *The Sea Beast*

Barrymore as Don Juan (1926)

Fairbanks-type role, leaping, riding, scaling balconies, descending on
vines with flashing rapier and ready dagger. Apart from the comic-book
quality of its script, *Don Juan* became a milestone: it was the fully syn-
chronized feature that along with a program of singing, talking, dancing
and short subjects, introduced Vitaphone to astonished and enthusiastic
crowds in New York City on August 6, 1926, at the Warner Theatre,
on Broadway between Fifty-first and Fifty-second streets. The shorts
included a song by Martinelli, solos by Mischa Elman, Efrem Zimbalist,
Harold Bauer and Marion Talley. There was a film talk by Will Hays,
a song by Anna Case with the dancing Cansinos in the background.
Rita Hayworth (then a Cansino) was in the group. The score for *Don
Juan*, recorded on Vitaphone discs, was played by the New York Philharmonic. It was a formidable array of talent, but it failed to smother
Mr. Barrymore's shadow. Some veteran critics agreed his was the worst
performance they had ever beheld. But watching it today, we know
how wrong the critics were. Barrymore was better than the music.

Barrymore was teamed with his lovely wife, Dolores Costello, in his next film, *When a Man Loves*. The scenario was the broadest imaginable adaptation of Abbé Prévost's detailing of the misadventures of those eternally star-crossed lovers in the eighteenth-century romance *Manon Lescaut*. Warner's scriptwriters stop short of the book's final tragedy in New Orleans but not before they have Barrymore as the maddened des Grieux inciting a whole cageful of casting directors' nightmares to take over the prison ship in a carnival of carnage that would surely have astounded the good Abbé author.

In 1927 John Barrymore joined Douglas Fairbanks, Mary Pickford and Charlie Chaplin in the United Artists. His first venture as a partner in that company was *The Beloved Rogue*, as François Villon, a role for which he was as eminently fitted as he would have been to play Byron. But the Justin Huntley McCarthy Villon that had so long dominated American theatre and popular fiction was bypassed to produce a wholly Barrymore creation that turned out to be more like Fairbanks' Robin Hood than McCarthy's Villon. The great German actor Conrad Veidt was brought to Hollywood to play Louis XI. But the real star of the production was William Cameron Menzies, designer of the fantastic settings for this film that never again found their counterpart in American cinema. Like the whole approach to the film, the sets are imaginatively grotesque. The entire picture in fact was far from the track that Hollywood was successfully beating, and the Fairbanksian style heartily adopted by Barrymore was so unexpected by his fans and so unanimously condemned by the critics that the film did not do well financially.

The year 1928 found Barrymore, at the age of forty-six, still able to convincingly play a youthful, dashing sergeant in the Russian Imperial Army. The 1928 film was called *Tempest*, and Murnau's blond star of *Faust*, Camilla Horn, was imported to be Barrymore's leading lady. Charles Rosher, one of Hollywood's most skillful cameramen, was responsible for making *Tempest* the most handsomely photographed of the Barrymore films.

The Barrymore family was well acquainted with the literary du Mauriers, and it sometimes seemed as though there must be some special affinity between John and the conception of du Maurier's Svengali. Not since the days of Mr. Hyde did Barrymore so revel in Grand Guignol as he did while mastering the young woman Trilby. *Svengali* was a project in which he was supplied imposing support by the almost Caligarian sets of Anton Grot, a gifted Polish art director, schooled in Ger-

Camilla Horn and Barrymore in *Tempest* (1928). Fraulein Horn was imported
after her moving performance as Gretchen in Murnau's *Faust* (1926).

many, who had been offering European designs to American filmmakers
ever since 1913.

In 1932 there happened a special film event: Irving Thalberg offered
John Barrymore a berth at MGM, enticing him with the first chance to
act with his brother, Lionel, since the two Barrymores had performed
on Broadway in *Peter Ibbetson* and *The Jest*. The film was *Arsene Lupin*,
with John cast as the gentleman crook, a sort of French Raffles, and
Lionel as the implacable detective out to catch him. The brotherly
reunion provided a delicious duel of stagecrafting one-upmanship—a
game that delighted both of them and provided special pleasure to Barrymore watchers as their teaming was repeated in three more MGM
superstar movies: *Grand Hotel, Night Flight* and *Rasputin and the Empress*.

These four Barrymore vehicles showed that Thalberg had correctly
estimated that having John Barrymore forgo his gothic tendencies and
trade again on his elegant charm and soigné style would be far more
effective at the box office than were the animated Gustave Doré creations. In *Grand Hotel* Garbo and Barrymore responded to each other
with genuine warmth and mutual respect—the result was to turn his
role of the baron into a major attraction of the film.

In *State's Attorney* Barrymore found the role of a criminal lawyer who turns against his support from the Mob and becomes district attorney to be his first serious, contemporary dramatic part in his entire dialogue-film career. In a way, it was almost a rehearsal for him for his magnificent performance a year later in *Counsellor-at-Law*.

Katharine Hepburn had scored a notable success on the stage as an Amazon in *The Warrior's Husband*. David Selznick lost no time in recruiting her in the same year, 1932, for RKO and casting her as the strong-minded daughter in *A Bill of Divorcement*. In this her first film, she began one of the most distinguished of American film careers, solidly holding her ground opposite John Barrymore as her anguished father. Friends of Barrymore felt that the actor was haunted by the notion of hereditary insanity. Perhaps it was a thought that colored very specially his moving performance as a shell-shocked war veteran who returns from an institution only to learn his wife is leaving him.

When MGM cast all three Barrymores in the 1932 *Rasputin and the Empress*, it was widely heralded—and still is—as a historic first time that both brothers appeared with their sister in any theatrical performance. Like most proclamations of firsts, it was quite wrong. John, Lionel and Ethel Barrymore had appeared together before, and in a film at that. The film that had brought them before the same camera was directed by Christy Cabanne in 1917, and it was called *The National Red Cross Pageant*. The claim for a Barrymore precedent generated much publicity for *Rasputin and the Empress*, but more than that, the production triggered an epic precedent-setting legal battle. Headed by Prince Yusopov himself, surviving Russian aristocrats materialized by the dozen to collect damages from film producers who imagined that the story of Rasputin's murder was a figment of their own scenario writers' always overheated inventions. It is miraculous that after all the court-awarded damages, any part of the film survives at all. It is not surprising that there have been many court-directed deletions tending to mitigate much of Rasputin's alleged nastiness toward various Russian princesses, countesses and ladies-in-waiting, most of whom, it turned out, were still alive in 1932, all very sensitive, all mortally wounded by the implications of the red monk's lusty behavior. And most of them, unfortunately for MGM, were the clients of some very effective lawyers.

A happier excursion by MGM into European modern history was *Reunion in Vienna*. The Alfred Lunt–Lynne Fontanne production of Robert Sherwood's exquisitely nostalgic Hapsburg reunion had been one of the bright spots of the 1931 theatrical season. As the dashing and ironic Rudolf, Barrymore found one of his most delicately balanced comedy roles, perfectly suited to his age, fifty, and seemingly created for his temperament. Frank Morgan, the Bunny of Barrymore's 1917 *Raffles*, rejoined him, a splendidly honed foil as the mildly outraged husband, victim of a one-night reprised romance between his wife and an utterly irresistible Hapsburg.

Dinner at Eight brought the poignant exposition of the last days of a once-popular actor in John Barrymore's portion of this episodic drama. It came in 1933, only a year before Barrymore's own collapse, which would finish his serious pursuit of his career. But before that happened there would be three more great performances by John Barrymore.

The high tide in Barrymore's film career proved to be 1933. His thirty-eighth film, *Counsellor-at-Law*, was one of his best. Elmer Rice fashioned the screenplay from his own hit theatre piece. For once a film version did not drift miles from the spirit of the play simply to become "filmic." For once Barrymore seemed to devote his total concentration to delivering a seriously distinguished performance, and the result was glowing perfection. As a principled Jewish lawyer who suddenly found both career and wife at moral crossroads, Barrymore never faltered, never was betrayed by the slightest excess.

In 1934 the great Barrymore film was *Twentieth Century*. As though all his aptitude for farce and buffoonery had been repressed in the serious roles of 1933, only to come bursting out like exploding fireworks, his bravura burlesque of a Belasco-like theatrical producer tangling with the glittering blond Carole Lombard was Barrymore unfettered. It was memorable comedy on a grand scale.

There was only one more fine performance remaining to him. It was in 1939 in *The Great Man Votes*. After being dismissed for years as a has-been, clinging desperately to the bread and butter of brief feature roles and a succession of low-budget B productions (there were three Bulldog Drummond movies with Barrymore cast as Inspector Nielson), a kind of miracle occurred. Responding to the taste of Garson Kanin, a respected theatre professional, John Barrymore magically shed his buffoonery and became once more the superb actor and gifted performer that he might have remained. A touching, heartwarming film, it became the last valid vehicle for the great gifts of John Barrymore.

Now, a half century after his death, there exists a devoted group of John Barrymore collectors and enthusiasts. They buy the biographies that still come from American publishers as though he were yet an active

As late as 1933, John Barrymore could still cut a romantic figure, as he did with Diana Wynyard in *Reunion in Vienna.*

celebrity. It is strange that most of these persistent followers are men, just as it seems odd that since Barry Paris' biography of Louise Brooks, all of the mail I have had expressing deep hunger to know about that vivid actress, categorized by Kenneth Tynan as a devastating sex symbol, is exclusively from women.

John Barrymore, after several dramatic dress rehearsals, died in the spring of 1942.

American cinema suffered a double loss in 1942: the death of John Barrymore and the retirement from the screen of Norma Shearer. In a period that lasted for only twenty-two years, Norma Shearer appeared in more than fifty movies. In forty-seven of those films she played the leading role. From 1925 she held her place as one of the foremost stars, through a time when film stardom provided America's equivalent of nineteenth-century European royalty. But the reign of Miss Shearer was different in many ways from that enjoyed by her peers. Neither scandal nor mystery encouraged the press or the journals of sensation to rely on her name to boost their sales. No flamboyant offscreen drama brought her notoriety beyond the renown of her professional activity, which was more than sufficient to make the name of Norma Shearer an international symbol of particularly American chic, youthful zest, urbane polish, intelligent good taste and, above all, a sense of steadfast inner worthiness.

Such qualities are not the usual attributes of an exceptionally successful actress. Nor did they encourage the kind of hysterical, swooning mass demonstrations that marked the multitude's admiration for some of our other stars. Those of us who counted ourselves among Miss Shearer's most ardent admirers during her career may have been guilty of taking for granted her inevitable ability to provide a splendid performance in whatever role she assumed.

Real astonishment over the profundity of her accomplishments was reserved for a 1970 retrospective look at fifteen of her films from a nineteen-year period, compressed into the space of seventeen nights of viewing. Seeing her films in chronological order was like watching time-lapse movies of the budding and blossoming of a lovely flower. Spectators at Eastman House, where the sessions were held, responded to this opportunity with growing fascination—and in increasing numbers until it became necessary to repeat showings toward the end of the series. Many arranged to attend every single screening, seven nights a week over two weeks. The films prompted enthusiastic letters to Miss Shearer, which must have reminded her of the days when fan mail was so very much a part of her life.

Apart from the most considerable emotional involvement the entire program inspired, most viewers were struck with the unsuspected versatility of an actress whose image in memory had somehow been frozen into the features of a particularly handsome, sleek, ultrasmart sophisticate. This concentrated exhibition of a long list of her films made it difficult to think of any other American star who brought more variety and demonstrated more genuine interpretive flexibility to her roles than did Norma Shearer.

Indeed, if one reflects on the film career of Norma Shearer, it becomes apparent that the qualities she brought to her work were absolutely unique. There was no other actress like Norma Shearer in the way that Clara Bow was a little like Colleen Moore or Tallulah Bankhead was rather like Constance Bennett. And the more one tries to isolate the qualities that made Norma Shearer unique, the more one heads into an area of a kind of gracious dignity—a serene purity of bearing and attitude that eludes sensible definition. For certainly she played a

The later Norma Shearer,
in 1931: sleek, chic and
sophisticated

good share of audacious, sometimes even wicked and often déclassé
women—but never without that special Shearer aura of wholesome
probity—along with most of the other positive attributes that have vanished wholly from a morally dismal world. The ghost flowers are gone—
the bluebirds are rare—the likes of Norma Shearer are nowhere to be
seen in contemporary film.

The film debut of Miss Shearer in 1920 is still to be observed in
D. W. Griffith's most financially successful movie, *Way Down East.*
Appropriately, it was shot in the East and provided extra work for the
young Canadian visitor to New York City who, accompanied by her
mother, was determinedly stalking the casting directors, taking model-
ing work and appearing at last in small parts in both plays and pictures.
Sharp-eyed film watchers can find her in the Tremont ball sequence, in
which Griffith, ever appreciative of fresh young beauty, granted one single close shot to Norma Shearer.

In the same year, 1920, she had a larger role in *The Flapper,* a film
that is a particular gem of Americana, as it was filmed in Florida, in the
Adirondacks and in snowy upstate New York. Not until 1922 did she

The early Norma
Shearer: ingenuous and
sweet; (below) Shearer in
His Secretary (1925)

In 1924 they were confident enough at MGM to essay Andreyev: Norma Shearer with Lon Chaney in *He Who Gets Slapped*.

Victor Seastrom directed Norma Shearer in *The Tower of Lies* (1925). Here she is with Lon Chaney and Ian Keith.

The Devil's Circus (1926) brought Shearer still another Scandinavian director. This time it was Benjamin Christensen. Charles Emmett Mack is her shy friend.

Norma Shearer in 1926: a confident and radiant star

Marriage to Irving
Thalberg, MGM's
brilliant production
chief, was no detriment
to Shearer's career.

begin playing ingenue leads. The next year found her at Warners, where in *Lucretia Lombard* she had advanced to playing "the other woman." The big turning point in the Shearer career came in 1924, when Irving Thalberg took over MGM along with Louis B. Mayer. She was cast opposite John Gilbert, also a rapidly ascending star, in the Victor Seastrom production of Andreyev's *He Who Gets Slapped*—a vehicle for Lon Chaney. This strange film was directed by the great Swedish master Victor Seastrom. He would use Norma Shearer in still another Lon Chaney production, *The Tower of Lies*, an adaptation of a Selma Lagerlöf novel. Most of Shearer's directors were American, but she did work with one other Scandinavian, Benjamin Christensen, in *The Devil's Circus*. The first American film of the Danish director, *The Devil's Circus* was long missing and ardently sought. It was an important find and restoration. The film brought a special European touch to Hollywood production, which worked quite differently from that of the gathering German immigrant artists. The film played at the Capitol Theatre in the spring of 1926 and moved Mordaunt Hall in the *New York Times* to comment:

This production is the first Mr. Christensen has made in this country and in it he displays a marked ability for introducing little human touches which do away with the necessity for many subtitles. The stage settings are natural and those in the circus reveal a keen eye for detail. . . . Norma Shearer impersonates Mary and she gives a highly creditable performance of the girl who never appeared to have a wrong thought.

The coming of dialogue only enhanced the ability of Norma Shearer to embody so many of the finest attributes of specifically American womanhood.

CHAPTER 9

Vanished Vampires

Women's revolt against being seen as sex objects has had some effect—some strange effects indeed. But change there has been. No more burlesque shows with their traditional rows of bald-headed men. No more Ziegfeld Follies glorifications or *George White's Scandals* or Earl Carroll's Vanities. To see partly nude beauties prancing about in feathery costumes, American males have to go all the way to Paris to patronize the Lido and Les Folies Bergère. What we have now are topless bars, go-go dancers and Madonna. Progress?

Early in the life of the movies it was seen with acute distress by some and with delight by others that the cinema was curiously effecive when it turned to eroticism. No one can understand how the theatre stars of the 1890s, chunky, matronly May Irwin and walrus-mustached John C. Rice, could stir up the censors in the 1896 Edison one-minute *The Kiss*. It had been simply intended as a souvenir shot from their Broadway show *The Widow Jones*. Or how it could be seen as a sex scandal inviting outraged protests and insistence on establishing a stern censorship for the shadow plays of the cinema.

Early film inherited the heroines of the Victorian theatre. Their essential quality was purity. They were the noble women whom men were expected to place on pedestals and court only with poetry and romantic protestations of eternal devotion. Heroic protagonists' chief function was to save these fragile creatures from fates worse than death. The photoplays welcomed Victorian theatrical womanhood, and many millions of feet of film were exposed before aggressive femininity was depicted on the screen—other than the literary wickednesses of Milady de Winters and Becky Sharp.

The idea of female sexual activity came to our puritanical land via

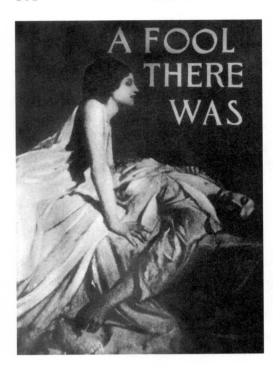

A copy of Burne-Jones' *The Vampire* was used on the cover of *A Fool There Was*, the novel that as a film made Theda Bara the most famous of movie vamps.

nasty notions from Great Britain. The most powerful subversive image came from the scandalous painting by Sir Philip Burne-Jones, first exhibited in London's New Gallery in 1897.

Calling his painting *The Vampire*, Sir Philip Burne-Jones, a highly respected painter, had been so audacious as to portray a sexually active woman (clad in a night gown) poised triumphantly over her quite obviously done-in male bed partner—or, as some professed to see him, her victim.

The notorious painting was also the acknowledged inspiration for a popular poem by Rudyard Kipling. It too was titled *The Vampire*, and it was published in 1897, the same year that the painting was on view. The poem was speedily well known in the United States, where Kipling was one of the most widely read British writers. The opening lines of *The Vampire*, rather more turgid than poetic, nevertheless set the tone for the long, long line of wicked women to afflict the movies in America:

> A fool there was and he made his prayer
> (Even as you and I!)
> To a rag and a bone and a hank of hair
> . . . .

But the fool he called her his lady fair—
(Even as you and I!)

. . . .

The fool was stripped to his foolish hide
(Even as you and I!)
Which she might have seen when she threw him aside—
(But it isn't on record the lady tried)
So some of him lived but the most of him died—
(Even as you and I!)

It took about thirteen years before the erotically destructive woman began turning up in American movies. Theda Bara's reign as the queen vampire of American films began in 1914. Her first film took its title directly from the first line of Kipling's poem: *A Fool There Was*. The Museum of Modern Art Film Library was apologetic about circulating *A Fool There Was*. Its catalogue erroneously stated, "This film is remembered because it introduced the vamp."

The word "vamp," as applied to "a woman who uses her charm or wiles to seduce and exploit men," is certainly a movie-inspired word. And although the raven-haired Theodosia Goodman, with her smouldering dark eyes, became the very embodiment of the wicked, scheming woman, she was not the film's first by several years. Selig had a film called *The Vampire* in 1910—four years before Theda Bara's 1914 debut. There were probably others, but the key film of the genre appeared in 1913. This was Kalem's *The Vampire*, filmed in Jacksonville, Florida, and directed by Robert Vignola, with the seductress played by Alice Hollister.

Scrawny Alice Hollister was far from anyone's ideal of a dragon lady. But the film is exceptional for the presence of dancers Alice Eis and Bert French. This dance team had choreographed a steamy, erotic dance directly from the Burne-Jones painting. One feature of the dance was a momentary tableau re-creating the exact positions of the man and the woman of the painting. The Eis and French *Vampire Dance* had successfully toured the entire vaudeville circuit of the United States before it was documented as part of the Vignola film.

Kalem's Jacksonville studio consisted of outdoor platforms. Sets of interiors built on them usually featured curtains and lamp shades fluttering and trembling in the Florida breezes. Bushes grew behind the stage of *The Vampire*, and the dancers were able to emerge from the shrubbery where they had already begun their dance. This production is a rare and revealing record of Florida filmmaking in 1913 quite apart

Alice Hollister, the femme fatale of *The Vampire* (1913)

The great feature of *The Vampire* was the *Vampire Dance* of Alice Eis and Bert French.

The Victor recording of Byron Gay's song hit *The Vamp* was a top seller in 1919.

from its impressive preservation of the Burne-Jones relic provided by Eis and French. The Eastman House collection incredibly holds the original negative of the Kalem *Vampire*, and prints struck from it are wonderfully sharp and clear.

From at least 1913 on, sex in films was permitted to rear its not always ugly head—but only in the shape of evil and designing women who had no business whatsoever on pedestals. The physical appearance of these wicked females improved considerably in the wake of Alice Hollister. Among those qualifying as vamps were Olga Petrova, *The Vampire*; Virginia Pearson, *Blazing Love*; Louise Glaum, *The Wolf Woman*; Betty Blythe, *Dust of Desire*; Nita Naldi, *The Common Sin*; Dagmar Godowsky, *The Marriage Pit*; Valeska Suratt, *The Siren*; Myrna Loy, *The Exquisite Sinner*.

A Coven of Movie Witches

Katherine Grant (above left)
Mae West, portrait (above)
Anna May Wong, portrait (1932)
(left)

Nita Naldi (above)
Brigitte Helm, *Metropolis* (1926) (above right)
Valeska Suratt with Eric Mayne, *The New York
Peacock* (1917) (left)

Betty Blythe in *Chu-Chin-Chow* (1925), and in *The Folly of Vanity* (1925) (below)

Jane Thomas, *Queen of the Moulin Rouge* (1922)

Sally Crute, *The Magic Skin* (1915)

Virginia Pearson

Louise Glaum, *The Return of Draw Egan* (1916)

Although she was far from the first of the screen sirens, Theda Bara (Theodosia Goodman) was the foremost.

But of course it is Theda Bara whose name survives as the definitive movie vamp. And there was never any question about her origin. In the July 1919 issue of the fan magazine *Classic*, she is described as "the famous Burne-Jones lady of the screen." Her last vamping was done in that year, 1919, with *The Siren's Song, When Men Desire* and *A Woman There Was.* But as late as 1923 she remained the legendary seductress. This fervent caption was printed beneath a rather fine drawing of her in the February 1923 issue of *Classic:*

THEDA BARA

Endless lure of pomegranate lips . . . red enemy of man . . . the sombre brooding beauty of a thousand Egyptian nights . . . black-browed and starry-eyed . . . infinite mystery in their smouldering depths, never to be revealed . . . Mona Lisa . . . Cleopatra . . . child of the Russian countryside . . . daughter of the new world . . . peasant . . . goddess . . . eternal woman

Pola Negri's early European triumph was in Max Reinhardt's *Sumurun*, directed by Ernst Lubitsch (1920).

Negri's greatest performance in the United States
was in *Barbed Wire* (1927).

Not until the end of World War I did American filmgoers realize
there was a deeper character existing within hot-blooded womanhood.
The revelation came from the first of the Ernst Lubitsch German productions to reach the United States. And it came from the stunning
image of the Polish actress Appolonia Chalupec—known to the mar-
quees of the world as Pola Negri. As Madame DuBarry and as Carmen,
Negri brought a wholly different kind of aggressive woman to the
American film audiences. The Negri women were sexy in every contemporary sense of the word. They were neither frail nor caricatures of
either evil or purity.

The German films of Pola Negri were soon followed by the actress
herself, who, signed by Paramount, with her vivid screen persona invited quite different approaches on the part of scriptwriters. Negri characters were strong and passionate. Her heroines were often thoughtful
and sometimes even allowed to have a sense of humor. Her performance
in *Barbed Wire* as a French peasant struggling against her love for a
German prisoner of war held in a camp on her own farm, foreshad-

Pola Negri as a French peasant in *Barbed Wire*, which Erich Pommer (below right) supervised

owed accurately similar tragedies enacted in reality when the Germans returned to France in 1940.

In *A Woman of the World* we see her gently rejecting the immature advances of a young small-town boy and then, in the same film, savagely horsewhipping the man she would immediately thereafter embrace with steaming passion.

The actors and actresses who contributed most to the predialogue cinema were eager to admit that no artist approached the lonely summit attained by Greta Garbo. And that she, having conquered so completely in the pantomime period, went on to dominate the vocal cinema as well marks Greta Garbo surely as the foremost actress of that universal theatre that only film has been able to give to the world. Probably the first notice in the United States of a Garbo film was in the June 1924 issue of *Motion Picture Classic*. Best of the fan magazines that proliferated through the 1920s, *Classic* ran a department on foreign films. There was a photo from Mauritz Stiller's *Gosta Berling* captioned "Above are Jenny Hasselquist and Greta Gustafson." The film is reviewed without singling out Garbo: "The carefully balanced and well-selected cast is headed by Jenny Hasselquist, Lars Hansson and Greta Gustafson," refuting the legend that Stiller had already invented the name Garbo for the release of *Gosta Berling*. It would thus seem that Greta Gustafson did not become Garbo until Pabst's *Joyless Street* or, perhaps, in the Swedish *Three Kings*, in which she had appeared with her sister.

Not until two years after *Gosta Berling* was finished did Louis B. Mayer see the film and find it exciting enough to sign both Garbo and Stiller to MGM contracts. There was more excitement when Pabst's *Joyless Street* opened in Berlin. Countess Agnes von Esterhazy and the great Danish tragedienne Asta Nielsen were in the cast along with Garbo, but Esterhazy has told of attending the opening, escorted by the then-prominent composer Kalman (*Countess Maritza*) who, much to the discomfiture of the charming lady by his side, almost fell out of their box in his enthusiasm for Greta Garbo.

It is odd that in her first three international hits—*Gosta Berling, The Joyless Street* and *Torrent*—there was nothing in Garbo's behavior to suggest that Hollywood should see her as a femme fatale. Yet in her second American movie, *The Temptress*, she was cast as an archetypal destroyer of noble manhood.

The Spanish novelist Ibanez and Hollywood seemed to have a disastrous lack of affinity—Ibanez's novels were never as bad as they appeared in their filmed versions, nor were Hollywood movies usually

Greta Garbo in her first American film, *Torrent* (1926)

Antonio Moreno and Garbo in *The Temptress* (1926)

as turgid as when they were based on Ibanez. Garbo's second American film was cursed, like her first, by an Ibanez-inspired script. Production began bravely with Stiller at the helm. But the Swedish director, perhaps jealous of Garbo's phenomenal success in *Torrent*, which had been made without his direction, was unable to cooperate with his American producers. After turbulent and costly quarrels, Stiller was replaced by Fred Niblo, a director secure at MGM in the reputation of his mighty *Ben-Hur*.

Again, the critical press protested the obvious idiocies of the story, the recounting of the vampire-temptress causing the deaths of four lovers and all but ruining the career of the hero, struggling to build none other than Hoover Dam. But those same reviewers were so swept along by the personality of Garbo that they found the film outstanding. The National Board of Review even rated it "exceptional," citing especially its impressive ending. This citation they revoked when the film was finally released with an altered "happy ending."

With *The Temptress* Garbo was definitely typed as a vamp. And so successful was that film that her producers were understandably reluctant to tamper with the formula that was proving golden for them, but extremely distasteful to Miss Garbo herself. For she was deeply concerned to establish herself in this country as the serious actress she had already proved herself to be in Europe.

Flesh and the Devil was based on a Hermann Sudermann work; Sudermann was a Teutonic Ibanez, and the role saw Garbo as another femme fatale. Nevertheless three new elements in the production were to prove fortunate for her career.

John Gilbert was the star. (Some of the publicity for *Flesh and the Devil* did not even mention Garbo!) Gilbert not only worked harmoniously with her on the set, but he took a dedicated interest in advancing her artistic career and used his considerable prestige and influence at MGM to telling advantage when Garbo began her determined campaign at the end of *Flesh and the Devil* to finish forever with her vamp image.

Clarence Brown, the director, was able to appreciate and exploit many of her rare gifts. He was considered so successful in directing her that the company entrusted seven of its Garbo films to him. And, finally, cinematographer William Daniels began to direct his cameras at her in a manner that was almost worshipful. The time was very nearly at hand to see a completely triumphant Garbo. That triumph came with the completion of the predialogue version of *Anna Karenina*, or, as MGM retitled it, *Love*.

Echoes of Burne-Jones? Garbo and Gilbert in *Flesh and the Devil* (1927)

Director Eddie Goulding had a way with his female stars: with Garbo in *Grand Hotel* (1932).

Love reached the screen only after three almost completed versions had been shelved, so insistent was Garbo on extricating herself from what she considered—so rightly—a slough of film banalities. Healer of *Love*'s serious ills was perceptive Edmund Goulding, who was later to achieve something of a phenomenon when he so readily handled both Barrymores along with Joan Crawford *and* Garbo in *Grand Hotel*. Goulding did what he could to stitch together a film from the remnants of the false starts. He replaced Ricardo Cortez as Vronsky with John Gilbert himself. Goulding wisely let his cameras remain on the faces of Garbo and Gilbert in giant close-ups for most of the footage. That would have been quite enough, but unhappily for the film, the forces of economics were brought to bear, and a ridiculously contrived happy ending reuniting Tolstoy's memorably unhappy lovers was allowed to wreck most of the effectiveness that the combined efforts of Goulding, Garbo and Gilbert had sustained throughout the production. Still, *Love* stands as Garbo's first American film in which she, by strength of untold battling with the studio, was able to perform in a role that was not insulting to her ability.

Not that she was altogether finished with femmes fatales. It was just that from that point on, her seductresses would be less crude than the

Anna Karenina was retitled *Love* (1927) for the MGM movie; MGM also reworked Tolstoy for Garbo and Gilbert.

Garbo as a silent Anna Karenina in *Love*

vamps of Sudermann or Ibanez. In her very next film, *The Mysterious Lady*, she was cast as a World War I spy using all her erotic equipment to pry military secrets from a hapless lover. Mitigating her return to the business of seduction was the fact that this film brought us the face of Garbo photographed more magnificently than it had ever been filmed before. By 1928 her directors finally realized that the Garbo Face was their most important business at hand, regardless of the story requirements.

Although Garbo had to put up with one more wartime spy in *Mata Hari*, she was rescued from the need to do any more overt vamp films by the very spirit of the time. In the age of gin, jazz and gasoline, there was no longer any room for the heavy-breathing destroyers of manhood that had been a Theda Bara specialty. Members of NOW these days would be astonished to know that by 1929 women had been liberated and had achieved sexual equality. Popular magazines were replete with discussions of the new morals, amateur competition and companionate marriage. The cinema, faithful—albeit sometimes highly polished—mirror of the social scene, reflected these movements of America's slipping puritanism. Garbo's screen characters were made to harmonize with the modern woman who made her own rules of sexual behavior. *The Single Standard* was based on a 1928 novel by Adela Rogers St. Johns, whose heroine insists on revised moral principles that would eliminate the double standard of sexual behavior and replace it with a single rule applying equally to men and to women. The Garbo character in *The Single Standard* refuses marriage, has affairs with a prizefighter and her chauffeur, a relationship that causes the latter to commit suicide.

Garbo enacted an even more promiscuous heroine in the same year with *A Woman of Affairs*. Michael Arlen (an Armenian immigrant) wrote a best-seller that was considered even more piquant than Elinor Glyn's *Three Weeks*. He was the Jacqueline Susann of his day, and the character Iris March of the book *The Green Hat* became the very symbol of the new sexual freedom of the raunchy end-of-the-decade era. Of course the Hays Office pursed its collective lips at plans to film Arlen's novel. But financial temptation proved too great. After all, in black-and-white film, no one could see that the hat Garbo wore was green. And they changed the character's name, for the original Iris March had become a popular symbol of amorality. Thus *The Green Hat* became *A Woman of Affairs*, and Iris March was renamed Diana Merrick. Again there was a male suicide in the film as a result of having skated on ice too thin. Readers of the novel knew the death was brought about by having contracted

Garbo tries to comfort a drunken brother, Douglas Fairbanks, Jr., in *A Woman of Affairs* (1928).

a sexual disease, although the film only noted that the boy "died for decency." And after having messed up several lives, Garbo finally kills herself (for everyone else's good, of course) by driving her sports car at high speed into a tree. Although the behavior was more free, the morality lesson was the same as that taught by the old-fashioned vamps: steaming sex brought deaths in its wake.

There was still a missing element of sex waiting to be supplied by the right woman—sex for fun. The most popular stars—Mary Pickford, Lillian Gish, Colleen Moore, Marion Davies, Patsy Ruth Miller— were reassuringly sexless. They were everyman's sisters. The most picturesquely beautiful and the most elegant leading ladies—Dolores Del Rio, Florence Vidor, Dolores Costello, Norma Talmadge and Norma Shearer—were all like animated magazine photos. They were much admired but hardly calculated to turn on male observers by their personalities or behavior. Yet the perfect fun-and-sex girl was on hand for a long time, just waiting for her audience to be born, when she would explode on the screen like a dazzling firework. That fully charged sex rocket was Clara Bow.

Clara Bow appeared in an incredible twenty-eight films (including a Tom Mix Western) between 1922 and 1926, when she began to attract special recognition in *Dancing Mothers* as the primary jazz-age flapper. The ubiquitous flapper was accepted as one of the definitive manifestations of the mad twenties, but again, it remained for a Briton to point out to Americans—and to the rest of the film world—that the Charleston-dancing, gin-guzzling young adult of the era was the primary vehicle for emancipated sex.

Back in 1897 it had been Sir Philip Burne-Jones who had alerted Americans to the idea that sex with certain dominant women could be dangerous to men. Now, in the 1920s, another British socialite, the sister of Lady Duff Gordon, invented the potent cult of It and became its high priestess. Using the name Elinor Glyn, as early as 1907 she had devised an international best-seller, *Three Weeks*. In this country, it was

Like no other star, Clara Bow could radiate joie de vivre.

Clara Bow not only understood the age of gin, jazz and gasoline—she typified it in *Dancing Mothers* (1926).

A distinguished visitor—Noel Coward, in overcoat—on the 1926 set of *Dancing Mothers*. Left to right: Herbert Brenon, the director; Norman Trevor; Elsie Lawson; Alice Joyce; Clara Bow; Dorothy Cumming; Conway Tearle.

more notorious than *Fanny Hill*. The book created a lively furor that lasted more than fifteen years. In American movies if a director wanted to show that one of the characters in his film was leading a racy life, all he had to do was to show her holding a copy of *Three Weeks* in her lap. She didn't have to be shown reading it—just holding the book was enough to tag her as modern and independent.

Elinor Glyn's 1936 autobiography was titled *Romantic Adventure*. In this work she explained that she wrote the controversial portions of *Three Weeks* while she was in Italy a year or so after her marriage. She felt rather neglected by her husband and wrote, "My romantic soul constantly sought in flights of unfettered imagination, an escape from the limitations and deprivations of my married life, and *Three Weeks* was the product. My head was a little turned, perhaps, by the amount of attention which almost all men except my husband gave me at that time."

In his 1947 study of best-sellers in the United States, *Golden Multitudes*, Frank Luther Mott comments: "It is a stirring thought that if Mr. Glyn had been more attentive on that holiday in Venice, the world might have been spared *Three Weeks*." It is even more stirring that in the year 1926, at the age of sixty-two, Elinor Glyn hit upon her most lasting of all contributions to the analyses of sexual attraction. Her redefinition of the neuter and neutral pronoun to the highly charged connotation of "It" first appeared in *Cosmopolitan* magazine in 1926.

The article became the talk of the season and inevitably begged for a film to be made and mounted on the national bandwagon that the piece had developed. Paramount signed Madame Glyn to write a screenplay, but fortunately for the film that did appear, she never delivered a script. What she did deliver was reams of copy for the publicity department. One release had it that Madame Glyn had personally chosen Clara Bow to embody her It girl. It was most unlikely that the decision was actually Elinor Glyn's. Clara Bow was then under contract to Paramount. She already had two flapper hits for Paramount to her credit, with *Dancing Mothers* and Sinclair Lewis' *Mantrap*. There was no other actress at Paramount with anything like the It possessed by Clara Bow.

Without the benefit of any titillating paragraphs from Elinor Glyn, the Paramount writers went cheerfully ahead, doing a Hollywood Cinderella story carefully tailored to the charms of Clara Bow. The producers made a wise choice in assigning Clarence Badger to direct the film. Badger's background for comedy was the best.

Although Badger knew his way around the filming of comedy all right, in making *It* he had another responsibility—keeping the famous

British authoress happy. This was no minor task. The noted writer was understandably miffed that the studio had concocted its own scenario without waiting for her to be inspired to produce more immortal verbiage of her own.

In an effort to placate her, Clarence Badger offered to write a scene in the movie for Madame Glyn herself. At first she demurred with regal outrage. He quoted her as protesting, "You ask the impossible. Do understand. I'd be ruined at court. My prestige, the esteem I command—gone."

Badger persisted. Now he had her on the defensive. "Shouldn't an authoress experience the things she writes about?"

"Please do not argue further. Even despite the possibility of increasing my own contractual interest in 'It's' takings by doing so—which you feel certain would be the case—I would never agree to!"

Here Badger saw his opening. "I'll build a beautiful set; one fitting for Madame's entrance. You shall be expertly made-up. Gorgeously gowned. You shall wear a diamond tiara sparkling in your hair—a diamond necklace. Your queenly appearance and majestic beauty will not only fascinate and win the praise of theater audiences, but will have, I am certain, a like effect on those of Royal Courts. Your personal definition of 'it' will—"

She interrupted him. "Oh, dear man, no more. What an alluring picture you do paint. Well now, forgetting your tinsel a moment—tell me—do you truly, honestly believe I would lend 'pecuniary enhancement'?"

"Not mere belief, Madame. I know you would."

"There is another condition necessary."

"Granted."

"I must be on a gentleman's arm as I make my entrance. For this purpose you must secure for me the most handsome gentleman in Hollywood."

"In America if necessary."

In the complete film, in a sequence that finds all the principals seated in an elegant dining room, Elinor Glyn makes the promised entrance. Apparently she was not altogether satisfied that the soigné dress extra on whose arm she made her showstopping entrance was really the most handsome man in America. For throughout the making of the picture she occupied herself in a search among the extras working everywhere within the Paramount studio, hoping to find one whom she felt really had It.

At last she did find her man and insisted that a part be written in for him. Gary Cooper's bit as a reporter is brief but effective. With the addition of Gary to the cast, Elinor gave the director no more trouble about shooting the studio version of *It*.

Writers have sometimes placed Clara Bow, along with Colleen Moore, Bessie Love and Marion Davies, as just another flapper of the type proliferating through the 1920s. But Clara Bow should more properly be compared with Greta Garbo than with any other film actress. Both Bow and Garbo were determined to be film actresses from childhood. Both were observant filmgoers as teenagers and studiously imitated the techniques they approved, as practiced by those players they admired. Although both achieved fabulous stardom, neither one became part of the usual social whirl of Hollywood top liners; Garbo remained an outsider by choice, Bow through the professional malice of her peers.

To an almost mystical degree, the images of Clara Bow and Greta Garbo emit powerful stimuli from the motion picture screen—Garbo registering ambiguous mystery, Bow assaulting the viewer with enormous vitality and breezy sexuality. Looking at *It* or *Mantrap* today, one is impressed by the positive dynamism that radiates from the shadow of Clara Bow on the screen. It is inexplicable magic that when the projected image is that of Clara Bow, so much energy and such highly charged personality can emanate from an optical illusion. One is confounded in any attempt to explain or analyze the phenomenon. The only recourse lies in Elinor Glyn's "it is nothing less than a matter of It."

Although the soul-and-body-destroying vampires created by the Valeska Suratts and Theda Baras of the pre-1920s movies have disappeared as serious screen characters, the movies have not completely relinquished the dragon lady, who does seem to fulfill a basic need of eroticism. Amanda Donohoe in *Lair of the White Worm* is every bit as deadly as any 1919 vampire, although Mel Brooks would have us regard her and her fiery serpents as high camp. And Anjelica Huston in *The Addams Family* is a figure of fun; Barbet Schroeder's dominatrix in *Maîtresse* is no joking matter.

Perhaps strangest of all has been the belated creation of a screen vampire from an actress who during her career was about as far removed from such a category as one could be. The linking of Louise Brooks with overpowering eroticism had already been established—at least in European circles, by Adou Kyrou in his *Amour-Erotisme et Cinema*. Kyrou

Louise Brooks in her American films might be coy, but she never acted the siren that Kenneth Tynan and Adou Kryou proclaimed her to be. Here she is in *Love 'Em and Leave 'Em* (1926).

chose Louise Brooks as his principal example of the theses suggested by his title. He wrote:

> Louise Brooks is the only woman who had the ability to transfigure no matter what film into a masterpiece. . . . Louise is the perfect apparition, the dream woman without whom the cinema would be a poor thing. She is much more than a myth, she is a magical presence, a real phantom, the magnetism of the cinema.

The extravagances of Kenneth Tynan and a score of other equally beguiled authors were mostly inspired by watching her in Pabst's *The Box of Pandora*. The role of Lulu in Franz Wedekind's drama was one of the most coveted by German actresses. The Danish star Asta Nielsen had played Lulu in the first film version, *Erdgeist.*

But Pabst was well aware of the hazards of casting Teutonic actresses so eager to demonstrate how wicked they could be. He began a long series of tests in a search for some girl who would be right for the part as Wedekind conceived it—an inadvertent femme fatale who could in no way be coquettish or even deliberately seductive.

When he saw Louise Brooks in Howard Hawks' *A Girl in Every Port,* he was convinced that she was ideal for Lulu. But involved with a Paramount contract, she was not available. Pabst's search continued. At last he settled on Marlene Dietrich, but before shooting began, Louise, in a contretemps with Paramount, did become available.

Pabst brought her to Germany to play Lulu, and as some consolation for Dietrich, he arranged with Kurt Bernhardt to cast her as the lead in *The Woman for Whom One Longs*—a role opposite the prestigious Fritz Kortner, the Dr. Schoen of *Pandora,* in a script that had many parallels to the misadventures of Lulu.

The pre–von Sternberg Dietrich in *Three Loves* (originally *The Woman for Whom One Longs,* 1929)

Marlene Dietrich being irresistible.

The Box of Pandora was not well liked in Germany, where there was resentment in having an unknown American play an important German dramatic role. Also, Louise's performance, having nothing to do with the prevailing acting styles of the time, was thought to be due simply to a lack of talent.

In the United States, the film had no chance at all. It was reedited by its importers to make it seem that Lulu was reformed by joining the Salvation Army, and henceforth all would be well with her. But *Pandora* was a long-running hit in Paris. Not without recutting. The French are sensitive about having a son involved with his father's mistress—for them a sin more heinous than incest. So they altered the relationship between Dr. Schoen and his son, having Franz Lederer as the son become Schoen's secretary instead. What then appeared to be a homo-sexual attachment did not seem nearly as distasteful to the French as rivalry between father and son over the paternal mistress.

It was with much very worthwhile trouble by fusing missing scenes from several different archive copies of the film in Denmark, France and Switzerland that I was able to assemble at Eastman House the original version of Pabst's important work. Watching his own editorial instead of the mangled and mutilated copies that had been available, one was able to appreciate at least two facets of Pabst's technique that separated his work from that of his contemporaries. His style of using subtitles has been noted in a previous chapter. But more unorthodox was his scorn of the usual establishing and reestablishing shots dear to directors anxious about allowing spectators to go astray. Pabst's was the keyhole system: I'll put your eye to the keyhole—become a voyeur of this scene and make of it what you will. A viewer is forced to participate intellectually in a Pabst film.

Contrary to the legends that have been forming like coral around the rediscovery of Louise Brooks, it was in 1951, *twenty-eight years* before the Tynan article in the *New Yorker*, that we began screening Louise Brooks' films at Eastman House. It was in 1953 that we imported (and restored) her three European films and began showing them in the Dry-den Theatre, where spectators enjoyed the undated charm and effective-ness of Louise Brooks as an actress. Apart from those screenings, the articles written about her nurtured the cult. Now all three of her Euro-pean films are widely circulated on videotape, and Louise Brooks has achieved a kind of immortality she never intended—that of an eternal movie vamp who has ensnared far more victims than ever seduced by Theda Bara herself.

Much of the disinformation about Louise, of course, was originated by her as part of her unstinting campaign to counteract any praise that came her way. In the Tynan profile, he claims Louise said she was drunk during the screening sessions when we looked at her films—so drunk she didn't know what was going on. Absolutely false! She knew so much about what was going on as we watched *The Box of Pandora* that she con-demned the music I had taped to go with it. "Syrupy and sentimental!" she castigated it. Working together, using nothing but Kurt Weill's Ger-man music, including some of his classical works, we finally arranged a score that she felt really fit. Others agreed, too. In *Saint Cinema*, Her-man Weinberg wrote:

Michael von Newlinsky carries a swooning Louise Brooks in *Diary of a Lost Girl* (1929).

> I like Jim Card's music scores for Pabst's "Pandora's Box" and "Diary of a Lost Girl," they are in fact perfectly splendid, and the Curator of the George Eastman House, that marvelous film archive in Rochester, has turned out a real labor of love.

What a pity Herman didn't know that both scores were largely the work of Louise Brooks, who most certainly and definitely was not drunk when she watched those films.

CHAPTER 10

Cecil B. DeMille

ecil B. DeMille was my first designated target on the 1953 worldwide safari on behalf of the Eastman House collection. Top priority for the hopeful bag was the private vault of Cecil B. DeMille. The rumor was that DeMille had hoarded one print of every film he had ever made. Why else would he have built on his elegant estate a nitrate-film vault more substantial than many of the industry's own film blockhouses?

Twenty-one years before, I had met DeMille at the Republican National Convention in Cleveland, Ohio. DeMille was there to promote the nomination of Alf Landon for president. My father had friends in the California delegation, and he knew it would be a major thrill for his movie-struck son of sixteen to meet the great DeMille. But at that age I had no idea just how great DeMille was considered to be. I knew he made movies, and I knew he had worked with stars who had long been in my eyes. That was enough to look on him with wonderment as he greeted me casually in his Statler Hotel suite, smoke and politician filled as it was.

In 1953 he was in the process of planning his second production of *The Ten Commandments*. He had first made it in 1923, and it had been his first enormous success. With sixty-nine films behind him, he was preparing his seventieth production, intending it to far surpass whatever he had done before. Even his most enthusiastic admirers felt that the seventy-five-year-old veteran was dreaming.

Ushered into his lair, I found him sitting at a desk placed at the far end of his Mussolini-sized office. Pressed by time as he must have been, he nevertheless received me graciously, seated me and proceeded with an instructive monologue for the next hour and thirty minutes.

Cecil B. DeMille set out to outdo the spectacles of the Italians, Griffith and Lubitsch with his first *Ten Commandments* (1923).

DeMille had surrounded himself with priceless collections of Egyptian art and what must have been one of the finest libraries of scholarly works on antiquities assembled outside of a university. He was then absorbed in the problem of how he could make the opening of the Red Sea cinematically believable. A biblical miracle was not enough for DeMille. He wanted to make the event visually acceptable with a combination of pseudoscience and Belasco theatricality. He showed me a series of sketches done after studies by a government hurricane expert. The sketches depicted two storms approaching the center of the Red Sea, colliding and discharging their fury downward with such concentrated energy that the waters were blown apart, clearing a dry path for the fleeing Israelites.

Always the showman, DeMille arranged his desk to make himself look very busy.

Next demonstration—lying on his desk was the jawbone of an ass. He brandished it as a weapon, showing me how Samson, even without the direction of Cecil B. DeMille, could have wielded it as lethally as did Victor Mature.

He then discussed his particular technique for evading censorship, which in the 1950s still afflicted the American screen. Among the pictures hanging on his wall was a large, framed blowup of Claudette Colbert as Cleopatra. She reclined, with what was then near nudity, on an Egyptian divan. In the foreground was a harp, the strings covering the entire background, which was devoted to the nearly naked Cleopatra. A male musician seemed to be playing for the recumbent queen. "Do you see," he asked, "what the harpist's fingers are doing to the body of Cleopatra lying there in the background?" I could indeed, since he had pointed it out to me, see the erotic suggestion of the perspective, but I didn't remember its having worked at all that way when I'd seen *Cleopatra*. Perhaps the Hays Office hadn't seen through the harp strings after all.

From time to time Henry Wilcoxon, promoted from actor to DeMille's production assistant, came into the office with some particular urgency. Like others who interrupted now and then, each time he left The Presence, he backed out all the way to the distant door. As author Crichton had observed at Joan Crawford's home, "Every cliché about Hollywood is true." As though I needed further proof, DeMille kept jangling coins in his pocket. Once or twice he brought some of them out to caress. They were his legendary lucky gold pieces.

At long last DeMille came to the matter that had brought me to see him. Eastman House was offering to make acetate copies of all his nitrate features in return for the privilege of keeping one print of each in the archive for study.

"Tell me again, Mr. Card, what you intend to do with my films if I should agree to your request."

"Make them available for study, Mr. DeMille. On the premises."

"For study? By whom?"

"By writers, film students, scholars—"

"Writers!" he exclaimed as though I had said "pirates." "Writers! Don't you realize my films represent some of the most valuable literary properties in this country? What's to prevent writers from studying my films and using the plots?"

I was dumbfounded. My face must have looked as stupid as I found his question to be. I simply could not get it through my head how a major filmmaker could apparently have so little awareness of the real world around him. Did he really believe writers couldn't steal his plots when those same films had been shown publicly? For me, a major, unlooked-for defeat: I did thank him sincerely for the time he had given me, and the lectures. But I certainly didn't walk backward to the door.

No famous film director has ever endured the critical contempt consistently heaped on DeMille through the last thirty-five years of his career. In 1926 a British critic wrote:

> I am not an admirer of Mr. Cecil B. DeMille, though I will admit that he has a perfect genius for vulgarity in every sense of the word. . . . I think his is the kind of picture which grips the eye at the moment, but which on reflection (and I believe that nearly everyone does reflect a little after seeing a picture) one is bound to shrug off as silly because his psychological values, even in their own convention, are false, and there is so little reason why any of his characters should do anything that they do. So afterwards one feels that one has been sold.

The writer was Iris Barry. Not surprisingly, during her curatorship of the Museum of Modern Art Film Library, of the seventy films made by DeMille, only one, *Male and Female*, found its way into the museum's collection.

DeMille's political enthusiasm for Republican causes and candidates did not endear him to the liberal press, and the media lost no chance to advertise their scorn. When I lectured about films to fairly well-informed adult groups, I found I was always able to produce snickering agreement in my audience by insisting that no individual operating on the mass taste of Americans had done more to corrupt and degrade both the art of motion pictures and the minds of millions of young people than Mr. DeMille with his phenomenally successful movies. But with DeMille's death in January of 1959, I had the sickening feeling, as a historian, that along with him, the last vestige of much that had made Hollywood great in the eyes of all the world would be buried.

DeMille's stature in the motion picture industry can be measured by the fact that in 1953, with Hollywood seriously on the ropes in its initial struggles with TV, DeMille was able to commit Paramount to an expenditure in excess of ten million dollars. There were not three movies in all the history of film at that time that had grossed that much. By 1953, his heart had already given him trouble. But he went to Egypt to make his picture and stomped around the desert at a characteristic speed that left all his young staff panting behind him.

Getting enough water to keep his hundreds of extras, his armies of technicians and his herds of animals operating in the intense heat was a mammoth problem. He ordered wells to be dug, and the Egyptian government laughed at him; they had been trying to find water in the desert for centuries, they told him. But DeMille was famous for using historical fact only when it suited his purposes. When history didn't make a good scene, he threw it out. And so it was with water. He needed it; he dug his wells; there was the water. If the desert in Egypt flowers where it never did before, it is thanks to Cecil B. DeMille.

In 1955, two years after that first interview with DeMille, I was back in his office again, taking another shot at persuading him to let Eastman House have copies of his films. This time he was juggling several hundred thousand feet of his new *Ten Commandments* in an effort to cut it down to about fourteen thousand feet, or three hours of running time. He was still trying to part the waters of the Red Sea properly and found he had to do some studio retakes with Yul Brynner, who had already started on a film at another studio.

Paramount was quaking in its fiscal boots with the costs on *The Ten Commandments* already past the twelve-million mark and still on the rise. If DeMille was worried about it, he gave not the slightest sign. He was gracious and talkative—as he had been two years before, coolly enthusiastic about finishing the film—sure that he could get Brynner back, confident that the miracle could be brought off in the special-effects department, with his supervision. Asked about the unprecedented costs, he laughed heartily. "The office is worried," he admitted. "They're trying to put a ceiling of fourteen million on the picture, but it may run to seventeen."

Here was a man working far beyond the realm of money. And working as such a spellbinder that the well-known practical businessmen and bankers were willing to stake more money than King Pharaoh himself had ever seen. And on what? Fourteen reels of tinted shadows—three hours of make-believe!

Where was the collateral? Only in the name and reputation of Cecil Blount DeMille—a man who had started in show business as a not-too-successful actor. DeMille's father had been a playwright and partner of David Belasco. After his father's death, DeMille's mother managed a play agency, and young Cecil attended the American Academy of Dramatic Arts. His first role was acted at the Garden Theatre in New York. Touring with E. H. Sothern, DeMille acted in some of the plays he was destined later to turn into movies.

Next he tried writing plays himself, then took charge of the family agency, the DeMille Play Company, and continued this active business until the history-making meeting with Jesse Lasky and Samuel Goldwyn in 1912. That meeting resulted in the Jesse L. Lasky Feature Play Company, which made as its first feature film the initial DeMille movie, *The Squaw Man*. Released in February 1914, *The Squaw Man* is traditionally listed as the first full-length movie to be made in the sunny, dusty little California community called Hollywood.

The early DeMille films were based on the theatre plays he knew so well. His beginning success had nothing to do with them, but can be measured at its start with his discovery—for the screen—of the American woman. With some inspiration, DeMille suddenly saw her not as the theatrical Belasco heroine of *Rose of the Rancho* or *Girl of the Golden West*, not as the Amazon queen he had made of Geraldine Farrar, or as the sunny, golden-haired, scarcely grown little girl that the whole world loved in Mary Pickford. Discarding both Farrar and Pickford as his heroines, DeMille turned to Gloria Swanson, and in her person presented the new and altogether-American woman.

What this new woman represented is clearly revealed by the titles of the DeMille-Swanson pictures: *For Better, for Worse; Don't Change Your Husband; Why Change Your Wife?; Male and Female; The Affairs of Anatol* and *Something to Think About*.

The lavish bathrooms in some of these films became a DeMille trademark that has been widely cited as having definitely aided and abetted the American obsession with gilded chambers for biological necessities. Louis B. Mayer once complained to Adolph Greene that King Vidor had wrongfully broken a taboo in *The Crowd* by allowing a character to be seen in a bathroom, actually seated on what Mayer carefully referred to as a "facility." Apparently outraged L.B. had missed seeing DeMille's *Why Change Your Wife?*, made eight whole years before *The Crowd*. In his film DeMille daringly had Tommy Meighan, playing Swanson's husband, not only sit on a similar "facility," but actually do so with a woman present in the bathroom!

But in truth, DeMille gave his watchers Something More to Think About than bathrooms. The something more was sex—and sex not in the Never Land of Theda Bara, but right there at home in the family circle itself. This, of course, was considered wickedness, and DeMille

The favorite locales for DeMille dramas: boudoir and bath. Thomas Meighan and Gloria Swanson in *Why Change Your Wife?* (1920).

As a savage captive of the Babylonian king, Gloria Swanson puts the bite on Thomas Meighan in *Male and Female* (1919)

realized that if he wanted to get away with it, he would have to do it by pointing out the immorality of the carryings-on that were making his films such box-office hits. He did this with a kind of standard flashback, often to biblical times, showing that sin and sex were historically prevalent, severely punished and theatrically splendid. His heroine, often Gloria Swanson, was mauled by lions or fed to fiery gods of vengeance in dream sequences. Or sometimes she was permitted, in the nick of time, to repent and reform in the modern story after having skated on the thinnest of improprieties for seven reels of silken-gowned magnificence.

Growing out of his flashbacks and dream sequences, the realization came to DeMille that the costume drama, particularly if it was associated with Old Testament material, offered him far more range for sex, violence and the preaching that would square it all with the censors. In *The Ten Commandments*, when Moses came down with the freshly minted Decalogue under his arm, he found the worshipers of the golden calf embroiled in a lusty saturnalia of epic proportions. Nudity abounded. And a monstrous wallowing in group sex prompted Moses to violate one of the Ten Commandments even before the clay was dry; Moses became a mass murderer albeit a dreadfully righteous one. The 1956 version of *The Ten Commandments* repeated it all, but in Technicolor with the resounding voice of Charlton Heston admonishing the sinners. In *The Sign of the Cross* not just one heroine was fed to the lions—whole groups of Christians, with especially nubile young martyrs among them, were torn to bloody shreds by the ravening beasts under the giddy direction of newcomer Charles Laughton as Nero. *Cleopatra* brought us Claudette Colbert turning her sexy attention to Julius Caesar, and the next year DeMille hurled Christian knights against the Saracens in *The Crusades*, with more blood than had ever before been shed in Hollywood. *Samson and Delilah* was a surefire winner—epic seduction brought the temples crashing down in the kind of spectacular disaster that DeMille's technicians were particularly adept at arranging. The 1927 *King of Kings* was in many ways DeMille's most successful biblical epic. It is still compelling to watch. Like *Caligari* it was shown many times, year after year—it is probably still being played in this cynical year, for, to the religious, DeMille's treatment of Christ was far more reverently done than in *Jesus Christ, Superstar*, for example. But still, reverent or not, C.B. couldn't resist turning Mary of Magdala into one of the screen's most elegant prostitutes in all the history of cinema. In the body of Jacqueline Logan,

Gloria Swanson is thrown to the lions in *Male and Female.*

all decked out in glistening luxury à la Cleopatra (one can almost smell the Egyptian perfume!), Mary makes love to her pet, a full grown leopard, while her admirers sit enviously awaiting what they hope will be their turns. And wouldn't you know it—one of her clients is none other than Judas Iscariot. So in all those big films, there was Mr. DeMille wallowing in sadistic sex but dodging recrimination with vast doses of historical nobility. These films were despised by serious critics, ridiculed by the few who bothered to discuss them, but as eagerly welcomed as the annual visit of Ringling Brothers, Barnum and Bailey. The analogy must have struck DeMille himself. His circus picture, *The Greatest Show on Earth*, the last work before the second *Ten Commandments*, outgrossed all real circuses.

There is no convenient niche in the history of motion pictures for Mr. DeMille. If he was not a great director, one has to qualify all existing conceptions of greatness. And yet he rarely made a great film, because, after the silent period, his motives were mean and vulgar in the more archaic sense of those words: mean in that he tried to appeal to the commonest of denominators; vulgar in that his audience was the widest possible mass of casual moviegoers. If cinematic circus can be acknowledged as a special kind of art, then in this field, DeMille was master of them all. Measured in terms of money and size and mass approval, he was, in fact, the greatest showman on earth.

DeMille's daughter, Cecilia, fortunately did not share her father's paranoia concerning the films kept in the family vault. Cecilia was far more interested in raising racing thoroughbreds than she was in motion pictures. Appearing as a child actress in some of her father's features had undoubtedly lessened the magic of the medium for her.

At a reasonable moment after DeMille's death in 1959, I approached Cecilia DeMille Harper for my third attempt to take on the DeMille collection. I found her to be charming, affable and fully receptive to the offer by Eastman House to preserve the entire surviving DeMille oeuvre. The vault doors swung open to us, and more than three thousand 35mm nitrate positives were shipped to Rochester. The trove included the DeMille masterpieces *The Cheat;* the Geraldine Farrar vehicles *Carmen, Joan the Woman, Maria Rosa* and *The Woman God Forgot;* the Mary Pickfords *A Romance of the Redwoods* and *The Little American,* with its alternate endings—the original in which she marries Jack Holt, the Prussian soldier, and the other that has her ending up with Raymond Hatton, the French soldier, DeMille hedging his bet depending on the outcome of the war. There were the Swansons *Old Wives for New; Don't Change Your Husband; For Better, for Worse; Male and Female; Something to Think About; Why Change Your Wife?* and *The Affairs of Anatol.* There were some big surprises too: *The Heart of Nora Flynn,* with the delectable Broadway-stage star Marie Doro; Blanche Sweet, impressive in *The Warrens of Virginia,* Wallace Reid in one of his best roles in *The Golden Chance* and, of course, the first *Ten Commandments.* Screening those films constituted a major surprise—the realization that in spite of all the box-office approval of most of DeMille's work, he had been shamefully shortchanged by all those who thought they were writing seriously about film after 1935.

Almost every film he had made before his first *Ten Commandments* in 1923 was highly creditable. Some of them were utterly fascinating, and others worthy to be ranked high above some tiresomely praised favorites of the pundits. But the biggest surprise to me was *The Cheat*—a towering masterpiece of 1915—the first original film to inspire both a play and an opera from its own scenario.

The Cheat shouldn't really have been such a surprise to me. One of the great pioneer film critics, France's Louis Delluc, had written:

Paris has received The Cheat with violent admiration. This has not failed to astonish the Americans. . . . But Paris has not been mistaken in admiring it for it sees here for the first time a film which merits the name of film.

Some American reviewers of the time did praise the film, but when they did, it was usually for the wrong reasons. For example, the *New York Dramatic Mirror* of December 25, 1915, usually reserving its comment for theatrical presentations, noted:

The Cheat is a mighty fine photoplay. . . . It contains one of the most realistic mob scenes that has ever been produced upon the screen and it would be interesting to know just what means the director used to work his characters up to such a convincing semblance of reality.

By December of 1915 everyone who looked at films at all had seen *The Birth of a Nation*, a film not without "mob scenes." But here is the

DeMille used Japanese screens to good effect in *The Cheat* (1915), with Fannie Ward and Sessue Hayakawa.

reviewer of a prestigious magazine, proclaiming DeMille's courtroom mob scene one of the most realistic "that has ever been produced upon the screen."

That courtroom scene is the least of *The Cheat*'s extraordinary qualities. The low-key, atmospheric lighting is sophisticated and effective far ahead of its time. The Japanese screens used to silhouette players, who are ripped apart in violence behind them, the screens suddenly spattered with blood, make the film look as though it could have been made by Kurosawa rather than by the unappreciated DeMille.

It would be hard to imagine a scenario more unlikely to be offered to the American public in a 1915 movie—or even at any time before 1945. The heroine is not only a cheat, she steals, she lies, she offers twice to prostitute herself and almost gets the Japanese leading man lynched by revealing to the entire courtroom that she had been branded by the man her husband tried to kill. Without the acting of Sessue Hayakawa, the film might go down as wild melodrama. But Hayakawa's technique of eloquent restraint and Oriental poise bring to an impossible role a quality of hypnotic authority that is consistently engrossing to watch.

After seeing the film, I felt an evangelistic compulsion to get it shown to skeptical audiences. It was screened at one of the New York Film Festivals (to endure, of course, the contempt of John Simon). I took it to London, and it was shown in the National Film Theatre. I took it to Berkeley where it was shown in the University Art Museum by the Pacific Film Archive as part of an extraordinary three-month program called "Treasures from the Eastman House," which featured the screening of no fewer than 104 films, all presented with laboriously researched program notes by Tom Luddy. This mammoth event took place in the fall of 1972, when Luddy was the tireless, enthusiastic curator of the Pacific Film Archive. Part of his notes for *The Cheat* follow:

> *The Cheat* will astonish anyone who thinks of Cecil B. DeMille only in terms of his sound spectaculars which at best were never much more than "showmanship" on an inflated scale (at worst, as in his greatest commercial success *The Ten Commandments* they were empty and inept, triumphs of sheer size and publicity.) *The Cheat*, which was made in the same year that saw *The Birth of a Nation* released, is another matter, perhaps even another DeMille. While Griffith's film gets all the textbook credit for "revolutionizing" the principles of narrative film-making, *The*

Cheat quietly influenced subsequent films and film-makers in a way perhaps more profound than Griffith's lesson in shot and scene construction. Only the French analyzed the shock waves caused by *The Cheat,* so that in 1919 Rene Clair could write: "*The Cheat* in 1915, *A Woman of Paris* in 1922—almost all the achievements of the American dramatic cinema are contained within those titles and dates." *The Cheat* set standards of acting, decor, frame composition and lighting which were not surpassed by years, not even by De Mille. Above all, it was the first modern film in content. In the silent period, De Mille was always furthest ahead in terms of dramatizing contemporary subjects from an equally up-to-date psychological viewpoint. . . . De Mille avoids all good and evil moralizing, and black-and-white stereotypes. Even the Japanese "villain" is shaded gray so that his sexual passion for the rich woman who cheats him is viewed as a more honest motive than the husband's desire to cover up the scandal. There is genuine pathos in *The Cheat,* deeply felt and conveyed by the near-stylized (but not theatrical) acting of Fannie Ward and Sessue Hayakawa. In some shots they play like dancers before a white abstract background (actually brightly lit Chinese panelled screens): there is one staggering shot in which De Mille focuses on *nothing* until the actors gesture into the frame from the side (the camera stays stationary). It seems incredible that a director could make a film this studied and controlled at the same time directing a second production, but it's true. After shooting *The Cheat* from 9 to 5, De Mille ate and rested for three hours, then worked on *The Golden Chance* from 8 p.m. to 2 or 3 a.m.

Incidentally, *The Golden Chance,* which starred Wallace Reid, falls far short of the masterpiece category, but was nevertheless a well-made, respectably watchable melodrama, and DeMille can be forgiven for not having turned out *two* chefs d'oeuvre in a single day!

Thanks to Cecilia DeMille Harper and the George Eastman House, most of the DeMille silents are available today. *The Cheat,* in particular, has been a black-market champion. Yet some refuse even to look at it. Why? Are they afraid they might have to revise their negative opinion of DeMille? In 1974, the late Dwight MacDonald and I went on a film-lecture tour of several Ivy League colleges. I was promoting the then newly acquired *L'Age d'Or* of Buñuel, and Dwight was showing and expounding on the charms and significance of Keaton's *Sherlock Jr.* Near the end of the expedition we were being entertained at an Amherst faculty luncheon, and the topic of DeMille came up. I climbed on my usual soapbox to praise *The Cheat.* MacDonald, who up to that moment had been an unfailingly charming and genial companion, snarled and with great heat insisted that *The Cheat* was intolerable garbage. Someone at the table asked, "Dwight, have you seen the film recently?"

"No! I would never look at it. I don't have to see a DeMille film to know it's garbage!"

In 1915 there were released thirteen feature films directed by Cecil B. DeMille. It was a year of prodigious activity for a director enthralled by so many unexplored avenues of creation beckoning to him. Among his wonders of that year was *Carmen*, with a lusty Geraldine Farrar recruited from the halls of the Metropolitan to mime her most famous role opposite Wallace Reid as Don José. DeMille realized he was hiring America's most popular diva, but to star a world-renowned singer in silent films posed a question. Farrar had studied voice in Germany, and it was there that she made her debut in opera. In Germany she became a sensation immediately. More than a sensation; it was whispered that she became the mistress of the Kaiser himself. Most unlikely. Geraldine Farrar could have tucked the Hohenzollern under one arm and carried him the entire length of Unter den Linden. Moreover, although it is uncertain whether or not Wilhelm was gay, his court was packed with homosexuals. Any affair with an American opera star might have induced a palace revolt.

But not even DeMille could have anticipated the scope of Farrar's popularity after the release of *Carmen*. Adoring teenage girls, proudly acknowledging themselves to be "Gerry-flappers," swarmed to her every film. When she returned to the Metropolitan to resume her operatic career, management was astonished to find her appearances sold out to youngsters; the Gerry-flappers put up with Bizet to enjoy seeing and hearing their heroine on the stage.

While Willard Van Dyke was the director of the Museum of Modern Art's film department, many of the original nitrate prints from Eastman House were shown at the museum in New York. The showing there of the DeMille *Carmen* evoked an enthusiastic review from Kirk Bond—the legendary writer who had directed my attention to early films decades before.

DeMille's twenty-ninth film, *The Whispering Chorus*, was his most audaciously experimental work and one of only two out of his seventy productions that was totally rejected by the film public. The whispering chorus of his film noir was pictured as disembodied heads composed of the consciences of the characters. The film had no admirable persons and no happy denouement. After four years of murderous world war, the film public was in no mood for a movie of black consciences.

Paramount's New York office was seriously alarmed to behold its champion director on the ropes. DeMille was ordered by them to film a current best-selling novel, *Old Wives for New*, by David Graham Phillips. The title plus the popularity of the book seemed to the bosses of Paramount to ensure a box-office hit. If DeMille felt chastened by having to work on a story not of his own choosing, he did not tackle the assignment with any lessened vigor, nor did he put the brakes on his determination for innovation. He cast Florence Vidor as his leading lady, and one of the most impressive and skillful actresses of the period, Camille Ankiewiscz (known as Marcia Manon), was entrusted with a role that challenged her abilities. Theodore Roberts, one of the movie public's most popular character men, an avuncular type never photographed without a comfortable cigar, was presented to his fans as a lecherous rake, a heartless womanizer. Even more sacrilegiously, the wife and mother of DeMille's film was a fat, slatternly, lazy, candy-gulping mess. If the watchers wondered how a man soigné and fastidious could ever have saddled himself with so appalling a frump, DeMille was eager to show them. In a DeMille flashback (a technique that was rapidly becoming one of his most favored devices) we saw what this slovenly woman had been when her husband first met and fell in love with her. We saw her as a wholesome, lovely country girl, and their encounter, in a sylvan stream, where he came upon her wading, was utterly idyllic.

But then the daring DeMille was not just satisfied with the usual flashback; he actually brought the woman as she had been into the living room, into the same scene occupied by the woman she had become. Not as a transparent memory, but as a solid participant on the set. This exceptional technique was, as far as I know, not to be seen again in any film until 1950, in Alf Sjøberg's deservedly praised *Miss Julie*.

Another astonishing scene in *Old Wives for New* broke with all clichés for movie murder and must have lingered for years in the memory of G. W. Pabst. The mature rake played by Theodore Roberts is shot in his bedroom by one of his outraged women. He does not fall to the floor, clutching his penetrated chest. Instead, DeMille has him walk carefully to the bed, sit on it with infinite caution, then lets us see the blood slowly beginning to ooze through the white pleats of his dress shirt. The director gives him time to think about it, then to die. Ten years later in *The Box of Pandora*, Pabst replays the scene with Fritz Kortner bemused by the realization that he has been shot by his mistress.

Indeed, Pabst and Sjøberg were not the only foreign directors to remember the early DeMille. In his first *Ten Commandments*, DeMille had Nita Naldi die a spectacular death behind a curtain. Instead of watching the sinister Sally Lung die, we saw the curtain being torn from its mooring, rung by rung, as she expired behind it. René Clement has Dalio die the same way in the French film *The Damned*—a great melodrama of Nazis fleeing retribution aboard a submarine. Alfred Hitchcock himself was not above swiping a scene from DeMille. He did it in *Psycho*.

The 1918 *Old Wives for New* became the first DeMille film in a major group of productions that provided the most valid sociological examination of sex and marriage that was ever undertaken in American silent motion pictures. The series ranged from light and engaging comedy to serious moralizing. The skill and brilliance of these domestic dramas are sure to secure the lasting fame of DeMille as a unique director far more firmly than a review of his spectacles. Other directors were able to conjure up impressive hordes of extras, but in his ability to convert parlor, bedroom and bath into arenas for the spectacle of the typically American battle of the sexes, DeMille had no competition.

If DeMille felt constrained by the task of shaping a film to conform to the outlines of a popular novel when he made *Old Wives for New*, he found full creative freedom in *Don't Change Your Husband*. In the May 1919 issue of *Photoplay* magazine the section "Reviews of Current Photoplays" was introduced with this comment:

> It does not seem too engrossing a statement to say that at the present moment the only director who shows a marked advance from what has been done before is Cecil B. DeMille. Here at least is a man who is not traveling in a rut. His photoplays—vivid, timely, pulsating life-dramas—show a perfection and artistic improvement with each new release. *Don't Change Your Husband* is the latest Cecil B. De Mille attraction and one of those seldom found but always appreciated productions, a photoplay that points a moral but doesn't bore. The story is an ungilded cross-section of life as it is lived.

It was with *Don't Change Your Husband* in 1919 that DeMille set out to present to the world film public a new and characteristically spectacular creation—the New American Woman, DeMille version. He chose Gloria Swanson to bring life to his vision, and thanks to this director-star combination, nothing quite like her had ever been seen before, nor is it likely that a comparable manifestation will ever appear again to beguile the millions into admiration and emulation.

DeMille wisely saw that in his films Miss Swanson was able to combine certain elements of her sprightly Sennett style along with the daringly gowned, provocatively coiffed, glamorous beauty that the master director surrounded with every sensuous setting and prop that his active imagination was able to conjure. Backed by DeMille's exploitation of her special talents, Gloria moved rapidly along the route to becoming the indisputable queen of Hollywood—an eminence that she managed to maintain longer than any other female star in American films.

It was symptomatic of DeMille to insist on placing scenes of these domestic dramas in the bathroom, forbidden territory to other directors. In *Why Change Your Wife?* the bathroom he shows us is neither the sleazy water closet of *Old Wives for New* nor the tile-and-porcelain temple of *Male and Female*. But it is the significant location of the opening scene of DeMille's most successfully realized social comedy. The husband is trying to shave and is constantly harassed by his wife, asking him to lace her up, trying to get into the medicine cabinet for items of her makeup: a flurry of domestic interruptions of the male rite of shaving.

Ernst Lubitsch did not arrive in the United States until 1923, three years after the release of *Why Change Your Wife?*, DeMille's best comedy-drama, yet it sparkles with infinitely more of the touches that have been traditionally attributed to Lubitsch than that German director ever achieved. Indeed, a strong case could be made that Lubitsch must have been influenced by the DeMille husband-and-wife movies in deciding to switch his own specialty from the historical spectacles *Madame DuBarry*, *Anna Boleyn* and *The Wife of the Pharaoh* to Kammerspiele, *The Marriage Circle*, *Three Woman*, *Kiss Me Again*, *Lady Windermere's Fan*, *So This Is Paris*, which were his first Hollywood movies. DeMille had exposed the slatternly wife in *Old Wives for New*, the seedy husband in *Don't Change Your Husband*; with *Why Change Your Wife?* it was the turn for the priggish Craig's Wife to be goaded into reformation. Gloria Swanson, in very top form, makes the metamorphosis hilarious, pictorial and one of the lasting delights of silent comedy. In a couturier's dressing room, being fitted for some dreary costumes, she overhears herself described by a woman in the next room as a drab. It is the turning point; she instructs the dress designer to outfit her in something sexy, wicked and altogether indecent. Gloria's wrath at realizing she's

Vivid and intense, Pola Negri's performance in Lubitsch's *Madame DuBarry* (1919) was extraordinary.

The Lubitsch touch. Recipient is May McAvoy with Pauline Frederick in *Three Women* (1924).

been considered a wimp is awesome to behold and irresistible comedy, too. Although working in a much lighter mood in this film, DeMille is still firmly the moralist. The subtitles become increasingly editorial from the start of 1918, but by 1920 and *Why Change Your Wife?*, DeMille was confident enough in his special mission to be able to lighten his observations with epigrammatic gaiety.

For any child who begins to see films at a very early age, there are bound to be inexplicable images of unforgotten power that remain to haunt dreams and induce nightmares for many years. One frightening scene haunted my childhood and puzzled me long into adulthood. I was fascinated in trying to reconstruct what combination of movie scenes could possibly have stamped in my memory a scene of a woman in her kitchen, placing the top crust on an apple pie only to be horror-struck at the sight of human fingers breaking through it and a contorted hand coming up from the pie. I had no idea whatsoever what kind of a film could have conjured up so unlikely a scene and finally concluded that my mind at some early point must have combined the two unlikely visuals into a single shocking vision.

Sitting alone in the theatre at Eastman House, screening for the first time the DeMille films that had just come to us, I had an indescribably powerful jolt. The film being projected was *Something to Think About*. Gloria Swanson was playing a housewife in her kitchen. When I saw her beginning to put the crust on an apple pie, I was seized with chills. Her husband was in a mine; the mine was caving in, burying him alive. And there came his fingers, breaking through the piecrust, spasmodically clutching at the air he was being denied as he died in the mine. DeMille!

Over and over again DeMille demonstrated that he was consciously furthering the career of Gloria Swanson with wisdom and understanding. He had used her as his leading lady in four consecutive films, and she was well established as an actress glamorously able to intrigue the female fans with her flair for far-out gowns and avant-garde style. If she were to win over the hearts of all ages, it was time to put her back into homespun and move her into a kitchen. This he did in *Something to Think About*, having her play a country blacksmith's daughter, a role that resolved the opinions of any doubters, very much in her favor.

The last DeMille film with Gloria Swanson was the 1921 *Affairs of Anatol*. Although the movie was ostensibly based on the play by Arthur Schnitzler, the variations and Americanization worked out by scenarist Jeannie MacPherson left absolutely nothing more of Schnitzler than the character names. Wallace Reid as Anatol, trapped in the spidery lair of a smouldering, steamy vampire who turns out to have a maternal heart of wax, is pure Hollywood. Bebe Daniels plays the vamp in a boa memorably designed by Paul Iribé, an art director of some note in the history of Broadway theatre. DeMille, delighted with Iribé's contributions, persuaded him to stay for many films of the future.

Erasing all traces of Schnitzler from *The Affairs of Anatol* was a task needing more than one scenario writer. Some veteran scriptwriters aided Miss MacPherson in this struggle: Beulah Marie Dix, Lorna Moon and Elmer Harris contributed episodes. Even Elinor Glyn was present, as an extra. But by way of topping the literary counterpoints to *Anatol*, Somerset Maugham, recently engaged by Jesse Lasky for Paramount, professed to see some of his own work emerge from the somewhat tangled tapestry of the filmed Schnitzler. The persuasive Mr. DeMille was able to convince Mr. Maugham "that there was only the remotest superficial resemblance between his story and ours." The same assurance could also have been given to Arthur Schnitzler.

Not until twenty-nine years later did Gloria Swanson and Cecil B. DeMille work together again—both in the cast of *Sunset Boulevard.*

DeMille's first *Ten Commandments* is the film on which his popular reputation as a superdirector is principally based. It is really two films: the biblical portion is impressive spectacle; the 1923 story is turgid claptrap as bad as anything that was made at the time.

Enlisting France's Paul Iribé to do his Egyptian settings and the statuesque Charles De Roche to play Pharoah ensured that parts of the film would have certain distinction.

But with Jeannie MacPherson doing the "modern" story and relying on the incredibly awful acting of so grotesque a performer as Edythe Chapman, DeMille totally negated any enduring, serious consideration of the film as an artistic achievement.

The parting of the Red Sea sequence is visually fabulous and dramatically exciting—better in fact than the technically superior sequence in the sound version, but so much of the film is so utterly deplorable that DeMille's hard-won respect based on fine works like *The Cheat* and *Old Wives for New* was effectively destroyed.

His later efforts and bigger, more sensational screen spectacles only augmented critical contempt for a filmmaker who had proved that he should, and once did, know much better.

DeMille professed to be baffled by the critical hostility most of his films encountered in spite of overwhelming popular approval signified by their vigorous box-office performance. He seemed to forget that the general public similarly approved the Nick Carter dime novels, Edgar Rice Burroughs' stories of Tarzan, Jiggs and Maggie and Mutt and Jeff in the funny papers—all without those successes having ever been designated great writing or lasting art. He longed almost desperately for intellectual approval, yet was unwilling or unable to offer the creative audacity he once possessed in order to astonish those who cared about film.

With DeMille, what began as a betrayal of his early abilities developed into an exploitation of the box office so habitual and so successful that he ultimately convinced himself his unworthy work was correct, right and the only proper way to make good motion pictures.

His capitulation was in every meaningful way tragic.

Cecil B. DeMille was not particularly renowned by those who knew him for modesty or humility. Eyebrows must have been raised when his associates read in his memoirs this observation:

> When the history of motion pictures is written a hundred years from now, Griffith will have his honored pages in it. I hope that DeMille may have a footnote.

But in the unlikely event the comment might have come from some little-known, obscure and sincere depth of DeMille, he might have been reassured to realize no proper historian of the future who looks at *The Cheat*, *Old Wives for New* and *Why Change Your Wife?* will fail to grant Mr. DeMille far more than a footnote.

CHAPTER 11

Josef von Sternberg

T he director of American films who I came to know rather well—certainly far better than any other director—was Josef von Sternberg. The closer one becomes acquainted with an artist, the less one understands his genius. As we become more aware of a friend's foibles and prejudices, it seems more and more mysterious to see a work of great power or sensitivity or beauty emerge from that mass of contradictions that inevitably make up the multiple layers of a creator's personality.

Youthfully ambitious Joe Stern was ideally prepared to become a great director. There is much truth to the Hollywood adage "A film is born at the cutting bench." Joe had tended the birth of many a movie working as a cutter in the old Fort Lee, New Jersey, World Film Studios in 1916 and 1917. He caught a free ride on his road to fame when director Louis Gasnier brought him to London to assist him on some films he was shooting there early in the 1920s. Gasnier, a French pioneer director who had been working in Hollywood, now faced with the need to class up the credits on a not-too-classy production, had an idea about his assistant, foreign-born Joe Stern. Gasnier was aware of a developing vogue in Hollywood for European directors in the wake of admiration for Lubitsch, Buchowetzki, Seastrom and Stroheim. He therefore decided to rename his assistant, Joe Stern, a much more impressive Josef von Sternberg.

Although Austrian-born Joe Stern had been an American much longer than Stroheim, he now shared with his fellow Austrian immigrant two useful items: a spurious "von" and a hustler's realization that insecure Hollywood provided Elysian fields for the con artist. Stroheim had been able to establish his chosen role of elegant Hapsburg officer

What more unlikely duo? Sergei Eisenstein and Josef von Sternberg.

in dozens of parts he played during World War I, swaggering as the arrogant, monocled Teutonic militarist. That image Stroheim heroically supplemented and augmented by his legendary budget excesses as a director. He knew that his producers, in spite of their anxiety and fury, would be impressed with a filmmaker who *could* spend so much of their company's money.

In 1924, new to Hollywood, the freshly designated von Sternberg had to find some other approach to making himself noticed. He began with his personal appearance. At a time when men's fashion demanded short, Wally Reid haircuts, Joe grew a shaggy mane. Then the elaborate mustache! His was one of the first ever of the menacing Fu Manchus.

In a community where hundreds were ever smiling and assenting, hoping to find places in the explosively expanding film world, Joe Stern set out to present himself as the meanest, nastiest and most insulting individual on the West Coast. There was a lot of natural-born competition. But his rivals in malevolence didn't look the part as magnificently as did Josef von Sternberg.

With a persona established that already had film folks murmuring about him, Joe urgently needed to make an outstanding movie. There was a great difficulty facing him. Although he had his assistant-directorship credit from London, he had succeeded so well in making himself notorious as an antisocial demon that the studios were firmly closed to him.

Georgia Hale and Bruce Guerin in Sternberg's *The Salvation Hunters* (1925)

They all had their share of monsters, and not one needed another who also looked the part.

Movie-style good fortune smiled on Joe when he met George K. Arthur. Arthur, a slightly built, moonfaced actor, was a most unlikely contender for film fame. But he had brought with him from England an asset few movie-struck hopefuls possessed: a bankroll. Hustler von Sternberg met the ingenuous Limey, and a historic partnership was formed. The result was, in 1925, *The Salvation Hunters*—Hollywood's first deliberately arty production. The film is immature, self-indulgent, incredibly slow moving, but one thing it is undeniably—it is art. Not good art, perhaps, but astonishingly impressive art. That was what Joe needed in 1925, and that is just what he got. The locations were carefully chosen to be as depressing as possible. A giant dredge, filmed to resemble a prehistoric monster, sinks its maw into the muck beneath the roily waters of a harbor, comes up dripping wet mud and swings over to dump its load on the banks. But the slimy wet stuff just slides down the bank, back into the water again—a perfect symbol of the frustration the film's boy and girl encounter in their efforts to get out of the grisly milieu that has them trapped.

Once released, the film found a formidable group of champions, with Chaplin at their head. It was he who arranged for the film's release with this praise:

> It gives me great pleasure to recommend *The Salvation Hunters.* To me it revealed a spontaneous and admirable film technique combined with artistic composition and rhythm of presentation. It's a great picture— and different.

The eminent Dutch conductor Willem van Hoogstraten was moved to rhapsodize:

> The handling of the theme is almost symphonic; its simplicity puts it on a plane rarely attained in the motion pictures.

Max Reinhardt, still in Germany, wrote of it rather chauvinistically:

> It is inconceivable that such cinematic greatness could have come from America.

Still more praise from the theatrical side of the world; producer Morris Gest went even further than the others:

> Wonderful! I'm wiring Douglas Fairbanks and Mary Pickford tonight that I think *The Salvation Hunters* is the greatest compliment to the American public ever paid them by an American director. I was reminded of Gorki's *Lower Depths* and felt that at last we had a Eugene O'Neill of the screen.

Extravagant as they are, these enthusiasms are understandable. Impossible to watch *The Salvation Hunters* and not realize that here, in a first film, the maker shows he has more eloquent style in composition than any other director then working in pictures. Impossible not to see that here is a revolutionary creator at work who validates his contempt for the contemporary clichés of filmmaking.

The other avowed artists of American films were quick to follow Chaplin's lead; Douglas Fairbanks and Mary Pickford were lavish in their praise for sullen Joe's initial effort. They both hailed *The Salvation Hunters* as a major work of art and cited Josef von Sternberg as the most important new discovery in the business. Most American critics reviewing the film were dubious, but a little cowed by the pronunciamentos of the Chaplin-Fairbanks-Pickford triumvirate. After all, *they* were already the United Artists. For a clue to the coming public response to the film, one must look to the fan-magazine reviews. *Photoplay*'s reviewer grumbled:

Josef von Sternberg's much discussed film is another adventure into the field of realism. . . . The tale moves almost in slow motion. Von Sternberg goes too far in taking the motion out of motion pictures. He starts with sonorous philosophic intent, piles on a lot of so-called symbolism—and drags to his immature conclusion. The direction is awkward, but there is a singular fine performance of the girl by Georgia Hale. Altogether this is an experiment. Take it or leave it. Personally, we look on life as more enjoyable than Von Sternberg sees it. There is comedy even in tragedy.

In a relatively short time, the bandwagon collapsed. Most of the objections cited by the *Photoplay* review were valid. Missed completely, however, was the powerful indication that a new, visually creative mind had come to the medium. The film is indeed unreasonably slow, but parts of it are absolutely hypnotic. It is von Sternberg the unique being born before one's eyes—a spectacle that at times is a little bit clinically boring, but, with the knowledge of what is to come of it in just two or three years, the birth is fascinating to observe in its several arresting moments.

Later, aware of the widespread hostility the film encountered, Chaplin actually repudiated his praise.

If most of the critics of the day were evasive, the filmgoing public was even more so; it avoided the film altogether. But Sternberg's champions were ready to put not only their prestige on the line, but their money as well. Mary Pickford signed Josef to make her next film. Charlie Chaplin hired von Sternberg to make *The Sea Gull* for him and, working on *The Gold Rush*, he fired his own wife in the lead and reshot most of the film with Sternberg's heroine from *The Salvation Hunters*, Georgia Hale, as his leading lady.

Now Sternberg was ready to out-Hollywood all the legendary industry beasts. He finished *The Sea Gull* for Chaplin. Charlie never released it. Perhaps it was too good. John Grierson, the great documentarian, one of the few private viewers who ever saw the film, maintained that it was superb. Probably too much so for Chaplin, who had had nothing to do with making it other than to provide the money, raw stock and studio space. Not only did Chaplin shelve *The Sea Gull*, he also publicly repudiated his praise for *The Salvation Hunters*. And Mary Pickford never did appear in the film she had planned to make with von Sternberg.

But meanwhile, Sternberg had not been thrown out of Hollywood in disgrace. Being spurned and scorned was his *linea de siempre*. He luxuriated in contumely. Hired by MGM to make *The Exquisite Sinner* as a vehicle for superstar Mae Murray, he walked off the set in the middle of a scene and departed from MGM. Now he *was* famous! Infamously.

Next stop—Paramount Pictures. The Museum of Modern Art Film Library made room for Josef von Sternberg in its pantheon of great directors by selecting two of his films for circulation: *Underworld* and *The Last Command*. And rightly so! Along with his growing concern for composition, in his early Paramount films Sternberg discovered what would become his most powerful trademark, overshadowing even his long, long dissolves and his crowded, overwhelmingly detailed frames. It was his close-ups.

The usual Hollywood close-up was a head-and-shoulders portrait. The Russian close-up was a dynamic, full-frame face, often cropping off the top of the head and the neck of the subject. But the Sternberg close-up was something of a mystical experience for the beholder, particularly if the subject was a woman. He usually had his actress smoking a cigarette. The translucent, drifting clouds of smoke wrapped the girl in a shimmering haze. Sternberg understood lighting better than any other director. He understood his camera lenses better than many a cinematographer. He was, in fact, the only Hollywood director who was a member of the American Society of Cinematographers. Any ordinary actress caught in Joe's idealizing compositions and his caressing lighting glowed like Garbo at her best.

Much too much importance has been attached to our annual tithing ceremony—the voodoo celebration of the Academy Awards. However much one may be aware of the ephemeral value of so many of these best-seller designations, it is noteworthy that it was Josef von Sternberg's *The Last Command* that was singled out in the first-ever batch of movie ventures to be Oscared. And it was in that film that Sternberg, with his close-ups of Emil Jannings, William Powell and Evelyn Brent, began to toy with transcendentalism in his screen-filling faces, which we can actually see "turning into poetry."

Iris Barry was quite right to include *The Last Command* and *Underworld* in the museum's collection, but totally wrong to have missed *The Docks of New York*, in which Sternberg reaches the apotheosis of his mysterious handling of the close-up—his technique that would bring international fame to Marlene Dietrich, whose face had been uninterestingly familiar on German screens before Joe transfigured it in *The Blue Angel*, *Morocco* and *Shanghai Express*.

A vintage year for silent films was 1928. Alas, most of the silent movies at the time were completely overlooked in the excitement of beginning dialogue. Ironically, 1928 was the year in which the silent cinema had reached its highest point of perfection. But its masterpieces were ignored by the public, entranced by the aural inanities of Jolson's *The Singing Fool* and the early talkies *Sal of Singapore, The Carnation Kid, Mother Knows Best, State Street Sadie, Tenderloin* and *The Terror.*

Perhaps the finest of all in 1928 was *The Docks of New York.* As he had rescued Evelyn Brent from a fading career by transforming an ordinary face into that of an earthy madonna, Sternberg chose Betty Compson, a former star about to drift out into darkness. Saving her literally and cinematically from drowning, Sternberg has his dockwalloper pull her out of murky waters and bring her into a kerosene-lighted, sleazy bedroom, and he shows us one of the most delicately intriguing faces of silent films. The word that defines the close-ups of Betty Compson is "luminous."

It is worth a trip to Rochester, New York, to see the Eastman House print of *The Docks of New York.* It was pulled from the original negative lent by Paramount. It was printed at Kodak with far more care than was ever given to making the original release prints. With the Sternberg obsessive concern over lighting and composition, the whole film shimmers and glows as though Ansel Adams had nursed it through his darkroom. Even the black-market dupes of that print, which now abound—even the 16mm reductions—are gorgeous. But to see the original 35mm print at Eastman House is to see black-and-white cinematography at its ultimate finest—both in the production of the negative and in the scrupulous lab work in the printing.

Of course the memorable qualities of *The Docks of New York* are far from limited to the effulgent close-ups. The entire film, save for the ending, immerses the viewer in a poetic idealization of the kind of place the New York waterfront ought to be—but certainly is not. The docks, fog-shrouded at night, and in daytime glistening in softened sunlight, are just what one might dream of finding where the big ships come into the great port of New York Harbor. The nights are moonwashed with mystery, and not even the daylight dispels Sternberg's pictorial magic.

The sustained rhythm of the film supports its dreamlike quality. The camera seems to have been cranked about thirty-two frames per second; the characters move smoothly, smoothly—at just the right side of slow motion; they undulate with surreal grace. And the camera travels along at the same even tempo. A quick movement (George Bancroft's

George Bancroft carries light-as-a-feather Betty Compson along the misty *Docks of New York* (1928).

sudden, savage punch, decking the bouncer) comes as a shock one almost feels physically.

After *The Blue Angel, Morocco* and *Shanghai Express* brought international fame to Sternberg, he often scoffed at his great silent films. *The Salvation Hunters*, he insisted, was a mistake, attributable to the inexperience of youth. (He was a youth in his thirties when he made it.) His films, he sneered, were made for fools, and only fools found value in them.

But when the Cinémathèque Française decided to do a homage to Sternberg in Paris, he accepted warily. He asked me to bring *The Docks of New York*, then the only print existing in the world, to Paris along with the Eastman House print of *Shanghai Express*—also printed from the original negative. The unique copy of *Docks* could not be risked in the cargo bays of either plane or ship. I booked a stateroom aboard the *Queen Elizabeth*, where I could watch the prints day and night in transit. Such elaborate concern for the safety of *Docks* put it in a jeopardy we had never imagined.

Day after day, almost every hour, I would leave the bar or the deck, go to my stateroom and check on the health of the films. In midocean, on one of those periodic inspections, I smelled smoke coming through the room's ventilator. I hurried out on deck to find an officer. I told the first one I encountered about the smoke and asked him to come to my room to check its source. In that kind of voice the British used to cow the Indians for three centuries, the officer snapped, "Just consult your room steward," and turned to walk away. The only way to respond to arrogance is with even more of the same. I stepped in front of him, assumed a von Stroheim stance and in the coldest tones I could manage said, "There is a fire aboard this ship. I am sure it is your duty to investigate it. I suggest you come with me to my quarters where the smoke is accumulating; you then may be able to determine its source before it becomes a serious hazard." With a contemptuous shrug, he reluctantly followed me to my room. Once there he sniffed the acrid air coming through the ventilator. "It's just your imagination," he snarled, turned on his heel and left the room.

Fifteen minutes later, with heavy black smoke pouring through the whole ship, the liner was stopped and swung around so that the wind would carry the smoke off the leeward side. In the staterooms across the corridor from mine, a frantic damage-control crew was busy tearing up the floorboards where the fire, ignited by bad wiring, was raging beneath their feet. Ten minutes later, the water from their fire hoses was up to their knees.

There was no alarm sounded. There was no reassuring announcement from the bridge. There was only heavy smoke, lots of water and much anxious speculation on the part of the passengers, a few of them closely approaching hysteria. When I realized that the fire was not burning underneath *The Docks of New York*, I returned to my post at the bar and reported on the progress of the damage party to the heroic bartender, who never deserted the scene of his critical responsibilities.

In two hours the crisis was over. The *Queen Elizabeth* was able to swing around and resume her eastward course. She was due to dock in Cherbourg before making her home port of Southampton. But on arrival in France, the captain thought better of docking in Cherbourg, and the passengers for that port were put ashore in a tender. After crossing the Channel to Southampton, we expected some sort of big reception with newsreel cameras and hordes of worried friends and relations awaiting the arrival of the singed *Queen*. But we had certainly underestimated the cover-up resources of the Cunard Line, practicing the art with skill learned from the sinking of the unsinkable *Titanic* with its too-few lifeboats back in 1912. There was no cheering reception.

There is no question but that the British are indeed the world's masters of understatement. On disembarking, the passengers were presented with a mimeographed sheet carrying this text:

R.M.S. *QUEEN ELIZABETH*

SUNDAY, 25TH SEPTEMBER 1960 THE COMMODORE TAKES THIS OPPORTUNITY TO TENDER HIS REGRETS TO ALL PASSENGERS WHO HAVE BEEN INCONVENIENCED BY THE ELECTRICAL FIRE WHICH HAPPENED TODAY, SUNDAY, ESPECIALLY TO THOSE PASSENGERS WHO HAVE SUFFERED DAMAGE TO CLOTHING ETC BY WATER.

Fire at sea was not the only hazard that threatened the showing of *The Docks of New York* at the Cinémathèque. At the Cinémathèque, the projectionists had been instructed to run every silent film at eighteen frames per second, no matter whether it had been made in 1915 or in 1929. Such a slow speed would make *The Docks of New York* look like a motion-analysis study. And the Sternberg homage was scheduled to begin with a showing of *The Docks of New York*, then, like *The Crowd*, playing its first return engagement in France since its original release. The theatre was filled with eager film buffs. Joe was present, bemused that all these young "fools" were bent on honoring him for something he'd done so long ago. Now his once-shaggy coiffure was white and clipped short, the menacing mustache meekly trimmed and as white as his hair. His eyes remained an electric blue—they had always made it hard for him to look as savage as he hoped.

I sat down next to him. "Joe, I need your help. They show all silents here at eighteen frames. They won't run your film at twenty-four as I've asked them, but they'll do it for you. Will you go back and ask the projectionist to run your film at sound speed?"

"At sound speed? But it's a silent."

"Yes, of course, Joe. But it's a 1928 silent. You know how you were shooting your pictures then."

"Of course I know how we were shooting them then. We were shooting them at silent speed."

I was dumbfounded. Could this be the same Josef von Sternberg who held membership in the American Society of Cinematographers? If he was indeed a genius, as he was about to be proclaimed that evening, he was a genius of cinematography. When I could speak, it was only weakly. "But, Joe, don't you remember? Your cameramen were cranking faster and faster those last years."

"Cranking? You must be crazy. Of course it should be run at silent speed. Where did you ever get such a crazy idea? Sound speed will ruin it!" Joe was pulled away to meet André Malraux, then the minister of culture. There were some introductory speeches. The lights began to go down. Joe came back to his seat, leaned over and urgently asked, "Do you know what you're talking about?" My assurance barely convinced him. "I still think you're crazy, but you've seen this film more often than I have. I'll go with you and ask the operator to run it at sound speed. But I'm sure you're wrong!"

The word from on high was given to the projectionist. The film was run at sound speed. Bancroft strolled leisurely through the smoky barroom. Betty Compson took forever to light each of her innumerable cigarettes, and the radiant smoke drifted and curled around her blond hair.

When the film ended, Josef von Sternberg received a standing ovation—unprecedented for the Cinémathèque Française. He leaned over and said one word to me: "Thanks."

It was in 1927, with *Underworld*, that Sternberg hit his magnificent stride. It was a most fortunate bit of casting that he was able to use George Bancroft as his charismatic gangster. Not only was Bancroft the Charles Bronson of the predialogue era, he was probably the very first of the screen villains who managed to have something really likable about him. (Wallace Beery was to develop that dual personality trait, exploiting it to the hilt as Long John Silver in Victor Fleming's magnificent rendition of *Treasure Island*, but it was George Bancroft who staked out the territory in 1925 in *The Pony Express*.) Bancroft had been working steadily as a Western bad man, sometimes opposite Tom Mix. His big hit came when he was cast as Jack Slade in Cruze's *The Pony Express*. The difference in his portrayal of Slade was that Bancroft had a visual laugh so hearty and robust that one felt sure it was being heard, though the film was silent. His craggy, rugged features would fragment into the merriest of laughter. In *The Pony Express*, Slade knowingly sends off a pioneer family with charming youngsters into an Indian ambush. Certain that they soon will be massacred, Slade stands waving good-bye to the children with the most benign smile ever to mask a bad chap's face.

George Bancroft's all-out laughter was an unusual characteristic for a screen bad man when he introduced it in *The Pony Express* (1925).

Sternberg enlisted big bruiser Bancroft to play the chief gangster in *Underworld*, a heavy given to great bursts of the kind of hilarity that Bancroft did so well. Then casting that smooth British performer Clive Brook as the gentleman drunk taken over by the gangster, he achieved an effective contrast to the beefy, extroverted American Attila.

Underworld gave Sternberg the opportunity to begin his special technique of glamorizing a rather ordinary female face. With magical lighting and a sense of camera angle, which he possessed to a greater degree than any other American director, Sternberg caressed the face of Evelyn Brent, playing the gangster's girl, Feathers. He made her features glow with a luminous translucence that went far deeper than ordinary makeup.

Underworld became the archetypal gangster film, with arresting touches that other directors did not hesitate to copy. When the rival gang leader, acted with vicious savagery by Fred Kohler, seeks to impress his girlfriend with his contempt for money, he crumples a ten-dollar bill into a wad, pitches it into a filthy spittoon and challenges the Clive Brook character to retrieve it. The incident showed up in a talkie. Another copied bit finds Bancroft besieged by the police, who are filling his hideout with a hail of machine-gun bullets. There is a kitten in the

Evelyn Brent as a Russian revolutionist rescues Emil Jannings, the enemy general, in *The Last Command* (1927).

room with the embattled gangster. In an abstracted way, he dips his finger in the cat's milk dish and allows the kitten to lap it while warily awaiting the next fusillade from the police.

The great success of *Underworld* gave Sternberg the studio prestige to achieve his masterpiece, *The Last Command*, a film that dared to be critical of Hollywood-studio attitudes. With Evelyn Brent in the cast again, *The Last Command* starred the great German actor Emil Jannings.

If ever there were a magnificent opportunity for an actor of gargantuan talent to exhibit vast skill, that superrole was created in the script of *The Last Command*. Von Sternberg has held that the idea of the Russian aristocrat-general become a palsied movie extra was his own.

In his autobiography, Jannings himself has claimed authorship, based on the experience of meeting, on the Paramount lot, an actual former Russian general officer penuriously existing in Hollywood on infrequent film extra work.

Except for the fact that most film directors were frustrated actors, one should tend to believe Jannings before accepting Sternberg's version: the whole conception of the part is that of a dedicated actor.

In any case, it was Jannings, not Sternberg, who won the Academy Award. And Jannings is unforgettable as the general, arrogant and brutal in his handling of a suspected revolutionist, charming and understanding as a lover and completely pathetic as the maimed and broken refugee.

Perspective is important in viewing a film of this sort. Now in the 1990s, the Russian Revolution seems a part of history far, far removed. When Sternberg's film was made, the bloodiest events of the Revolution were only ten years earlier. White Russian refugees were to be found in every capital city: making movies and driving taxis in Paris; running restaurants and shooting films in Berlin; and acting as extras in Hollywood.

Sternberg tells about Jannings during the making of the film. From Berlin Jannings had brought his ancient and trusted valet. When they were shooting the portion of the film with the actor playing the dazed, bewildered extra, teased and taunted by his fellow players, Jannings would almost creep home after work, totter up the walk to his house and scratch beseechingly on his front door. When his valet opened it for him, Jannings would slink apologetically inside.

But when they were working on the portions with Jannings as the general at the height of his power and authority, Jannings would go home, swaggering up his walk, pound furiously on the door with his riding crop and thrust his valet unceremoniously aside as he strode belligerently indoors.

When Sternberg went to Germany with Jannings to film *The Blue Angel*, a curious sea change took place in his technique. Marlene Dietrich, perfectly cast as Lola-Lola, a vulgar barroom chanteuse, was actually deglamorized by the director, who was already noted for changing veteran actresses Evelyn Brent and Betty Compson into photogenic rivals of Greta Garbo. Dietrich was presented as a brassy, raucous, cheap entertainer who was ready for a good laugh and was generally good-natured, but no candidate for soft-focus lenses and flattering backlighting. In Marlene Dietrich's two major German silent movies, *I Kiss Your Hand Madame* and *The Woman for Whom One Longs*, she had been photographed by the directors Land and Bernhard with gauzy shots that made her look much as she would in the American-made films *Morocco* and *Shanghai Express*, wherein Sternberg idealized her. In his Hollywood talkies, Sternberg used more and more the long, lingering mixes that turned his transitional shots from one sequence to another into the likes of nonobjective paintings with the superimpositions of unrelated images that seemed to fascinate him.

I had great affection for Joe Stern and deep admiration for all his silent films. His first sound films are cinematically impressive and great fun to watch. But in his last years of activity his films and his ideas were more astounding than admirable. Often it is disillusioning to learn of a great director's own favorites among his creations. Sternberg told me his own favorite work was *The Devil Is a Woman*—a film almost totally devoid of any action, and, told entirely in flashbacks, it is without any sense of forward progression. Worst of all, Marlene Dietrich performs in it with what Louise Brooks described as "having the cutes." Dietrich herself has acknowledged this trite movie as containing her own favorite role.

Unfortunately the list of von Sternberg's incredible lapses does not end with *The Devil Is a Woman*—it only begins there. His *Crime and Punishment* is undoubtedly one of the most flagrant examples of almost sacrilegious miscasting in all American films. Pudgy Peter Lorre as Dostoevsky's haggard and haunted Raskolnikov? Apple-pie-American

Peter Lorre as Raskolnikov with Edward Arnold as Porfiry in *Crime and Punishment* (1935)

Edward Arnold as Raskolnikov's nemesis Porfiry? These atrocities were committed in Sternberg's version of *Crime and Punishment*. For Sternberg, punishment for that crime was *Jet Pilot*, made for Howard Hughes in 1950. But Hughes, only a little less flaky than Sternberg himself, did not release the film for seven years. By that time, jet-propelled aircraft had become commonplace, and so had the star of the film, Duke Wayne. The only part of the film critics found of interest was an in-flight refueling scene, which reviewers noted that Sternberg had managed to make look somewhat pornographic.

There exists at Eastman House an extraordinary tape interview done in Sternberg's Hollywood home in 1957 by George Pratt, then assistant to the film curator. Sternberg tells of having returned to his homeland, Austria, and beginning work there on a vast film epic that would summarize the creative accomplishments of Jewish artists over the centuries. On that tape, the voice of Josef von Sternberg seriously maintains that Adolf Hitler, learning of the Sternberg project in Austria, invaded that country to stop the production.

If that claim seems extravagant, have a look at Sternberg's last film. *Anatahan* was made in Japan with an all-Japanese cast. It was a good story idea about Japanese soldiers on a remote island, unaware that the war was over, and their involvement with a gorgeous Japanese siren and her husband. The actor playing the seriously outnumbered husband had probably been cast because of his striking resemblance to the Sternberg of 1925, complete with Fu Manchu mustache and an unvaryingly truculent expression. Good enough. But the sound track! On the track is a narration by von Sternberg; it runs right over the Japanese dialogue, most of the time having nothing to do either with what the Japanese are saying or with the action going on in the visuals. Instead, the narration, in the director's own voice, is a long-winded discussion of Sternberg's philosophy bearing on almost every aspect of life other than those portions of it being enacted on the screen.

If *Anatahan* were not a peculiar-enough hybrid of incongruent vocalization and dramatization, think about Joe's last request. At Eastman House we had the original 35mm camera negative of *The Blue Angel*. We had already furnished Joe with a beautiful 16mm print of his film. Months afterward, he asked us for another.

"What happened to the 16mm print we gave you?" I asked him.

"Not a thing," he explained. "But it's bothered me that creatively, making a film has nothing to do with real art. Real art means the artist must have *laid his hands physically* on his work. I want another print so

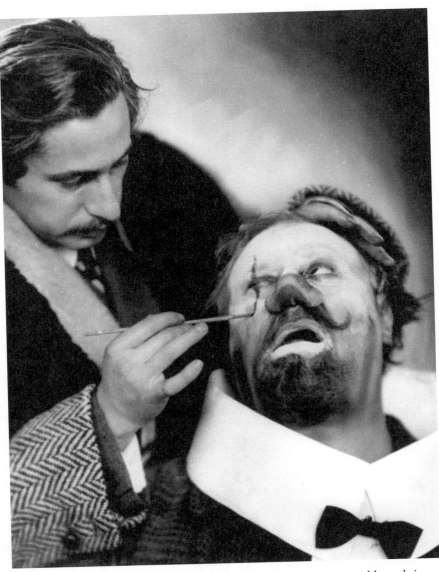

Josef von Sternberg believed that only actual hands-on activity could result in art. Here he makes up Emil Jannings for *The Blue Angel* (1930).

Von Sternberg with his Japanese cast and crew for *Anatahan*

Josef von Sternberg, hands on the camera. Von Sternberg was the only major director to be also a member of the American Society of Cinematographers.

that with a sharp stylus I can cut designs into the actual emulsion of the film, over the images that I have already put onto it. When the film is projected, then superimposed over the *camera* images will be the designs that I have, with my own hand, created on those frames of film."

Alas, I have never learned what happened to this original von Sternberg. It would have been something to see—but not too much of a box-office winner.

CHAPTER 12

King Vidor

All the major features directed by D. W. Griffith and all but one by Stroheim are available for viewing and study. Of the silent films made by directors of arguably comparable, perhaps greater, stature, too many have been allowed to slip into the limbo of missing films. There are serious gaps in the existing oeuvre of Sternberg. And for many years the reputation of King Vidor as a significant pioneer in early film history has been ignored in favor of his deserved renown for *The Big Parade*.

Vidor reached his greatness before the arrival of dialogue. He had honed his skills in bringing pantomime to brilliant visual eloquence, to razor sharpness. The sound track blunted much that he had achieved. King Vidor was not a man of the theatre. His whole career had developed as he more and more effectively dealt with the mysteries peculiar to a silent medium. The King Vidor of *The Crowd* could never have produced a *War and Peace* with Henry Fonda as a Tolstoy character.

The Crowd is undeniably an essential work of genuine Americana and, minus the grand-scale spectacular nature of *The Big Parade*, is an even richer exposition of valid human responses particular to the twenties era. But along with *The Crowd* there are four other Vidor silents restored to view that should be watched in attempting to appraise the Vidor style. The earliest of these distinguished works is *The Jack-Knife Man* of 1920.

Vidor's career began in Texas as a freelance newsreel cameraman. Scenting an inviting future for film in California, he brought his exquisitely beautiful wife, Florence Arto, along with him to Hollywood. Once there, he wisely moved to the side of the camera to direct. One of his first features brought praise from a source that would be important to

King Vidor in the 1920s

him. In those days before films had achieved respectability, the best critical writing usually was to be found in the fan magazines rather than in the *Literary Digest*, *Theatre Arts* or *Mentor*. Among the best reviewers were Burns Mantle, writing for *Photoplay*, and Frederick James Smith, film critic for *Motion Picture Classic*.

The promise of King Vidor's work had not escaped Mr. Smith. In his September 1920 *Classic* review of *The Jack-Knife Man* he wrote:

> King Vidor has proved himself again. Mr. Vidor it was who startled the celluloid world somewhat over a year ago with his *Turn in the Road* which revealed its producer as possessing a singularly human touch.

Being sure of his ability, we have waited for Mr. Vidor to do something bigger. The bigger thing has occurred—Ellis Parker Butler's *The Jack-Knife Man*. Here is a gently drawn little genre study, finely conceived and done with admirable workmanship and an excellently restrained sympathy. . . . *The Jack-Knife Man* is worthy of your attention for it belongs to the photoplay school of tomorrow. No pasteboard melodramatic characters, no machine made plot development, no trite methods of screen telling are here. For Mr. Vidor—we are sure of it now—is just finding himself and before long he is going to turn out a big and human celluloid document.

The story that Butler had written was a homespun tale, much in the tradition of Mark Twain. Vidor shot his film in authentic Mark Twain country, along the Mississippi River. The rural, outdoor setting of barns, stables, country roads, buggies, country stores and snowy village streets doesn't simply bring authenticity to the film, but with the passing of years, those actualities have made the picture a precious document of a kind of countryside lost to us forever.

A good part of the action is confined to a primitive river shanty boat,

Bobby Kelso and Harry Todd in *The Jack-Knife Man* (1920), an early Vidor masterpiece

and the shots of it floating down the river are visually so satisfying that we know we're seeing the daily reality of 1920. The lonely river bum is played with grizzled accuracy by Fred Turner. Claire McDowell, a Griffith actress from the early Biograph days, is memorable as a homeless, dying mother, drenched and wandering, who finds refuge from the cold and the rain in the old man's shanty boat. Five years later, Vidor would cast her as the mother in *The Big Parade*, welcoming her maimed son back from the war that didn't end all wars.

Trying to steal the boat, a tramp joins the skipper and the motherless little boy, and the two old men compete for the child's affection. With a story like this, one could expect treatment of cloying sentimentality or outright hokum. But Vidor avoids the syrupy sequences that so often mar the work of John Ford. With wry humor, he keeps his people honestly human—a skill that marked Vidor's best work throughout the whole time of his predialogue period. This film, devoid of sentimentality, is the earliest example we have of Vidor's greatest strength—his ability to use professional players, strip them of their standard theatrical-behavior specialties and allow them to perform with the naturalism that Vittorio De Sica achieved from his auto-worker star of *The Bicycle Thief*.

In 1924 recognition arrived and rapidly increased for King Vidor and marked his occupancy of the top rung of American directors. He would continue to hold that place through the end of the predialogue era. Preserved twenty-eight years later by Eastman House and highly recommended is Vidor's second film starring Laurette Taylor, *Happiness*.

Vidor had encountered Laurette Taylor two years before. His assignment then was hazardous—to make a film version of the formidable Broadway star's *Peg o' My Heart*. That play, by her then husband, J. Hartley Manners, was to her career what *Rain* was to that of Jeanne Eagels. But the situation of Laurette Taylor was quite different from that of Jeanne Eagels when the latter went to MGM later on. Eagels had already played the lead in a half-dozen films of the 1918–1919 period. Laurette Taylor's whole acting career had been limited to live theatre. *Peg* represented the peak of her theatrical success, and stardom in living theatre was then accounted—by theatre people—to be a far greater achievement than renown in the movies. Like every successful stage star, Taylor was a perfectionist, cherishing the technique that had brought her to the top of her profession. She was not ready to modify her acting for the benefit of the motion picture camera. In the past, comparable stubbornness on the part of theatre actors proved to be disastrous if their film directors,

Laurette Taylor in a 1924
publicity portrait for
Vidor's *Happiness*

cowed by the stage performers' prestige, were unable to persuade them
that film acting required quite different techniques.

To his great credit, King Vidor was not willing to be directed by
Laurette Taylor. The first weeks of work on *Peg o' My Heart* produced a
continuing battle between stage star and film director that presaged the
impossibility of bringing in a film version of *Peg* with Laurette in her
famous role. At last Vidor resorted to the device of shooting several
scenes just as she wanted them. He had her look at the tests, and, luckily for cinema, she readily recognized that her stage mannerisms were
just too extravagant for the intimate eye of the motion picture camera.
She started to pay close attention to Vidor's suggestions. And the results
were startling.

Taylor's readiness to accept his direction did not solve all Vidor's
problems in working with a legendary theatrical star. In both *Happiness*
and *Peg o' My Heart* Laurette Taylor was cast as a teenager. She was a
woman in her middle thirties, and the vast discrepancy between the
characters' age and her own threatened the most willing suspension of
disbelief on the part of film audiences. Her visual appearance on the

screen had to be offset by a personality so bubbling with appeal that demanding film watchers would ignore her slight heaviness and her obvious lack of the youthful freshness that American film fans seemed to demand as a special fetish.

In *Happiness*, both her performance and Vidor's sensitive handling of so great a hazard overwhelmed the problem. It was an achievement of major proportions for both star and director. Once again King Vidor showed that his special forte was keeping his shadow players magically human—even when some of them, by long movie habit, fought hard against it.

Happiness is an irresistible film. In almost the same way that Cher shed years and a long-established mystique in *Moonstruck*, Laurette Taylor was able to charm film fans devoted to the likes of Norma Talmadge and Gloria Swanson, even Mary Pickford, to accept the live theatre's Laurette Taylor as an exception—a nonmovie queen worthy of their warm response.

The unlikely project was aided by an exceptional cast assembled by Vidor to support his difficult challenge. Hedda Hopper is exquisitely right playing a bored socialite who becomes bemused and finally enchanted by a schlemperish hoyden, more radiant than anyone she had ever encountered. Hopper's equally enervated gentleman friend, suffering similarly cosmic ennui, is done with delicious precision by the British actor Cyril Chadwick, who, like Henry Daniell, could register regal disapproval with icy perfection.

But the performance that, along with that of Laurette Taylor herself, tips the film over into the area of the exceptional is the endearing behavior of Edith Yorke as the abandoned mother of the heroine. With the kind of delicacy Mae Marsh at her best brought to her sweet-old-lady roles, Edith Yorke, again, without sentimentality, hunts her missing husband, whom she is convinced is an amnesia victim, on long excursions "in the cars," subjecting every mature male to her questing gaze, all the time taking in stride the wild eccentricities of her astonishing daughter.

In the same year Vidor made *Wine of Youth*, a film that strikes positive resonance with today's youthful viewers far more than most silent films. Women's liberation has provided a perpetual theme in novels, dramas and films. A concomitant of course is sexual liberation. The Hays Office was far from ready to allow a film to be made showing young people living together, no matter that the notion was being discussed widely in that era of gin, jazz and gasoline, short skirts, short hair and young women eager and curious to find out what being liberated might mean to them.

For the scenario of *Wine of Youth*, screenwriter Carey Wilson adapted a popular Rachel Crothers play of the preceding year. *Mary III* had taken into account the fashionable interest in the possibilities of a more permissive society. In *Wine of Youth*, the way of life that has become standard in the 1990s was presented with King Vidor's firmly developed style of breathing believable life into his players. Led by Eleanor Boardman, an actress exuding intelligence and integrity rather than movie glamor (the Meryl Streep of the silents), the young people challenge the hypocrisy of their parents and revolt to the extent of going on a unisex camping trip. Put up in outdoor tents, they evade the taboos of the Production Code, which in those days frowned on male and female even walking into the same bedroom.

The experimenting kids provide an entertaining mix of flappers and sheiks along with some serious idealists trying to discover what this thing called life is all about.

Four years later the same problem would be explored again by an MGM film that brought stardom to Joan Crawford, *Our Dancing Daughters*. In the Crawford film, the young folks are not so young, much wealthier and they inhabit a Never Land of big money and endless privilege that is accurately located in Carmel. The Vidor morality play, much more believable, involves upper-middle-class families without the benefits of the more flexible yacht-and-country-club social ambience.

Vidor's *Wild Oranges* was also released in 1924, although he had made it for Goldwyn just before that company merged with Metro. It is a lively melodrama that attests to the director's skill as an editor, for almost the entire film had to be reshot with Frank Mayo replacing the original leading man. It is doubtful, with all the trouble he had in restitching it together plus the raging viciousness of the plot, that King Vidor would ever have cited *Wild Oranges* as one of his best silent films. But the fact is that in making so effective a thriller, far outside the style of his developing work, he established a dependable versatility that removed him from the kind of specialization that marked a director like Frank Borzage.

As horror films go, this one is more genuinely frightening than many of the Tod Browning Grand Guignol pieces. Shot mostly on location, Vidor's own adaptation of a Joseph Hergesheimer short story involves the nightmare of a girl and her grandfather held captive in a crumbling Southern mansion isolated on a tiny offshore island of Georgia. Their jailer is a homicidal maniac, and their only hope comes from a yachtsman who puts in to the island out of casual curiosity.

The ensuing violence and terror are enough to nearly satisfy Stallone and Schwarzenegger fans of current cinema, but the style of King Vidor in developing the tale is far more elegant than encountered in the Golan and Globus' Michael Winner bloodlettings. After the frail grandfather is done in as brutally as has ever been accomplished in the movies, there is a fabulous chase through fearful swamp waters. The outcome seems highly doubtful to the last moment, when one of filmdom's most ravenous-looking and ferocious mastiffs becomes the deus ex machina to save a parlous day. Lovely Virginia Valli manages to remain supremely attractive throughout frantic action. Whatever her salary, she more than earned it with King Vidor putting her through paces that could only have been totally exhausting.

There has been much deserved praise and recognition for the enduring value of *The Crowd*. Happily, film lovers of the world did not wait for King Vidor to leave the scene before acclaiming his contributions. There were many festivals and award ceremonies in his honor. One of the earliest took place at the second Telluride Festival in Colorado in 1975.

Telluride came about in this way: Bill Pence, a good friend and fellow collector, owned several marvelous repertory houses in the West—in Denver, Aspen, Telluride and other historical mountain towns. He asked me to organize a lecture-and-film program at the Wheeler, his Aspen theater, in 1973. The show was to be repeated in his Telluride showplace. When I saw that jewel box of a film theatre, I importuned Bill to organize a yearly festival to allow fellow film lovers to watch exceptional movies in so delicious a theatre and in so exciting a landscape as offered by Telluride, Colorado. The first Telluride Festival took place in 1974, when we honored that surprising triumvirate Leni Riefenstahl, Gloria Swanson and Francis Ford Coppola. For its first years, the festival was guided by Tom Luddy, Bill Pence and me. Subsequent honorees included Viola Dana, Jack Nicholson, Werner Herzog, Henry King and King Vidor. When I left Eastman House in 1977, Bill Everson took my place as one of the three codirectors. Serge Losique was a fan of Telluride. Together we plotted to do a superfestival in Montreal: the World Film Festival. Serge took that ball and ran with it in a spectacular way. Today it is the biggest festival in the world, larger even than Cannes.

While King Vidor was in Telluride he told us how he was fascinated by the tragic ironies that befell his unheroic hero of *The Crowd*, James

Card introduces Gloria
Swanson at the first
Telluride Film
Festival, in 1974.

Leni Riefenstahl, one
of the first three
honorees at the
Telluride Film Festival

Henry King, honored at the
second Telluride Film
Festival, in 1975

Henry King as an actor
in 1917

Viola Dana (right) and King Vidor (below) were both honored at the Telluride Film Festival in 1976.

Murray. After seeing *The Crowd*, who could forget the scene where that born loser, intent on suicide, is dissuaded from the act by his small son? As they walk along the bridge over the railroad tracks, the father weeping, the little kid reaches up and takes his dad's hand. Vittorio De Sica did that moment again at the end of *The Bicycle Thief*. Certainly the Vidor scenes had impressed the Italian directors. Roberto Rossellini in *Open City* remembered Mélisande in *The Big Parade* trying to hold back the truck that was rushing Jim to the front, when he had Anna Magnani in the same sort of desperate protest.

Neither could King Vidor forget Murray's performance. Some months after *The Crowd* had been released, King Vidor offered him another part. By then Murray had made a mess of himself with booze. Vidor told him to slim down, wash up and report for work. Instead, Murray disappeared from Hollywood. Not much later, back in New York, Murray's body was found floating in the East River. King Vidor, in his last years, kept hoping to do a film about James Murray. He never got to it.

CHAPTER 13

Monta Bell

The films restored and preserved at Eastman House were shown regularly to the public and to writers who trekked to Rochester, beginning with the opening of the Dryden Theatre in 1951. But showing films in Rochester, New York, is almost as limited a project as writing in Danish. One of the earliest large-scale exhibitions of the results of my iconoclastic collecting was the 1972 program at the Pacific Film Archive in Berkeley. From September through November, 104 features from Eastman House were shown to the outside world—or at least that portion of it known as the West Coast. All films were covered by the magnificent program notes by Tom Luddy, then curator of the California archive. Seventy-five of those titles were silent pictures from 1915 to 1930. Twenty years later, some of those films are just being "discovered."

During that memorable fall of 1972, along with *The Cheat*, the film that brought about most surprised admiration was Monta Bell's superb *Man, Woman, and Sin*, revealing Jeanne Eagels as a superior film actress, and a John Gilbert so restrained and ingenuous as to be almost unrecognizable. Some of the excitement attached to seeing the film was that it had been designated as one of the lost films in the Museum of Modern Art's monograph published in 1970. In fact, the film never had been lost at all. The original negative had lain in the vaults of MGM ever since the film had been made. Before 1950, no one had ever asked for it.

Of the half-dozen truly extraordinary personalities among the actresses of American silent films—a group that includes Garbo, Clara Bow, Pola Negri, Gloria Swanson and Louise Brooks—in some ways more exceptional than any of the others was Jeanne Eagels. Long before she had played Sadie Thompson in *Rain*, the 1922 hit that made her famous in the American theatre, Jeanne Eagels had played leads in five films. In the MGM publicity for *Man, Woman, and Sin*, it was proclaimed that film would be the celebrated Sadie Thompson's first film appearance! Her first film role was an early one—in the 1915 *The House of Fear*, a detective movie devoted to the exploits of an American Sherlock Holmes, one Ashton Kirk, an amateur detective who had bowed to the public in 1910. In her next film, *The World and the Woman*, she played a prostitute who discovers she has healing powers. Her role as the hooker was thoroughly believable, wonderfully understated and a distinct foreshadowing of the histrionic integrity that would make her Sadie Thompson so impressive on the stage when *Rain* became the biggest Broadway success of 1922.

Her next two films were made for Thanhouser. *Fires of Youth* was released in 1917. It was one of those exposés of fearful factory conditions, much like Thanhouser's famous short film *The Cry of the Children* had been in 1912. *Under False Colors* was a melodrama with Eagels acting as a Russian countess fleeing revolutionaries. In March 1918 she played the lead in a big film that premiered in Carnegie Hall. It was *The Cross Bearer*, a World War I drama that allegedly contained actual documentary footage of German troops in Belgium where the action of the movie took place.

Eagels was exposed to the public in five leading roles in her films, and it is something of a mystery as to why popular stardom eluded her as a result of her film persona, when she would make such an enormous hit on the stage as Sadie Thompson, four years after her last film role. Probably her film acting was received with the same indifference as that of Louise Brooks had been. Their performances just did not fit the style and acting clichés that had solidified by the mid-1920s. Their perfectly natural behavior seemed in those days to be not acting at all, and film watchers, used to standard dramatic posturing by their favorites, did not respond with any excitement to the screen presence of either Jeanne Eagels or Louise Brooks.

That same indifference prevailed when Eagels returned to films in 1927, a world-famous actress, thanks to *Rain*, to make *Man, Woman, and Sin*, cast opposite John Gilbert, at that time the most popular and highest-paid actor in films. Gilbert's fans were counting on seeing him as the dynamic, confidently smiling matinee idol, easily overcoming every hazard and obstacle set up to frustrate the character he usually played. But Monta Bell would have none of that. His role for Gilbert was that of a naive, insecure mama's boy, infatuated, in all the force of

Jeanne Eagels wears "something more comfortable" in *Man, Woman, and Sin* (1927).

immaturity, with the boss's kept woman—a steamy, unwholesome gardenia of a disillusioned sophisticate who radiated sexuality.

Casting Jeanne Eagels in such a role was perfect. Already worn and coming apart after long acquaintance with too much alcohol and too many drugs, she was still bewitchingly beautiful, but in her cynical eyes there resided that powerful challenge of a woman who knows too much—a look possessed by Greta Garbo, by Marlene Dietrich, by Tallulah Bankhead, but by none of them to quite the unfathomable depths of the tragic eyes of Jeanne Eagels.

Man, Woman, and Sin is a film that could *only* be savored, understood

and appreciated in an era long after its release, when there exists infinitely more understanding sympathy for and interest in the plight of a
ruined woman than could be found among the film watchers of 1927
and 1928.

Monta Bell brought much more to *Man, Woman, and Sin* than the
unforgettable Jeanne Eagels. Those familiar with the taboos of the 1920s
in American films will be surprised to see the interior of a bordello portrayed without apology or hedging. Even more unusual (and quite probably unique) was the use of blacks in the film. Gilbert and his mother are
shown to be whites living in a Washington ghetto, surrounded by blacks.
Their black neighbors are friendly and on intimate terms with them; they
are caricatured neither as grotesque comedians nor as dancing plantation
types. Later in the film Gilbert is shown in a diner—the man eating next
to him is black and ordinary, not a drunk, not a hoodlum, not funny—he's
just another customer eating in a diner. Such treatment just did not happen in other Hollywood films in those days.

After the Berkeley showing, *Man, Woman, and Sin* was taken to London in 1975 for a program at the National Film Theatre. Again it provoked a large measure of astonishment. After watching this film, many
began to speculate about Monta Bell. How much influence did he have
as an assistant to Chaplin, some wondered, in the making of that un-
Chaplinesque *A Woman of Paris?*

Monta Bell was born in Washington and had worked for a newspaper
there before acting in a stock company for two years. Like Luis Buñuel,
Monta Bell had his *linea de siempre*, but unlike the great, obsessed Spanish master, Bell never spoke about his special interest in any interview,
nor was it noticed at the time his films were released. Only in a review of
all the Bell films that have been restored does there emerge a startling
repetition that has no comparable example in the work of any other
American director. The Monta Bell protagonist was often a mother-
obsessed misfit, an unadmirable, immature character who invariably
brought grief and embarrassment, sometimes tragedy, to any woman
foolish enough to allow herself to become involved with him. At least
three times, John Gilbert was the actor embodying the Bell antihero.

In 1924, three years before the appearance of *Man, Woman, and Sin*,
Monta Bell had made *The Snob*, with John Gilbert and Norma Shearer.
Gilbert plays an obnoxious schoolteacher who shuns his Mennonite parents, hoping to impress an attractive teacher, enacted by the already
resplendent star Norma Shearer. The ambitious cad marries his lovely

colleague, but promptly ignores her in favor of a wealthy socialite. The marriage is wrecked. When this charmer learns that his wife has become an heiress with an income that surpasses that of his rich inamorata, he tries to repair the ruined marriage. But this film, in an era when all movies were supposed to have happy endings, has the wife determined to go through with a divorce that leaves the Gilbert character a complete loser.

John Gilbert himself created the apotheosis of Monta Bell's anti-hero, writing the script for Bell's 1932 dialogue film *Downstairs*. The enduring Hollywood legend is that Gilbert was unable to continue his career in the talkies after the disaster of the 1929 *His Glorious Night*. Even King Vidor, who certainly should have known better, implies that that failure kept Gilbert from making further dialogue productions when he describes the damage done to stars by sound in his book *A Tree Is a Tree*. But the fact is that other than the acknowledged bomb *His Glorious Night*, John Gilbert appeared in ten dialogue features, earning $250,000 each for most of them. That amount was in excess of the entire Depression-era budget for many films.

The legend, as false as most legends, ignores Gilbert's role in *Queen Christina*, playing the lead opposite Greta Garbo. If his appearance in *Christina* is mentioned at all, it is usually explained away by claiming that Garbo insisted on his playing the part as an auld-lang-syne gesture. Rouben Mamoulian directed that film, and I once asked him about the choice of Gilbert after Laurence Olivier had been tested for the role. "Was it really on Garbo's insistence?" I asked.

"Nonsense," said Mamoulian. "The decision was mine. Olivier simply disappeared on the screen alongside Garbo."

In *Downstairs* Gilbert plays a character without one single admirable quality. He seduces and breaks the heart of the married maid of the establishment where he works as a chauffeur. He picks his nose and wipes his finger on his trousers. He gooses the elderly cook and moves on the lady of the house. When he is finally fired after physically fighting with the husband of the wronged maid, he is, at last, shown applying for another job in another wealthy household, about to begin the cycle all over again. No suggestion of retribution here and no happy ending for the abused women.

When Bell applied this favored formula to Garbo's first American film, *Torrent*, objecting critics seemed to blame Blasco-Ibanez, the author of the turgid novel on which the film was based. It was Ricardo

Cortez who this time had to suffer through a thoroughly ignominious role. As the pampered son of a vicious, wealthy, landowning Spanish termagant, Cortez is made ridiculous throughout the film. He is spineless and feckless, and his mother talks him out of his romance with his sweetheart, played with haunting ambiguity by a young Garbo, who understood not a word of Bell's directions. The unheroic Cortez has his horse run away from him as he lopes awkwardly in pursuit. Banished from her Spanish home, his sweetheart goes to Paris and becomes a celebrated diva, with the former boyfriend showing up at inopportune moments at crucial stages of her career. Garbo, on one such occasion, jams his hat down around his ears, and Cortez makes an exit like Harpo Marx.

Ultimately, with his mother's drive, the Cortez character becomes a successful politician, married, with a loving wife and two adorable children. In the final sequence, potbellied and rabbit cheeked, he makes one last effort to renew his affair with the diva. Garbo, slimmed down and looking more magnificent than ever, ridicules him unmercifully. The slob is left, at home, gazing forlornly at a triumphant-looking portrait of his mother—a scene duplicated exactly at the finish of Alf Sjöberg's masterpiece, *Miss Julie*.

One of the strangest pieces by Monta Bell is *Lady of the Night*, which offered the dual role of madonna and whore to Norma Shearer. The film begins with one of the most effective opening scenes in all the history of silent movies. Shearer, as the prostitute at night, comes out of the gates of a penitentiary. In probably the only scene in American films where a major star is shot without any makeup at all, we behold an almost unrecognizable Norma Shearer standing alone on a city sidewalk. A hearse draws up in front of her. It is one of those old-fashioned hearses, with a glass window in the coffin compartment. As the hearse pauses there in front of her, Shearer takes out her compact and, using the window as a mirror, puts on her makeup to resume her trade.

A rich role for any actress: a prostitute who longs for respectability and a socialite who wants to be wicked. And Norma Shearer playing both roles. It is the usual dream of an actress tagged as a "wholesome" character, as happened to Ingrid Bergman and Julie Andrews.

But suppose that making-up-in-the-hearse-window scene had been done by Stroheim. It would have been cited in more textbooks than the wedding with the funeral in the background of *Greed*.

A bulgy, past-middle-age lover tries in vain to rekindle a past affair: Garbo and Ricardo Cortez in Monta Bell's *The Torrent* (1926).

CHAPTER 14

Discoveries

F or the collector or archivist who hunts for surviving prints of silent films there are two categories that rank as purest gold. Original, 35mm, tinted prints without decomposition are the most rare, the most desirable of all. Next come the 16mm Kodascope prints made by the Eastman Kodak Company throughout the 1920s and rented and sometimes sold through their international subsidiary, the Kodascope Film Libraries.

It was never easy to collect 35mm prints, and with every passing year the likelihood of discovering more of them is lessening. Gone are the wonderful days when James Mason, moving into the former home of Buster Keaton, found a cache of most of the Keaton features in mint 35mm prints. Or Edgar Bergen, having bought the former house of John Barrymore, coming across 35mm tinted prints of the Barrymore features in the basement.

The Keaton features found their way to the late Raymond Rohauer, who, to his credit, took Buster along on world tours with the Keaton films, making it possible in the process for a down-and-out Keaton to enjoy a whole new career in his last years. The Barrymore trove passed through Philip Chamberlin, an enterprising film buff, and wound up being copied and preserved at Eastman House.

In my own collection, before Eastman House became an archive, I had a number of cherished 35mm prints among the eight hundred titles that I'd accumulated over many years. Showing the 35mm nitrate films was always a hazardous problem, although most collectors tended to disregard the ominous flammability and noxious emanations associated with nitrate of cellulose. My childhood Moviegraph with its homemade extension arms had long been gone with kid-stuff paraphernalia. When we moved to Rochester after the big war was over, our first home was on Marion Street, in a modest neighborhood on the outskirts of the city. The little house has a big place in my memory, for it saw the birth of our two daughters and the establishment of our first permanent home film theatre.

The Moviegraph had been replaced by a Holmes Portable, madly set up right next to the coal-burning furnace. Often the projectionist was John Allen, coolly running the nitrate while puffing on a pipe that gave off smoke and sparks like a locomotive on a mountain upgrade. After several years of living thus dangerously, the projector was donated to Eastman House, and the screening room moved up to the attic. That third-floor retreat became a mecca for film people from Chicago, Manhattan, Berlin and Paris. Bob Youngson was among them when he only weighed 350, stomping the floor so that the walls trembled in his unrestrained hilarity as he watched some rare comedy. Bob gained great success editing extant footage into shorts and features for Warner Brothers. One of those two-reelers brought him an Academy Award. Later Bob would work for MGM and, at more than six hundred pounds, grow too unwieldy to leave his prestigious 1 Fifth Avenue address.

Among the Marion Street regulars was a young British publicist for Allied Artists—Bill Everson—the same who has become the most prolific writer of film histories, who is the world's most peripatetic international lecturer, carrying more films with him than any other human being could handle. Even after our theatre was moved up to the third floor, the basement was not without its attraction for our visitors. There was a fruit cellar, its racks filled not with preserves, but with hundreds of the genuine brass cans holding original Kodascope prints. The Kodascope films were the most wanted of 16mm jewels. Printed at Kodak's own Rochester laboratory, they were the sharpest, clearest tinted 16mm films available. The fruit cellar contained not one each of most of the Kodascope releases, but five or six complete prints of each title, and part of the Marion Street hospitality was to invite guests to visit the fruit cellar and help themselves to whichever titles they fancied. Mr. Everson is now the possessor of one of the greatest film collections in private hands. The seeds of his collection came from the Marion Street fruit cellar.

The most impressive-looking of our attic guests from Manhattan was a lean-faced fellow with an almost alarmingly haunted look in his deep-set eyes. He brought along with him a film he had stitched together from sundry 16mm prints: there was the erupting-volcano scene from *The Lost World* intercut with shots of various actresses in peculiar predicaments. He discoursed mysteriously on his quest for "the myth of the Kineto-scope." I knew that his name was Joseph Cornell, but only years later and after his death did I realize his fame and stature as a unique artist of col-lage. He gave our daughter Callista a present—a strange item he had constructed. It was a colorful howling dervish—the mouth opening was backed up by a kind of box. We thought it was a toy, used by throwing spitballs into the target mouth.

The Cornell dervish bounced around the house for many years. Once it was even displayed as an offering in a garage sale. Luckily there were no takers. Callista grew up, married and was living in Evanston, Illinois, when we first learned of the value of the Cornell creations. Cal-lista's husband was a documentary filmmaker. They needed money. She called to ask if we could find her Cornell dervish. We rescued him from the coal bin and sent him to Callista. In Chicago it was appraised for seven thousand dollars. Her husband promptly sold it.

While Eastman House was being converted to a museum and before the Dryden Theatre was built, there was a deprived period when I was without any 35mm equipment to show accumulating 35mm prints in the Card collection. One that I acquired and had to wait for five years to look at was a 1916 Edison, *The Cossack Whip*, starring Viola Dana. I had no clear memory of Viola Dana from the old days, but examining single frames here and there with a loupe made the film a beckoning fas-cination. When finally I was able to have *The Cossack Whip* projected on the screen of the new Dryden Theatre, the amazement was shattering. I had never heard of director John Collins. I would never have imagined that the Edison Company, legendarily stuffy, would have produced a film championing the Russian revolutionists in 1916. But apart from the ideological stand, the visuals and the cutting were so advanced over Griffith's *The Birth of a Nation* that not to have heard of John Collins was absolutely inexplicable. Collins had bloodthirsty cossacks galloping along the horizon, enfilading down hillsides in breathtaking battle patterns.

Viola Dana and John Collins were husband and wife working together in the Edison studios. Viola was already a veteran film actress; she had been making movies since 1910. Like their fellow pioneers Pick-ford, the Gishes and Blanche Sweet, Viola Dana and her sister, Shirley

Viola Dana at the peak of her stardom for Metro

Mason, had been in show business since early childhood. Viola was particularly trained as a dancer, and in *The Cossack Whip* her role finds her
first as a peasant girl whose family is slaughtered by the tsar's cossacks.
Later in the film she becomes a dancer, and the scenes of her dancing are
beautifully photographed by Collins' ace cameraman, John Arnold.

The excitement over this fine 1916 film spurred some very urgent
research. First off, there was the sad explanation for the dearth of information about the career of John Collins. Along with his wife and John
Arnold, he had gone to California in 1918 to work for Metro, but died
in the flu epidemic of that year. His widow went on to become one of the
most popular stars of the early silent period. John Arnold distinguished
himself with the kind of cinematography that helped make *The Big
Parade* one of the most impressive American films. In the 1950s John
Arnold was the head of MGM's camera department.

The heated search for surviving Collins films turned up even greater
creations than *The Cossack Whip*. Most outstanding was an earlier Edison Company film, the 1915 *Children of Eve*. This moving work was

Viola Dana reenacts the Triangle Shirtwaist Company fire in *Children of Eve* (1915).

inspired by the notorious Triangle Shirtwaist Company fire of 1911. In that tragic disaster 146 sweatshop workers died. Most of them were underage girls. The Collins drama was an uncompromising film noir. There was no last-minute rescue for the heroine played by Viola Dana. She had been persuaded by her crusading boyfriend, an idealistic social worker, to take a job in one of the sweatshops as an undercover worker gathering evidence of the outrages being committed by the exploiting owners. The fire scene was harrowing and realistic, and the Dana character is shown dying with all the others.

Our Collins dragnet turned up one of his greatest hits in the Czechoslovak Archive. It was *Blue Jeans*, made for Metro in 1918—just at the end of John Collins' career. Again the film starred Viola Dana, this time in an adaptation of one of the popular old melodramas of the nineteenth-century stage. In this movie, instead of being tied to railroad tracks (as he was in Agustin Daly's *Under the Gaslight*), the hero, after an epic soul fight with the villain, is tied to the log feeder in a sawmill and advanced to a hair's breadth of the giant buzz-saw blade.

The rural locations of *Blue Jeans* are hauntingly picturesque. D. W. Griffith has no more stalwart champion than historian Bill Everson (Bill named his son Griffith Everson), but in his excellent 1978 book, Everson wrote:

> All of Collins' films were splendidly cut and photographed with a mobility, pace and sense of pictorial beauty perhaps found only in the films of Tourneur and Griffith. "Blue Jeans" is an especially stunning film since it invades Griffith's "Way Down East" territory of rural melodrama several years before Griffith did. . . . Collins' unerring sense of place and people, the perfectly selected rural locations and the absolutely "right" faces was quite remarkable.

Of all John Collins' wonderful players' faces, none was more "right" than that of Viola Dana. Her enormous, haunting eyes were often featured in John Arnold's great full-frame close-ups as dynamically as those that much later would be created by the Russian cameraman Edward Tissé—close-ups that brought so much of the power and intensity to the masterpieces of Sergei Eisenstein.

Collins' *The Girl Without a Soul* offered Viola Dana an actress's dream part—a dual role as twin sisters—along with a challenge to the cameraman to solve the technical problems of split-screen sequences with the same actress confronting herself in portraying another character. The year 1917 was early for bringing about this kind of camera magic successfully, and Arnold was able to manage it without a glitch.

Immersed in the newfound wonders of the Collins films, I had the added joy of learning that in the mid-1970s, Viola Dana was very much alive and living with her sister, Shirley Mason, in Marina del Rey. Visiting with her, I found her in her eighties, in lively good health, wittily articulate, with all her memories intact and readily recalled. Viola was invited to the second Telluride Film Festival, where she was one of the guests to be honored along with King Vidor. Later she appeared at Eastman House and the Pacific Film Archive in Berkeley—always discoursing with animated brilliance. Lonely after the loss of her sister, she moved to the Motion Picture Country Home, where she spent her last years in the company of Mary Astor and other colleagues of the silent days. Viola Dana's sparkling personality was undimmed at ninety, when she died in July of 1987.

Although the discovery of the Collins films was the most important in recent years, there were an encouraging number of others as exciting. For a long time historians have mourned the fact that much more than

95 percent of the American predialogue films are irretrievably lost. Still, thanks to the growing number of collectors, archives and lovers of the silents, hardly a year goes by without someone finding a 35mm original nitrate print of a film sixty or seventy-five years old. Sometimes these finds are great disappointments to those who may remember them as having been quite different. But in every case, good, bad or magnificent as the film itself might be, each restoration adds to our knowledge and is as significant to film history as the unearthing of one more ancient human skull is to the paleontologist.

Probably the most spectacular of recent restorations is Raoul Walsh's 1915 *Regeneration*. This early film noir is as dark as a movie ever got to be. Dealing with attempted rape, murder, gangsters, battered children and violent drunkenness, it stars one of filmdom's early Scandinavian imports, Anna Q. Nilsson. Like so many early films shot on location, it is an inadvertent documentary, filmed on the Bowery, in Chinatown and in dreary tenements of Manhattan's already distressed Lower East Side.

Almost as surprising is Christy Cabanne's 1916 *Sold for Marriage*, in that it presents the usually docile Lillian Gish as a fiery, feisty Russian immigrant.

The 1917 *A Girl's Folly* is an invaluable find. Directed by Maurice Tourneur, working with Clarence Brown, this amazing film was shot in the World Film Corporation's Long Island studios, and since the story is about filmmaking, we are treated to perhaps the most complete demonstration of filming on revolving stages, with multiple movies being shot simultaneously, that has ever been recorded. Tourneur plays a movie director himself, and the star, Robert Warwick as a matinee-idol actor, performs with restrained dignity that is unexpectedly admirable. With wry humor, the film is rational, distinguished and altogether admirable.

For Clara Bow fans, two more of her films were added to the growing list of saved movies: *The Plastic Age* and *Helen's Babies*. Brooks cultists could add Mal St. Clair's 1926 *The Show Off* to the list of her available pictures. And Lon Chaney buffs had another thrill when the 1917 *Scarlet Car* surfaced. Colleen Moore in the Limehouse-district movie *Twinkletoes* of 1926 achieved a performance differing from the flapper type she was making a symbol of the 1920s. And recently Cinecon members in a Hollywood meeting were impressed by the 1927 *Valley of the Giants*, with Milton Sills and Doris Kenyon.

Rockliffe Fellowes and Anna Q. Nilsson in Raoul Walsh's 1915 *Regeneration*

Anna Q. Nilsson endures a fatal attack by William Sheer in Walsh's early film noir (1915).

Kevin Brownlow came upon a curious movie of special fascination for historians of the American theatre. *How Molly Malone Made Good* was given a gala premiere in November 1915 at the Metropolitan Opera House in Philadelphia. The film was a project of Burns Mantle, distinguished dramatic critic of the *New York Evening Mail*. The script involved a neophyte young lady reporter scooping a regular reviewer by interviewing the foremost theatrical celebrities of 1915. Appearing in the film were May Robson, Henry Kolker, Cyril Scott, Julian Eltinge (a famous female impersonator), Robert Edeson, Leo Dietrichstein, Henrietta Crosman and the then-celebrated opera star Madame Fjorde, of the Royal Opera of Berlin.

Marguerite Clark was one of the most prominent stars of the pre-1920s. For years none of her films seemed to have survived, but only recently her 1918 *Miss Hoover* was found and restored, a fine film directed by John Robertson with Eugene O'Brien and Hal Reid, the father of Wallace Reid, supporting Miss Clark.

In the raging fires of America's retaliation against Japan during World War II, much of Japan's cinematic history was destroyed. A curious and fascinating survivor was Kinugasa's *A Page Out of Order*. The film had been made in 1926. He stored the original negative in a rice barrel on his country retreat. Printed up with an arresting music score in the 1970s, the film is a mind-boggling masterpiece. Set in an insane asylum, the film is an intriguing cross between *Caligari* and *One Flew over the Cuckoo's Nest*. It begs the question, What of the other Japanese films of the silent period? Its flirtation with expressionism and impressionism is exciting but what of its fellows? We do have Ozu's charming *I Was Born But* as another tantalizing indication of the richness of Japanese cinema of the early days, but two films are not enough for a rational appraisal.

These accidental survivals should cause serious historians to wonder about the silent films of Hungary, Egypt, Turkey and all the countries of South America. In Spain, Ricardo Banos was shooting pictures with Raquel Meller before she went to France and engaged in a much more publicized film career.

In the late 1980s there occurred an event of paramount importance toward a new understanding of film history. For the first time in three quarters of a century, the outside world was given a look at the Russian prerevolution films. Glasnost enabled us to see the films that the Soviets had carefully preserved but had forbidden to show. What revelations! We should not have been so surprised. The traditions of the Moscow

Art Theatre and the teachings of Stanislavsky should have prepared us
to see the same high standards of acting carried over into Russian cinema. But the films of Eisentein, with their utterly dehumanized characters, had misled us. Now, as the prerevolutionary films are being widely
circulated in the United States, we gasp at the subtleties of so masterful
a director as Evgenij Bauer and the sophistication of superstar actress
Vera Kholodnaya in dramas as early as 1915 and as finely crafted as anything emanating from Scandinavia or anywhere else in the film world.

Even more surprising than the superior quality of the films is the
information being circulated along with the pictures about the extent of
Russian film fandom before the revolution. According to the recently
communicative Russian film historians, the popularity of Vera Kholodnaya far outstripped the adulation evoked in this country by Garbo or
Valentino. When Kholodnaya died at the very height of her career, a
national day of mourning took place. Business and official offices were
closed and transportation came to a halt! The 1915 film *Children of the
Age* directed by Bauer is an excellent sample of Kholodnaya's acting,
outstanding for its intense restraint.

Still another Bauer production, *For Luck* of 1917, presents us with
an ironic fact. Prominent in the cast of this film noir is none other than
Lev Kuleshov, one of the prime instigators of the revolutionary Russian
cinema with its dynamic cutting, startling close-ups and caricatured,
politically correct characters.

From barns, abandoned warehouses, attics, basements, even from
bedroom closets, these old nitrate prints are still being discovered, for
every good silent-film historian is a film hunter as well. One reads much
about the deterioration of nitrate prints. But it is still possible to find
absolutely healthy nitrate film today. In the vault of Eastman House
there are Lumière originals of 1898 without the slightest hint of decomposition. Motion picture film, health-wise, is much like human beings.
Some films fall apart at age forty. Some, like the Lumières, are bright
and undiminished at ninety-five. There will be other discoveries this
year. What will they be? Dare we hope for Greta Garbo in *The Divine
Woman* or John Barrymore with Colleen Moore in *The Lotus Eater*?

CHAPTER 15

The Festivals of Film Artists

I n 1955, film festivals were proliferating throughout the entire film-watching world. I had often wondered about how our PR-conscious director, Oscar Solbert, felt about the Academy Awards each year appropriating his given name for the golden statuettes that are awarded. I should have anticipated that eventually he would counter with some award of his own. Thus I was not entirely surprised when he called me into his office one day and ordered me to set up a film festival for Eastman House. "We will award Georges," he announced. I firmly believe he was confident that in a matter of time, the Oscars would be superseded by Georges.

Usually I was reluctant to work very hard on any project that was not of my own inception. But this one was proposed at just the right time for me. I'd been brooding over the suicide of Clyde Bruckman. The pioneer director and the one chosen by Buster Keaton to guide his greatest films was reported to have killed himself in despondency over being bypassed and forgotten. Yet his Keaton films were even then the favorites of film societies and museums. More people, in fact, were look-ing at the Keaton-Bruckman films at the time he killed himself than there had been in the 1920s when Keaton comedies occupied a niche only slightly higher than the Westerns. I had been wondering how best to give belated recognition to the film artists who were still alive, whose work was beginning to be really appreciated as creative accomplish-ments to cherish as part of our cultural heritage, rather than simply exploit as cute curiosities of a naive past. The general's festivals might be just the proper vehicles.

So I gave him the pitch that had been fermenting since Bruckman's passing. "General, the success of any film festival depends not on the movies that are shown, but on the guest celebrities that are lured to attend. Let's meet this fact head-on. Our festival should not be just of films, but a festival of film artists. Suppose we give awards to the greatest living actresses, actors, directors and cameramen of specific periods of the past. Let's go back as far as we dare, as far as we can find great people of the early days still alive. And let's include cameramen. They're always being left out of the big events. We're committed to photography—so why don't we honor the cinematographers on the same basis as the other artists?"

The general bought it—and with his customary enthusiasm. "It's a great idea. Will you pick the people to be honored?"

"Of course not. We'll let them choose themselves. Suppose we begin with the 1915 to 1925 period. We'll have Kodak's people in LA get us the addresses of every film actress, actor, director and cameraman who ever worked during that decade. We'll get Earl Blackwell and his celebrity service to do the same for those in the East. Then we send them ballots with every single survivor's name on it. We let them pick the five top players, directors and cameramen. Then the five winners in each category we bring to Eastman House and give them the George Award."

The general was a traditionalist. Eastman House as a museum had opened to the public November 9, 1949. The first Festival of Film Artists was announced for November 9, 1955. The operatives east and west had assembled more than five hundred names of professionals who had worked in American films during the designated decade. Each was mailed a numbered ballot.

When the ballots came back to us, some of the stars had signed their supposedly anonymous choices. Mae Murray just wrote all over the face of hers that Mae Murray was the greatest of all, then autographed it. Among the stars, the winners were not surprising, but the choices of top directors were unexpected.

Among the actresses of that period, Mary Pickford easily outstripped all the others. Next came Lillian Gish, Gloria Swanson and, to our delight, Mae Marsh! Norma Talmadge also finished among the top five.

Of the winning actors, Chaplin easily outpolled all the others. Then came Buster Keaton, Harold Lloyd, Richard Barthelmess and Ronald Colman.

The five directors chosen were Cecil B. DeMille, high at the top of the list, then Henry King, John Ford, Marshall Neilan and Frank Borzage. Three of those directors had begun their film careers as actors: Borzage, King and the exquisitely handsome Mickey Neilan. Neilan was the great surprise choice. Writers and film historians rarely mentioned Mickey Neilan. He was, in fact, one of the early victims of the dreaded Hollywood unlisted blacklist. Make that roster, and your work in American films was finished. Even worse, as an unperson, persona non grata, the individual became socially invisible in Los Angeles. The wonderful thing was that Neilan's coartists had not forgotten that he had made *Tess of the d'Urbervilles* in 1924, or that he had directed Mary Pickford in eight of the films that had brought her such lasting fame, that he had directed John Barrymore in *The Lotus Eater* and Lon Chaney in *Bits of Life* or that he had contributed the original story for *Hell's Angels*. Mickey Neilan's unenviable spot on the blacklist had come about gradually, over a long period of refusal to give such studio heads as Louis B. Mayer the respect he didn't think they deserved. Mickey had a sharp Irish tongue and throughout his career was never a bit shy about using it both freely and publicly. Nevertheless, his colleagues of the 1915–1925 decade chose him readily along with those recognized giants DeMille, Henry King and John Ford.

The choices of cameramen were, of course, not as exciting as the singling out of glamorous stars, but certainly revealing of the respect the winners had earned from the people they had so basically helped to stardom. The winners were Charles Rosher, who had filmed sixteen of Mary Pickford's vehicles, and Arthur Edeson, who had three great Fairbanks epics to his credit: *The Three Musketeers, Robin Hood* and *The Thief of Bagdad.* Hal Rosson was remembered for the 1916 *Oliver Twist* and Gloria Swanson's 1924 hit, *Manhandled.* Although no one was aware of it at the festival, Hal Rosson was also the first ever to film Louise Brooks; it was in *The Street of Forgotten Men.* Lee Garmes had begun filming in 1918. He, too, had shot a Louise Brooks feature in 1926—*A Social Celebrity,* although I'm sure his winning votes were more thanks to the 1927 *Garden of Allah* and George Arliss' *Disraeli.* But it was John Seitz who was the real champion cinematographer. His credits were amazing: *The Four Horsemen of the Apocalypse, The Prisoner of Zenda, Scaramouche* and *Mare Nostrum.* Seitz had been shooting features since 1917.

All the winners were invited to come to Rochester for the event. The percentage of acceptances of course would be crucial to the success of the whole enterprise. Chaplin was overseas, and he had already been denied a visa to return to the United States on grounds of "moral turpitude." This outrage, by the way, was perpetrated during a Democratic administration, the group that likes to think of itself as more liberal than their reactionary opponents. Ronald Colman and Norma Tal-

Blanche Sweet and Stuart Holmes in Mickey Neilan's *Tess of the d'Urbervilles* (1924), a lost film

John Barrymore and Colleen Moore in *The Lotus Eater* (1921), another major film of Marshall Neilan that remains lost.

madge were seriously ill, and DeMille was seriously busy with *The Ten Commandments*. Mickey Neilan, along with Buster Keaton, was supposed to be nearly drowned in alcohol and despair. But we tried hard to get them all to come to Rochester. We chose Jesse Lasky to be master of ceremonies.

I was sent to Hollywood to confer with the Kodak people in Los Angeles—they were footing the bill for Eastman House's festival. Kodak's Hollywood man in charge told me that even though Chaplin was far and away the top winner, he was not to be considered for any award or even to be mentioned in any of the publicity. This charming executive also sought to ban the participation of Marshall Neilan. "Neilan's a vicious drunk," he warned. "If you bring him to Rochester, he'll disgrace you all and ruin your whole festival."

I was proud of the general; he brushed aside these objections with the contempt they deserved, and invitations went to all the winners. He even tried to work out a deal with the State Department for Chaplin, and I'm sure he would have succeeded, but Chaplin, deeply wounded by his political rejection, refused to accept any special deal.

Gloria Swanson couldn't make the scene—she was in Rome acting with Vittorio De Sica and Brigitte Bardot on *Nero's Mistress*. But those who did show up made for a dazzling event. On hand were Lillian Gish, Dick Barthelmess, Mary Pickford, Buster Keaton, Harold Lloyd, Mae Marsh, Frank Borzage and, the most soigné, self-possessed and distinguished-looking man in the group, Marshall Neilan. Cameramen Arthur Edeson and Hal Rosson were there. And master of ceremonies Jesse Lasky, himself so much a basic part of Hollywood history that he seemed a very legend, and one was surprised to find him actually still alive.

There were more than three thousand people in the Eastman Theatre that night helping to create an occasion both sentimental and warm with dignity, informality and fun, for the audience was somehow taken into the party. They were warmed up by a series of excerpts from the most memorable films of the prizewinners. Harold Lloyd as that freshman football hero, winning the big game in the very last seconds of play; Mary Pickford both feisty and wholesomely beautiful as *Little Annie Rooney;* Lillian Gish being snatched from the brink of Niagara Falls by Richard Barthelmess, floating on a chunk of ice in *Way Down East;* Gloria Swanson as an embattled subway rider in *Manhandled;* Barthelmess getting the mail through although nearly beaten to death by the vicious sadistic mountaineer (played by Ernest Torrence in his screen debut) in

At the first Festival of Film Artists, in 1955: Jesse Lasky, Frank Borzage, Mary Pickford and Marshall Neilan

Tol'able David; Buster Keaton struggling desperately to save a beloved cow from the slaughterhouse in *Go West;* exquisitely delicate Mae Marsh in *White Rose:* they were a visual treasury of memorable moments that delighted the guests and kept the folks from Hollywood laughing louder than anyone else at the shots of high comedy. The clips brought opinions from both Jesse Lasky and Mary Pickford that the scenes reminded them that films had lost much of the wholesome fun that had existed in the 1920s. Lillian Gish went further to lament "We took the wrong turn when we married films to words instead of music."

The November 9 opening of Eastman House in 1949 had been a day of ideal fall weather. The November 9 of the 1955 Festival of Film Artists was visited with a savage blizzard that made the attendance of more than three thousand Rochesterians at the event an almost heroic response.

Not able to leave Hollywood at that time, DeMille sent his current Moses, Charlton Heston, to pick up his George. The publicity department of Paramount had sent me a copy of the talk Heston was planning to make in accepting the award for his boss. Thinking it was simply an informational copy, I left it on my desk. From Eastman House, just about nine blocks from the Eastman Theatre, it's normally a three-minute trip. The blizzard that night made it a half-hour mush. I first met Heston in the wings of the Eastman Theatre stage. Brushing the snow from his hair, he approached me somewhat desperately. "Card, they tell me you have my script! Let me have it, quick!" He was on next.

"Your script? They sent me a copy of what you were going to say. I didn't think you'd be *reading* it! It's back at my office."

"Your office! You'd better damned well get on the hexenreiter and get it over here for me right now!"

"Sorry, Mr. Heston. It took me a half hour of snow fighting to get over here. And you're on next. You'll just have to ad lib." Moses cursed me.

But Heston went on without his script and won the audience over immediately by confessing, "I feel a little damp behind the ears." He then continued with observations infinitely better than those that had been written by the publicity department.

The euphoria of having so many fabulous people on hand was tremendous. But so was the fury ignited by the sometimes deliberate false accounts of the event in the media.

Our anger at the State Department's banning of Chaplin (not just because it kept him from our festival!) spilled over into my remarks to the audience when I introduced the film clips. Impossible for Clyde Gilmour, a Canadian film critic who had been invited, not to have heard my denunciation of Chaplin's mistreatment. But in his account of the event in Toronto, he wrote that the very name of the top winner, Charles Chaplin, was never mentioned. This false accusation was picked up by Gilbert Seldes, who was not present in Rochester, but in a savage piece in *Variety* chided us for completely censoring all mention of Chaplin.

Other than that nastiness, all of us at Eastman House were enormously pleased by the outcome of the festival. But no one was more delighted than Jesse Lasky. Jesse had been for too many years one of the almost forgotten has-beens in Hollywood. The festival brought him media attention and pictures of himself with the stars in the major journals. Jesse wanted to take the show on the road; he wanted it to play in Los Angeles, where he needed rediscovery. His thought was that if we did it again in his hometown, we could have the too-busy ones on hand—Cecil B. DeMille (himself!) and John Ford and Henry King. I was absolutely against a repeat performance but was overruled, and off we went for the reprise. First of all I had a brutal battle with Lasky over Chaplin. Jesse insisted that Chaplin's name not appear on the new elaborate program being prepared for what rapidly became a Jesse Lasky

Plotting in the Paramount commissary: James Card, Jesse Lasky, Cecil DeMille and Oscar Solbert (1955)

production. I lost again. But with Cecil B. DeMille, Henry King and John Ford on hand with the others this time, on the night of the show I again made a strong point of declaring Charlie Chaplin the winner of winners and deploring the situation that prevented his being with us. Once again, my remarks were ignored by the press. Mary Pickford gave a moving tribute to Chaplin and wished him well "wherever he might be." (He was living in Vevey, Switzerland, where, in fact, he ended his days.) Louella Parsons in her report of the festival *did* note Mary's mention of Chaplin, but in this snide way: "Only sour note in the otherwise warm and nostalgic 'Festival of Film Artists' was Mary Pickford's mentioning the name of Charlie Chaplin." I had been absolutely right. The festival may have been a big hit in Rochester. In Hollywood, it was only a raindrop in a big puddle of mud.

As far as General Solbert was concerned, there was no turning back. The next year, 1956, was spent in getting ready for the second Festival of Film Artists, scheduled for October 1957 to escape the possibility of a second major blizzard. The period to be covered was 1926 through 1930. This time there were many more film artists of that span still living to get ballots and vote for five top actors, actresses, directors and cinematographers. In tabulating the votes, we found many repeaters from the first festival selections. Among them, Harold Lloyd, Richard Barthelmess, Mary Pickford, Lillian Gish, Gloria Swanson, Frank Borzage, Cecil B. DeMille and the cameramen Charles Rosher, Lee Garmes and Arthur Edeson. Newly elected were Greta Garbo (who topped all others by a wide, wide margin), Janet Gaynor, Joan Crawford, Maurice Chevalier, Ramon Novarro. Of the directors, only Josef von Sternberg and Frank Borzage made it to Rochester. The other winners were King Vidor, Frank Capra, Clarence Brown, Frank Lloyd and John Ford, but they were all busy, still working on films in Hollywood. Winning stars absent were Clara Bow, Norma Shearer, William Powell, Fredric March, Gary Cooper, Ronald Colman and, again, Charlie Chaplin. New to the cinematographer group were James Wong Howe, William Daniels (who shot almost every one of Garbo's Hollywood films), George Folsey, Peverell Marley and Hal Mohr.

This time the general hosted a gala luncheon in the Genesee Valley Club, Rochester's equivalent of the Union Clubs of other cities. The luncheon was dramatic in that it marked the first meeting of Mary Pickford and her former daughter-in-law, Joan Crawford, since their long-ago contretemps over Joan's marriage to Douglas Fairbanks, Jr. The Royal Family of Pickfair had strenuously objected to that union of the prince to the former Lucille LeSueur, professional Charleston dancer. They should have saved their annoyance—the marriage didn't last long. But everyone at the luncheon watched breathlessly as the reunion took place. They were probably disappointed. Mary and Joan were scrupulously cordial and even friendly to each other, Mary even leaning over a table to give her former daughter-in-law a kiss. Having played out that scene, Joan took her George Award under her arm and, with her current husband, Al Steele, Pepsi-Cola tycoon, left right after lunch without waiting for the formal doings in the theatre. Later that afternoon, at Eastman House, Chevalier and Swanson delighted everyone with a camera by staging a great love scene at the foot of the grand staircase.

For the second festival we asked Rouben Mamoulian to be the master of ceremonies. We thought it would be an appropriate bit of nostalgia to bring Mamoulian back to the theatre where George Eastman had installed him in 1923 to produce and direct the elaborate stage prologues to the movies. After the Eastman Theatre began to run sound films in 1929, Rouben Mamoulian left for Hollywood to begin his distinguished film career by directing Helen Morgan in *Applause*. The 1957 festival marked his first return to Rochester and the theatre he had known so well twenty-eight years before.

Mamoulian's wife came with him. She was a gorgeous, glamorous Hollywood type, and although the Mamoulians were only to stay overnight, she brought so much ponderous luggage that it couldn't all be squeezed into the spartan room they were assigned in the Rochester Treadway Inn. Mrs. Mamoulian ordered an immediate transfer to a more commodious hotel.

Other celebrity arrivals were also not without their own problems. In 1957 there were direct flights from Los Angeles to Rochester. It was in the good old days before hub airports. I was at the Rochester airport to meet a plane that carried more than any usual share of VIPs. On that flight were the director Frank Borzage, Ramon Novarro and Maurice Chevalier, who traveled with an entourage of no fewer than three comely female attendants. The plane arrived at 1:30 a.m., Rochester time. When I greeted the group, Chevalier let out a whoop and pumped Novarro's hand. Ramon was astonished. "I've been wanting to meet you for years—ever since *Ben-Hur*," Chevalier exulted. The two great stars not only had never met before, but had flown all the way from Los Angeles without recognizing each other. Also, they all let me know, they had had nothing to eat since before boarding the plane in California. First bit of business was to get them to food. Rochester is not known to be a swinging town after midnight. But there was a restaurant right on East Avenue, not far from the theatre itself, run by an ambitious restaurateur who thought of himself and his establishment as several cuts above the small-town reputation of Rochester. His boîte he called the Five O'Clock Club, and its marquee boasted that it was "Just like New York." I parked the car with its illustrious guests and rushed in to see if they had any food left. The owner was sitting with some friends at a booth near the door. I knew who he was—he was big in self-advertising. It was obvious at once that he didn't know me. "We're closed, Mac," he snarled at me.

"Can't we just get a quick sandwich or something?"

"I told you we're closed. The chef's gone."

"Look, Leo, can't you have a waiter go into the kitchen and fix three or four simple sandwiches? I have Maurice Chevalier and Ramon Novarro out here in the car. They haven't had a thing to eat all day, and every place but yours is closed."

At Eastman House for the second Festival of Film Artists, in 1957: James Card, Lillian Gish, Janet Gaynor and Mary Pickford

The proprietor turned to his friends. "After all that trouble we had with that guy tonight, here's another one—this one has Maurice Chevalier out in his car!"

I went back to our guests. Across the street was a White Tower hamburger place (forerunner of the MacDonald's and Burger Kings to come). It was there that I had to take Borzage, Novarro and that noted French bon vivant and gourmet Maurice Chevalier for hamburgers. I noted that Maurice disguised his burger with a complete dousing of mustard. Without much shame, I confess to elation when, only a few months later, the Five O'Clock Club that was "Just like New York" went out of business.

Our cast on the stage of the Eastman Theatre almost made the event look like a rerun of 1955, for there, again, were Lillian Gish, Harold Lloyd, Mary Pickford, Frank Borzage, Dick Barthelmess and Charles Rosher, but with the added attractions of Gloria Swanson, Josef von Sternberg, Janet Gaynor, Ramon Novarro and Maurice Chevalier, who, of course, stole the show. Chevalier's onstage technique was unforgettable. Offstage, standing or sitting surrounded by his personal entourage, he looked almost asleep, gloomy and brooding. But in the instant before he stepped on the stage, his face would light up as though he'd turned on a set of bulbs. His whole body seemed to have been electrified; his face was flushed with energy and breezy enthusiasm. When he stepped off the stage, the appearance of somnolence fell over him like a curtain. Chevalier's off-and-on act reminded me of Buster Keaton at the first festival. Offstage, of course, he smiled—and often. He was a cheerful, friendly charmer. And everywhere he went, both amateur photographers and newspaper cameramen would try to ambush one of those smiles. But Buster teased them with an almost supernatural sense of timing: he could sense just the instant they were about to fire their cameras, the smile would snap off his face, and the trademark, solemn Keaton look would be all they'd catch.

The second Festival of Film Artists was the last. Before we could do another, General Solbert died. As of this writing, every other actor,

Winners of the second Festival of Film Artists. Top row: Lee Garmes, Frank Borzage, Charles Rosher, Maurice Chevalier. Middle row: Josef von Sternberg, Robert Edeson, Richard Barthelmess, James Wong Howe, Ramon Novarro, William Daniels. Bottom row: John Seitz, Harold Lloyd, unidentified, Gloria Swanson, Lillian Gish, Janet Gaynor, Mary Pickford.

actress and director who won awards in those festivals has also departed.

General Oscar Solbert was an exceptional individual. He exasperated me to the point of my resigning three times. Three times he tore up my letter of resignation. I miss him the way I miss my own father.

Subsequent directors of Eastman House have tried to have festivals of film artists. But they miss the salient point of the two originals—that the artists chosen for the Georges were chosen entirely by their fellow film people. The later, spurious awards have been given to celebrities chosen by Rochester socialites.

The Movies Matriculate

A t first it looked to be a good thing that cinema was at last sufficiently recognized as an art to be admitted to the curricula of most colleges and universities. But both lovers of film and makers of motion pictures are having increasingly grave doubts about the nature of teaching that comes under the nebulous heading of "semiology."

The efforts that led to the establishment of a film studies program at the University of Rochester are probably not much different from the steps taken to inject cinema studies into other institutions of higher education. In New York there had to be approval by the State Board of Regents. For such authoritative regulatory bodies of the bureaucracy to acknowledge the academic worthiness of film was a major breakthrough for cinema.

By 1952 the combination of the Dryden Theatre and the Eastman House motion-picture-study collection made it possible for any student or historian to have films screened. But in that year there was not a single film course being offered by the University of Rochester. Such myopic inattention to "the most wanted art" was rectified largely through the prodigious efforts of a most extraordinary woman, Marion Gleason. Mrs. Gleason was formerly the wife of Harold Gleason, George Eastman's in-house organist. She was well acquainted with Mr. Eastman, was, in fact, his guest on several trips. Marion Gleason joined the staff of Eastman House after it had become a museum and had been chartered as an educational institution. Mrs. Gleason's job was to act as a kind of saleswoman to persuade local schools to tour student groups through the House, with the hope of learning something of the history of photography and motion pictures. In the latter field, Marion Gleason had unique qualifi-

cations. When 16mm amateur movie film was introduced by Kodak in
1922, she became a producer and director of the demonstration movies
made to show customers how easy it was to make pictures. But Marion
had her sights set on higher education. She wanted university students to
be able to explore the history of motion pictures.

Tirelessly and patiently, Mrs. Gleason proselytized the university
department heads, finally succeeding in getting some of them to send
their professors with their classes to look at films having a bearing on
their subjects. Once in a while, the film bore too heavily on their cherished notions. The chairman of the history department was wildly outraged when he got a look at the documentary *From the Tsar to Lenin*. The
chairman was a noted authority on the Russian Revolution. It was his
field, and he had published extensively in that field. Although every
image in the film was limited to actuality footage, the arrangement of
the scenes and the reality of the action conflicted so violently with his
own professorial version of what had happened in the Revolution that
he just couldn't stand to have others in his department or any of their
students watch the film.

Another disaster happened when the head of the English department chose to bring her class in American literature to see the John
Barrymore–Dolores Costello silent version of *Moby Dick*, a title Warner
Brothers had changed to *The Sea Beast*. And the title was not all that
Warner had changed. In the film Captain Ahab was far more intent on
pursuing the fair daughter of a missionary halfway around the world
than he was on hunting the great white whale. The professor of English
suffered acutely watching the violence done to Melville in that movie. I
heard that she never went to another film the rest of her life. Probably it
was a good thing; she might have been tricked into seeing *Moby Dick*, the
Warners' second swing at Melville. In that one there was dialogue (none
of it Melville's), and once again there was John Barrymore turning Ahab
into something all his own. Now Joan Bennett was the whale's competition for Ahab's attention. That experience the professor might not have
survived.

At last it was recognized that an intermediary was essential, someone
who could guide the professors away from the more devastating devia-
tions in cinematic versions of literary masterpieces. I had been teaching
a film course at Syracuse University, and in 1966 I was recruited to
become the University of Rochester's first-ever professor of motion pictures and charged to devise its initial course in cinema, within the gentle
embrace of the fine arts department.

In those early days, Bill Everson, David Bradley and I were peons with no academic degrees advanced beyond the minimal bachelor of arts to support our names in the university catalogue. We were tolerated first because Bradley and I had made films, but mostly since the three of us possessed vast personal film collections. And in my case, I also had available the gigantic Eastman House collection.

What happened to film when it went to college depended largely upon which discipline received the foundling art. If cinema was taken within the fairly tolerant theatre department or even into fine arts, it usually was a reasonably symbiotic placement. But too often after the deans discovered there were such things as written film scripts, the English departments would pounce on the medium. It was there that serious mutilation could take place.

Oftentimes the individual professors were blameless. Some of them liked movies quite apart from their academic lives. Others just liked the idea of using films and being spared having to teach for the hour and a half it might take for the film to run. Fourteen years after my lone, precedent-setting course at the University of Rochester, twenty-four professors had jumped on the bandwagon, teaching two or more film courses apiece. None of these professors was trained in any aspect of motion pictures. But they had been reading about films! Qualification enough to teach—at the college level. Eleven of these pundits were professors of English; two were French instructors; five were history professors; three were from fine arts (there was no drama department at the University of Rochester—and little drama). One professor of psychiatry taught film classes, so, of course, there had to be a professor of psychology in the act, too. In addition there was a professor from the School of Music, and sociology and political science had their representatives. There was even a professor of religious studies, one who taught Japanese literature and a professor of Jewish studies. Among the film courses taught were these offerings: History 353, Myth and Theory of Female Personality; History 288, Saints and Devils in History and Film; Sociology 197, Sociology as an Art Form; Religion 229, The Transcendental Film.

With the possible exception of History 353, all these courses, really being taught by amateurs, were rather ingenuous. The real inquisition started when the university began to hire genuine professors of cinema from the outside world—graduates brought from the simmering campuses of Berkeley and Madison, Wisconsin. These mercenaries arrived armed with doctorates backed by unintelligible dissertations and determination to destroy any real love of film their students might bring with them to their classes. They were nothing like the simple, old-school, aging professors they were replacing. They were survivors of Jack Kerouac's beat generation, and they had a big hand in creating the turned-off generation of the 1960s. If one had much to do pedagogically with them when they were teenagers, it will be remembered that no one of them would ever make a positive statement. Instead of saying "I'm going to get a haircut this afternoon," they would invariably say "It's like I'm going to get a haircut this afternoon"—except, of course, that they never did get that haircut. Nothing was ever something. Everything was always *like* something. They used "like" the way this generation of students uses "Uhmmm." When they became graduate students, they discovered semiology. What a revelation to them! Here was a philosophy that made it possible for them to use syntactics and metonymies to go right on saying everything was *like* something else, and nothing was really just itself, but to say it without sounding like undergraduates.

In order to perpetuate this scam, they had to find a body of printed literature to use as a springboard to develop their own theoretical writing, which ultimately would give the semiological approach to cinema its academic authority. For those able to read French, the appearance in 1951 of *Cahiers du Cinema* in France provided an early feeding ground. Later, when *Cahiers* began appearing in English, nourishment was provided aplenty. In the interim, there was some published assistance. In 1957 Princeton published Siegfried Kracauer's *From Caligari to Hitler, A Psychological History of the German Film*. This was not the real thing—yet. But a *psychological* history was "on the road."

Kracauer had been a music critic on the *Frankfurter Zeitung*. In the 1920s and the pre-Hitler 1930s the *Frankfurter Zeitung* had been to Germany what *The New York Times* and the Paris *Herald-Tribune* have been for years to the United States. I would even throw in the London *Economist* and the *Wall Street Journal* for full measure. The point is that however unqualified a journalist might be, if he wrote for any length of time for any of the aforementioned newspapers, his credentials were impeccable. When Hitler made things unbearable for liberal journalists in Germany, they went elsewhere—if they could. Kracauer went to New York, where the Museum of Modern Art Film Library made him welcome (as it had also received Luis Buñuel as a kind of visitor–staff member). Spending time at the museum, Kracauer began to write about film. Back in Frankfurt, Kracauer knew and cared so little about cinema that when, as the paper's music critic, he reviewed Pabst's film version of the

Brecht-Weill *Dreigroschenoper*, throughout his review he referred to Pabst, who had been Germany's top film director since 1925, as "Herr Papst." Setting up in business as an authority on the history of German films, Kracauer wrote his *From Caligari to Hitler* offering the peculiar theory that most of the famous German films were somehow symptomatic of what were to become the horrors of Nazism. A curious notion indeed, since the majority of the films he cited as ominous examples were largely the creative work of Jewish artists. The popular light soap operettas that were the bread and butter of the German film industry were for the most part ignored by Kracauer in favor of the dark, imaginative pictures that he accused of harboring the sinister principles of National Socialism. Kracauer, of course, was not writing in his native language. Sometimes, as with Joseph Conrad, that fact could become a positive attribute. In Kracauer's case, his English was just sufficiently obscure to make his points ambiguous enough to delight the pipe-smoking elbow-patch English professors of our universities. After all, ambiguity is their way of life.

The late Bosley Crowther had been the film critic for *The New York Times* for close to thirty years. Writing with a lucidity that would be unfashionable today, Bosley Crowther was not shy about pointing out the emperor's clothing that adorned *From Caligari to Hitler*—though perhaps it was a little unkind of him to label Kracauer's book "a refugee's revenge."

Of all the academic disciplines that took cinema under their wings, it was in the departments of English that the medium has been most viciously savaged. Once those professors were able to get their hands on printed scenarios, they were able to bat the texts around, toss them like a cat destroying its prey, breaking their spines, tearing out their throats and leaving their corpses alone after the blood stopped flowing. Dissecting the motion picture with syntactics, the semiologists are spattering the art of cinema with more gobbledygook than any other art form has ever had to endure. It is brutal for a filmmaker whenever he is trapped as a guest in a seminar of semiologists discussing his work. He doesn't get a chance to tell them anything of his intentions. The baffled director or scenarist must often wonder whether he'd errantly wandered into a psychiatric ward rather than a college classroom. The filmmakers hear interpretations of their work so fantastically obscure it is difficult for them not to believe they're not being put on. If they speak up, their sometimes angry protests of being completely innocent of having arranged all those signs and symbols fraught with significances far from intended themes are unheeded. Film writers and directors are considered by semiologists to be lacking in intellectual depth. The film students are quick to forgive them—the artists don't really understand the *meaning* of what they've done.

Some professors have been writing protests against the system. Bill Everson decries "structuralism," but semiology is much worse than that relatively mild form of torturing literature. Kevin Brownlow wrote a trenchant piece in *The New York Times*, warning that semiology was turning into a kind of theology. David Bradley, who directed a film for MGM along with being the greatest of the collectors, was able to teach in California without invoking "the formal relations between signs or expressions in abstraction from their significance and their interpreter."

And Professor William K. Everson has now taught film history to generations of devoted students without once directing their attention to the signs and symbols that deal with their functions in artificially constructed compromises and pragmatics.

In the syntax of semiologists, the word "signifying" appears frequently. There is a bemusing similarity in the repeated use of "signifying" in black male oral poetry called toasts. Dr. Bruce Jackson, eminent criminologist, distinguished professor of English and director of the Center for Studies in American Culture, State University of New York at Buffalo, has made a valuable study and collection of this unique living form of oral narrative poetry. The toasts are a little-known branch of black folklore and come from low sources: jails, street-corner hangouts and hobo camps. Ponder one of the most popular that has multiple variations and innumerable verses. It is called *Signifying Monkey*.

> Say deep down in the jungle in the coconut grove
> lay the Signifying Monkey in his one-button roll.
> Now the hat he wore was on the Esquire fold.
> his shoes was on a triple-A last

H. Rap Brown has discussed *Signifying Monkey* in his *Die Nigger Die!*:

> Signifying at its best can be heard when brothers are exchanging tales. I used to hang out in bars just to hear the old men "talking shit." By the time I was nine, I could talk Shine and Titanic, Signifying Monkey three different ways.

In all the examination of these toasts that have been made, there is no explanation of what the Signifying Monkey signifies. Can a parallel be found between the popularity of that Signifying Monkey and semiologists' signs and symbols that also signify? That monkey for the blacks was born and flourishes in the meanest of circumstances: the holding cells of county jails, the hobo jungles, ghetto street corners and sleazy bars where the men's only hopes of superiority lie in folklore. Are the semiologists likewise prisoners of inferiority, their fears causing them to hide themselves in the jungles of jargon, where they are protected from the awful responsibilities of lucidity?

If that is the case, they are not safe there. In his autobiography, *My Last Sigh*, Luis Buñuel, one of the greatest of all film directors, writes of this incident:

> As the honorary president of the Centro de Capacitación Cinematográfica in Mexico City, I once went to visit the school and was introduced to several professors, including a young man in a suit and tie who blushed a good deal. When I asked him what he taught, he replied, "The semiology of the Clone Image." I could have murdered him on the spot.

Iris, what did you do with that revolver?

CHAPTER 17

Silent Film in a State of Grace

T oday the silent film exists surrounded by love—old loves like mine—but best of all, by the fresh loves of people who have *chosen* silent cinema. Not those who simply had silent movies in their youth because there were no others. But the fine people who welcome atavistic nostalgia. Their genes were swimming around in the warm pools of great-grandparents' blood, awaiting the time when they would be gathered into the makings of individuals of later generations and born with the secret memories of what pleased their forebears. Such folks may be surprised by their own response to the music of Kid Ory, to a painting by George Bellows, to a building by Frank Lloyd Wright. Among them are the enthusiasts who work long, hard hours without pay to restore grand theatres built long before their own parents' birth. Their deep love for what they never really knew themselves has brought back to life great movie theatres such as the State and the Palace in Cleveland, the Riviera in Tonawanda, the Smith in Geneva, the Landmark in Syracuse—great old houses in Palo Alto and Seattle. There they happily enjoy silent movies screened with an organist playing old scores or even with a fully reconstructed theatre orchestra. My heart overflows with warmth for these fans of the great pictures of the past.

Kevin Brownlow has brought silents like Abel Gance's *Napoleon* and Douglas Fairbanks' *Thief of Bagdad* in good 35mm prints, on big screens, in large theatres, with orchestral music so that people today can participate in the thrill of the basic films.

The resonance augments from year to year. After the death of John Hampton, whose silent-movie theatre had been a landmark of Hollywood for decades, his theatre stood dark and decaying until his widow, with the enthusiastic help of the son of silent-movie actor William Austin, restored the theatre and relighted the screen with wonderful movies. There is a group in Hollywood that shows early films in the Lasky barn, where Cecil B. DeMille made his first pictures. David Bradley, former MGM director, supreme collector and professor, each year in his Hollywood home brings together surviving film stars and directors to watch their own work along with fervent admirers. The Bradley sessions have seen Anna Sten, Rouben Mamoulian, von Sternberg, Mary Philbin, Margery Wilson, Madge Bellamy and dozens of others watch their own work in the generous company of one another. In Los Angeles, in Dayton, Ohio, and Moorhead, Minnesota, the yearly cinefests of the Cinecon groups pull in afficionados from Munich, Paris, Berlin, Luxembourg and Tokyo along with others from every state to enjoy film together. And every year the organizers are happy to offer some of the rediscovered and newly restored silents to often wildly appreciative viewers. In Italy the Podornone Silent Film Festival celebrated its eleventh year.

In these days of dialogue, like the amazing blossoming of the hardy century plant, there can still be a new silent film produced. In 1962 the Japanese astonished us with *The Island*. There will be others—not enough to make them commonplace—but eventually there will be more.

Kaneto Shindo's *The Island* (1962)

Evelyn Brent with the look von Sternberg gave her

What is the key to the seduction of silence? Is it the remoteness from cacophony of heavy metal and the ceaseless garrulousness of the TV tubes? Probably much of the special quality of silent cinema is a matter of participation. A talkie can be experienced by simply sitting and allowing the sound to wash over one. But to see and make any sense at all of a silent movie, we *have* to *participate*. Just reading the dialogue titles in itself is active participation. We give the dialogue the inflections that qualify the meaning of the words. (Some watchers, in fact, participated too completely—they read the titles aloud and made unbearable nuisances of themselves.) Perhaps this act of partaking—of sharing in the illusion that is cinema—involves us in a far more subtle response than we have supposed. Some thirty years ago a team of medical researchers decided, on the basis of their experiments, that image retention was not simply a physical characteristic of the eye's retina. But instead, the ability to perceive individual still images of an action as action itself was centered not in the retina, but in the central nervous system. Hurrah! That would place our emotional response to film on a basis comparable to our thrill over certain combinations of musical notes when a symphony orchestra brings us to tears or to exaltation.

I cannot conceive of living without showing films. Movies have been the ambrosia of my life. To offer that gift to others, sharing in their enjoyment of the movies I love, is my greatest joy.

Once, when Sternberg's *Underworld* was being screened and the shimmering close-ups of Evelyn Brent as Feathers, the gangster's moll, were on the screen, one young man fell off his seat, writhing ecstatically in the aisle, happily moaning, "O Feathers! Feathers!"

Much as I applaud so enthusiastic a response, it really would not do

Evelyn Brent as Feathers in *Underworld* (1927): capable of rendering a man helpless

to have a theatre filled with the whole audience in the aisles. Still, if one is able to submit to a séance offering one of the really fine predialogue films and can leave all cynical notions of superiority outside the dark of the screening room, if the film is shown with the harmony of music in tune with the message of the images, and one is willing to suspend disbelief for an hour or two, the experience may very well seduce a viewer into that delightful state that can come very close to one's private definition of love.

INDEX

A NOTE ON THE TYPE

This book was set in a digitized version of Janson. The hot metal version of Janson was a recutting made direct from type cast from matrices long thought to have been made by the Dutchman Anton Janson, who was a practicing type founder in Leipzig during the years 1668–1687. However, it has been conclusively demonstrated that these types are actually the work of Nicholas Kis (1650–1702), a Hungarian, who most probably learned his trade from the master Dutch type founder Dirk Voskens. The type is an excellent example of the influential and sturdy Dutch types that prevailed in England up to the time William Caslon (1692–1766) developed his own incomparable designs from them.

Printed and bound by Arcata Graphics/Martinsburg,
Martinsburg, West Virginia

Designed and composed by Cassandra J. Pappas